No Price Too High

Victimless Crimes and the Ninth Amendment

ROBERT M. HARDAWAY

Forewords by Gary E. Johnson,
Former Governor of New Mexico
and John L. Kane, Jr.,
U.S. Senior
District Judge, Denver, Colorado

Westport, Connecticut
London

Library of Congress Cataloging-in-Publication Data

Hardaway, Robert M., 1946-
  No price too high : victimless crimes and the Ninth Amendment /
  Robert M. Hardaway; forewords by Gary E. Johnson and John L. Kane, Jr.
    p.   cm.
  Includes bibliographical references and index.
  ISBN 0–275–95056–5 (alk. paper)
  1. Narcotic laws—United States—Criminal provisions.
  2. Decriminalization—United States. 3. Drug abuse—United States—
  Prevention. I. Title.
KF3890.H37   2003
345.73′0277—dc21   2003040373

British Library Cataloging in Publication Data is available.

Library of Congress Catalog Card Number: 2003040373
ISBN: 0–275–95056–5

First published in 2003

Praeger Publishers, 88 Post Road West, Westport, CT 06881
An imprint of Greenwood Publishing Group, Inc.
www.praeger.com

Printed in the United States of America

The paper used in this book complies with the
Permanent Paper Standard issued by the National
Information Standards Organization (Z39.48–1984).

10 9 8 7 6 5 4 3 2 1

Dedicated to Judy Swearingen

Contents

Foreword

This book, *No Price Too High*, by Robert Hardaway, debates the effectiveness of the criminalization of illicit drugs. In an argument against the war on drugs, Hardaway refers to the results of the criminalization of prostitution and gambling. Although both are viewed as wrong, they are also seen as personal problems, not as crimes, which hurt other people. Hardaway confesses that the use of drugs will have harmful results, but only to the person using them. Thus, drug addiction is clearly a health issue, not a criminal issue.

The title of this book, *No Price Too High* sarcastically implies that, to our law and judicial system, there is "no price too high" to make something illegal, even if that only makes the problem worse. Using extensive references, Hardaway proves that the drug problem has only increased since its criminalization.

I found this book to be both interesting and enlightening. Hardaway shows the historical mistakes we made from the criminalization of personal problems such as prostitution and gambling. By making these acts illegal, prostitutes and gamblers received no solution to their problems; in fact, their problems worsened. When these issues were decriminalized in some states, prostitutes were protected and gamblers were treated—the problems declined. Hardaway states that the only way the drug problem will decrease is if drugs are decriminalized so addicts can be treated and rehabilitated.

Former Governor of New Mexico Gary E. Johnson

Foreword

We are indebted to Professor Robert Hardaway for bringing together the common effects of the so-called victimless crimes of drugs, prostitution and gambling and demonstrating quite persuasively that such laws produce unintended consequences far more damaging to our society than the defined crimes themselves. Of course, it is essential to understand just what a victimless crime is. In a sense, every crime has a victim, whether it is an individual or society at large, if for no other reason than because the law making certain conduct criminal says so. Properly understood, however, a victimless crime is proscribed consensual conduct that causes no direct harm or threat of direct harm to others not engaged in the consensual activity.

The law provides that some individuals are incapable of giving consent under any circumstances and therefore need protection. Children, mentally ill or severely limited individuals, and those under legal restraint, are incapacitated. In some instances, consent is categorically prohibited. At common law and under certain antiquated statutes, suicide is a crime. At first glance, such a law is absurd because the perpetrator cannot be penalized. I surmise the justification for the offense originates in ancient property law rather than religious objection. Dueling was likewise outlawed because consent was forced upon one challenged by the threat of being branded a coward for refusing to engage in such self-defeating activity. Other than these exceptions, the law presumes consent, which of course is an exercise of freedom.

The prohibition of any activity categorically restricts freedom and enforcing such a restriction necessarily invades privacy. Such invasions include annoying and truly shameful activities ranging from the construction of peepholes in public toilets to the more pernicious practices of surveillance and monitoring of conversations, to betrayal by informants. Because privacy is essential to freedom, it is a value the legal process must measure as a cost of criminalizing certain kinds of activity. How that cost is measured is always a matter of dispute, primarily between those who most value freedom and those who place greater weight on order.

There are three basic matrices for resolving these disputes: The first deals with questions of fact, matters of what is and can be known, calling upon the courts to practice the discipline of epistemology. The second is the application of principles to those facts through the use of reason, which requires the discipline of logic. The third and most problematic is definition, calling for mastery of rhetoric. Professor Hardaway quotes John Stuart Mill that "wrong opinions and practices gradually yield to fact and argument." Only, he might have added, if the language used is shared. Eventually truth and reason will out.

Behind the problems of so-called victimless crimes is an absence of general legal philosophy which, in the words of Roscoe Pound, "gives us petty tinkering where comprehensive reform is needed." Professor Hardaway gives us that much needed comprehension in this book. *No Price Too High* provides a sense of the heft and purpose of the Ninth Amendment, a source of wisdom in this age of folly.

John L. Kane, Jr.

Acknowledgments

Although my name appears as author of this book, much of its content is the result of the collaborative efforts of a small army of research assistants and staff at the University of Denver College of Law who labored over a period of ten years to research and ferret out sources, data, statistics, and authorities which provide the basis for the conclusions set forth within. The following student research assistants were particularly contributive and in some cases submitted preliminary drafts of several sections of the final four chapters: Ted Burton, Molly Jensen, Holly Panetta, Chuck Piekanski, Chris Rossi, Corlese Henecke, Brook Woodward, Jennifer Cortese, Karina Condra, Steve Wienczkowski, Blake Harrison, and Jeremy Stevens. In particular I would like to thank my current student research assistant, Steven Camden, who not only provided invaluable research assistance, but also made extraordinary efforts checking citations and updating data during the final phases of the editorial process. Final conclusions expressed in the book are not necessarily those of these research assistants, and any errors in the text are mine alone.

I also thank Thistle Hill Publishing Services for helpful editorial guidance, and express my deepest appreciation and gratitude to former governor Gary E. Johnson of New Mexico and Federal Judge John Kane for taking time from their busy schedules to write the forewords.

Finally, I wish to express my deep gratitude for the research support provided by the University of Denver College of Law, and in particular both Chancellor Dean Ritchie of the University of Denver and Dean Mary Ricketson of the University of Denver College of Law.

CHAPTER 1

Defining the Victimless Crime

He who knows only his side of the case, knows little of that...(but) wrong opinions and practices gradually yield to fact and argument.

—John Stuart Mill [1]

Every year, more than 400,000 Americans die as the result of tobacco use.[2] In the last quarter of the twentieth century, alcohol use resulted in the deaths of another 110,640 Americans,[3] including 16,653 alcohol-related traffic deaths,[4] and was the major factor in 50.2 percent of all homicides, 52 percent of all rapes, 62 percent of assaults, and 30 percent of suicides. Illegal drug use caused 3,562 deaths.[5] Translated into deaths per 100,000 users, "tobacco kills 650, alcohol 150, heroin 80, cocaine 4."[6]

If a Martian were to visit the United States tomorrow and confront these statistics, the Martian might be surprised to learn that of these three substances, only drugs are criminalized. The Martian might also be surprised, indeed bewildered, to learn that although alcohol and tobacco are legal and even subsidized, American society willingly spends $80 billion annually, arrests and incarcerates hundreds of thousands of American citizens for drug offenses (utilizing more than half of America's jail capacity and thereby necessitating the early release of many murderers, rapists, and child-molesters), conducts thousands of wiretaps, imposes sentences up to and including life imprisonment without parole for possession of less than 1.5 pounds of certain illegal drugs,[7] forfeits billions of dollars in potential tax revenues to organized crime, and tolerates corruption and undermining of the political system—all to implement a drug war that has resulted in greater drug use after criminalization than before.

One might try to explain to the Martian that such extravagant human, social, and financial costs of criminalization (including thousands of drug-related murders and assaults) are fully justified in order to keep 3,562 Americans from possibly jeopardizing their health. After honestly conceding, however, that the harm done to most of those 3,562 Americans resulted from the effects of drug prohibition (such as contaminated drugs and unsterilized needles) rather than from the drug itself, the Martian might express even greater amazement.

We would have to admit that more than a fifth of all property crime (exceeding $4 billion in 1974) was committed by addicts seeking money for drugs made artificially expensive by prohibition (the profits going to finance organized crime and to corrupt public officials). Nor would we dare admit that 243 addicts committed more than 473,738 crimes and that 26 addicts (denied their drug by prohibitionists) commit 22 major crimes per day.[8] If we dared, we might attempt to lessen the strain on credibility by simply stating the moral conviction that no price is too high to pay to protect those 3,562 Americans from choosing to take drugs and possibly jeopardizing their health. (One observer has whimsically remarked that whoever those 3,562 privileged Americans are, they have launched more ships and caused the mobilization of more resources than the legendary Helen of Troy.)

America's drug laws might be difficult to explain to a Martian, but American policymakers have apparently had little difficulty in explaining them to American voters, the majority of whom overwhelmingly support such laws, or at least say they do. Although more than ninety million Americans, about 40 percent of the population, have used illegal drugs (including a former president, a former vice-president of the United States, and a former Speaker of the House),[9] and allegedly more than twenty-three million Americans have used them during the past month,[10] the American people's professed support continues for drug laws that include punishments as severe as life imprisonment without parole for possession of small amounts of drugs.[11]

In fact, as the chapters within will reveal, the vast majority of researchers and scholars who have addressed criminalization of victimless crimes have found the costs of criminalization too great and the results not only minimal but actually counterproductive to the professed goal. Indeed, the research for this book revealed a ratio greater than ten to one in scholarly articles advocating the legalization of drugs and prostitution.

Professor James Inciardi of the University of Delaware, one of the few American academics to oppose drug legalization, recently complained that former federal drug czar William Bennett "has virtually no (scholars) helping him" in opposing drug legalization.[12] Ethan Nadelmann, a Princeton professor, complains that it is harder and harder to find opponents to drug legalization to debate him.[13]

Politicians hardly need academic support to curry electoral favor in opposing drug law reform. Politicians find simplistic slogans far easier to dispense to constituents than the results of extensive empirical and scholarly research, and comparative studies. In 1994, former president Clinton was obliged to fire his surgeon general, Jocelyn Elders, for, among other offenses, suggesting that the scholarly debate over drug reform and legalization be discussed openly as a matter of public policy. George Schultz, former secretary of state under President Reagan, gave a speech on October 7, 1989, in which he said, "We need at least to consider and examine forms of controlled legalization of drugs."[14] Although Secretary Schultz was not fired for this sin, he did later add, "I find it very difficult to say that sometimes at a reception or cocktail party I advance these views and people head for somebody else. They don't even want to talk to you."[15]

So politically sensitive is the issue of drug legalization that when a 1979 congressional fact-finding committee looked into the properties of cocaine, a congressman interrupted a testifying expert about to volunteer his opinion about drug legalization by snapping, "I won't ask you that."[16] Apparently, the congressman could not risk the press reporting an expert's opinion on drug legalization expressed at a congressional hearing.

In view of present public perceptions, the evolution of sound policy for drug legalization may take as long as, or longer than the evolution of alcohol and tobacco legalization. Although today's generation takes for granted the legalization of liquor and tobacco, the prospects for legalizing liquor were once considered far more remote than today's prospects for drug legalization. The Prohibition Amendment to the Constitution passed on a wave of popular support. In 1930, Senator Morris Sheppard of Texas scoffed at those who urged alcohol legalization by asserting, "There is as much chance of repealing the Eighteenth Amendment as there is for a hummingbird to fly to the planet Mars with the Washington Monument tied to its tail."[17] Similar pronouncements were made with regard to legalizing tobacco by officials in those sixteen states that, prior to 1922, prohibited tobacco use.[18] Nevertheless, the path toward legalization of alcohol and tobacco in those states was a long and arduous one, completed only when the most obstinate opponents were finally convinced that prohibition's costs to society were too high, and the rewards of criminalization to organized crime too great.

The question remains how to explain American policy on victimless crimes, of which drug policy is but one. Many books and articles have been written on the individual topics of drugs, prostitution, and gambling. All three of these societal problems have occasioned vigorous debate on whether criminalization of each serves the interests of society. However, few scholarly and popular works now available have looked at all three problems from a common perspective. This book will compare the policy rationales for each of these societal problems with a view toward creating a general theory of decriminalization.

On the issue of decriminalization, proponents and opponents alike usually begin with a general discussion of the harm each creates in society. In this respect, useful historical comparisons can be made to past debates over such other victimless crimes as consensual homosexual conduct and contraceptive use.

CONTRACEPTIVE POLICY

Contraceptives, for example, were banned in the United States for many years. The U.S. Tariff Act of 1930 forbade the import of, among other articles, any writing urging treason, murder and, "...any drug or medicine or any article whatever for causing unlawful abortion...."[19] The fact that private use of contraceptive devices by consenting adults was considered a societal evil akin to murder reveals our society's frequent priority on keeping its members from engaging in private and consensual conduct the majority considers "immoral." Many state laws banning contraceptive use were even stricter than the federal law.[20] Laws against contraceptive use would probably still be in effect today if not for the 1965 Supreme Court case of *Griswold* v. *Connecticut,* which struck down a Connecticut law that made it a crime for consenting adults to use a contraceptive device. The Court held that such a ban violated a "zone of privacy created by several constitutional guarantees."[21] Despite the Griswold case, however, many state legislatures found contraceptive use so abhorrent that they made it a felony to "exhibit" contraceptive devices. In 1972, for example, a Massachusetts court convicted a man of a felony for giving a lecture on contraception to students at Boston University and for exhibiting and distributing a sample of Emko vaginal foam. The U.S. Supreme Court reversed the conviction for giving the lecture on contraception (on free speech grounds), but upheld the conviction for distributing the foam.[22]

As recently as 1971, the federal Comstock Act defined contraceptive material as "filthy and vile."[23] The Comstock law was named after Anthony Comstock, who introduced in Congress a bill to outlaw as unmailable any writing describing contraceptive methods and was later appointed as U.S. Postal Inspector. Comstock zealously pursued citizens whom he suspected of engaging in conduct which, though consensual, offended the morality of society. According to one historian, he enjoyed baiting doctors who engaged in promoting such activity. In one instance, he had two women associates write to a Midwestern physician, claiming that their husbands were insane and that they feared that any children might inherit their insanity. When the doctor wrote them simple advice (about contraceptive methods), Comstock had him arrested and sentenced to seven years of hard labor."[24]

The vigorous defenders of such anticontraception laws, much like those who defend drug laws today, strongly believed that preserving the very fabric of society depended upon preventing consenting adults from behaviors that, though voluntary, might harm themselves and potential life. Such views were apparent in laws that revealed a greater fear of what consenting adults might do in privacy than of harm to an unwilling victim. Blackstone, for example, wrote in his epic treatise on common law that the act of anal intercourse between consenting adults was a heinous offense of " ...deeper malignity than rape."[25] In 1986, Chief Justice Warren Burger of the U.S. Supreme Court approvingly cited this Blackstone quote in upholding a Georgia statute that imposed a twenty-year prison term at hard labor on any person who engaged in consensual anal intercourse with another person (including one's heterosexual spouse).[26]

SODOMY LAWS

As with laws against contraception, sodomy laws assume that a private act between consenting adults poses a more serious threat to society than acts of wanton violence upon unwilling victims. The former's theory of harm rests on a perceived societal need to free citizens from the very thought that others might be engaging in mutually agreeable but immoral conduct. Clearly, the common law doctrine that an act of anal intercourse between consenting adults is a greater threat to society than an act of brutal rape upon an unwilling victim is based on such a premise.

Were this common law premise a matter of theory only, the issue of decriminalization of victimless crimes would be of little but academic interest. In fact, however, the enforcement of most laws in the United States today is based on this very premise. In 1989, more than half of all scarce U.S. prison space held those convicted of crimes involving consensual conduct.[27] The cost of incarcerating more than one-third of a million inmates convicted of engaging in consensual acts related to drugs alone exceeded $8 billion (not counting the lost productivity and ruined lives of those incarcerated).[28] Arrests for consensual sexual acts between prostitutes and willing customers constitute half the total arrests in many major cities.[29]

SOCIETAL PRIORITIES

So committed are law enforcement officials to enforcing crimes involving consensual conduct, that they are prepared to give early release to the most vicious murderers and rapists to make in America's overcrowded prisons for those convicted of crimes involving consensual conduct. In many cases, even the most vicious and violent offenders receive probation or reduced charges or sentences to find room in the prisons for those convicted of such crimes as possessing a small amount of drugs.

In 1991, the U.S. Supreme Court upheld the mandatory sentence of a Michigan man sentenced to life imprisonment without possibility of parole for mere possession of a pound and a half of cocaine.[30] The fact that first-degree murderers often receive parole in as few as three and a half years, in order to make room for drug users, has little effect on the policy-makers responsible for protecting society. According to these policymak-ers, citizens suffer greater harm thinking about another citizen who is harming himself through willful drug use than citizens who are made per-sonally vulnerable to the ravages of the released murderer or rapist. The drug user and his family are believed less harmed by life imprisonment without parole than by the drug itself (although at much greater cost to the taxpayer).

EFFECTS ON LAW ENFORCEMENT

Randy Barnett, a former prosecutor and assistant state's attorney for Cook County, Illinois, recently described the devastating effect the "War on Drugs" had on the prosecution of violent crimes in his district. In 1979, before the crackdown on drug users, he handled between 125 and 135 cases. With such a relatively low caseload, he took to trial those charged with the most vicious and violent crimes, offering only those plea bargains that involved fair and correct sentences for those crimes. When the war on drugs set a new priority of cracking down on drug users, however, his caseload skyrocketed to more than 400. He then had no choice but to offer "giveaway" plea bargains to even the most violent offenders. He later con-cluded, "There is no such thing as a free crime. Every enforcement effort consumes scarce resources. The more conduct we define as criminal, the more that scarce resources have to be allocated selectively among different crimes."[31]

Unlike countries in which drugs and prostitution have been legalized, the United States has deliberately placed higher priority on enforcing con-sensual crimes than crimes involving helpless and brutalized victims. Two poignant cases that took place less than one year apart serve to illustrate this point.

In 1991, four popular students at a middle-class high school in Madison, Wisconsin, became jealous of another classmate's new blue jeans. They took her out in a car, locked her in the trunk, and for several hours amused themselves by beating, stabbing, and sodomizing her with a sharp tire iron. When their victim dared to beg for mercy and call out for her mother, her four classmates dragged her out of the trunk, sprayed Windex on her wounds, poured gasoline over her, and then burned their screaming class-mate to death. The ringleader later described what they had done by say-ing, "You should have seen it. It was so funny."[32] After the perpetrators were convicted of first-degree murder, the judge decided to relieve the burden on the overcrowded prison system by promising the chief perpe-trator of the crime that she "could do something useful with her life after being released from prison."[33] In response to a relatively light sentence received, one perpetrator said, "It's so stupid when you think about it. I don't blame me. We just need a little growing up."[34]

Under this nation's existing priorities, the early release of such defendants provides needed prison space for people like J. Harmelin. He was sentenced, the year before the Madison torture murders, by a Michigan court to a mandatory sentence of life imprisonment without the possibility of parole for possession of less than a pound and a half of cocaine.[35] Apparently, Mr. Harmelin could do nothing useful with his life after prison; policymakers decided it was necessary to incarcerate him for life in order to protect society. A half-million dollars was better spent incarcerating drug user Harmelin for life, it seems, than to parole him and make room for such violent offenders as the Madison torture murderers.

Indeed, under existing public attitudes, Mr. Harmelin may even have been fortunate to receive only a life sentence without parole. In 1989, federal drug czar William Bennett responded to a question about the feasibility of beheading drug offenders by stating, "Morally, I don't have any problem with it."[36] In the 1970s, several states' laws (including Georgia, Louisiana, and Missouri) proscribed the death penalty for youths older than eighteen who sold a marijuana cigarette to a youth under eighteen.[37] In Missouri, the sentence for a second possession of marijuana was life imprisonment without parole.[38] In California, a first offense of selling a marijuana cigarette carried a sentence of life imprisonment.[39]

THE RESULTS OF STIFF PENALTIES AND ENFORCEMENT

Those committed to continued criminalization of victimless crimes theorize that heavier penalties and enforcement of such laws will result in greater compliance. In this regard, it may be useful to again make some historical comparisons.

Consider the issue of legalized abortions. Setting aside, for the moment, the question of whether abortion is a societal evil requiring suppression, consider only the question of how suppression might best be accomplished. The Netherlands, for example, with contraception and abortion legal and available on demand, has the lowest abortion rate in the world.

Contrast this low rate, however, with the abortion rate in Romania under dictator Nicolae Ceausescu, who decreed abortion a serious state crime to be enforced by the secret police. (Indeed his abortion laws appeared to have been modeled after those of Nazi Germany, the only country in history to impose the death penalty for abortion.) Under Ceausescu's brutal regime, government agents (dubbed the "menstrual police" by some Romanians) rounded up women under the age of forty-five every three months and examined them for signs of pregnancy in the presence of agents. A pregnant woman who later failed to produce a baby at the proper time could expect to be summoned for investigation and interrogation by the secret police. Not surprisingly, abortion rates in Romania skyrocketed to the highest in Europe, with more than 60 percent of pregnancies ending in illegal abortion. In 1990, after Ceausescu was overthrown and the harsh abortion law overturned, *Newsweek* reported the poignant case of a young Romanian woman who was recovering from a self-induced abortion. "I could have killed Ceausescu for that (antiabortion) law alone," the suffering woman told a *Newsweek* reporter. "Now that it's possible to be a woman again, I'm mutilated."[40]

The effects of harsh U.S. drug laws and enforcement have had similar results. During the "Drug War" of the 1980s, the federal government extracted more than $20 billion from hapless taxpayers to fund antidrug activities and harsh law enforcement.[41] When millions of children went unvaccinated and millions of Americans were homeless, more than $10 billion was spent on drug enforcement in 1990 alone. The armed forces, including coast guard and air force auxiliaries, were mobilized in search and destroy missions and in radar and helicopter searches. U.S. troops were deployed to Colombia, and army helicopters dispatched to Bolivia. The Central Intelligence Agency and National Security Agency used spy satellites as part of the drug war. Drug arrests of American citizens doubled to more than 852,000 in 1989, causing the already bursting U.S. prison system to turn away violent offenders and give early release to many murderers, rapists, and child molesters.[42] When the National Guard was mobilized in forty-one states, domestic wiretap authorizations skyrocketed. Similar to Ceausescu's antiabortion laws, U.S. drug laws became progressively stricter in congressional legislation enacted in 1984, 1986, and 1988.

And what was the result of such massive expenditures of public treasure, wiretaps, privacy intrusions, early release of violent offenders, and incarceration of hundreds of thousands of American citizens for drug use? Like the increased number of abortions that resulted from Ceausescu's harsh antiabortion laws, drug use increased dramatically. In 1990, the U.S. State Department reported that world production and consumption of drugs had climbed to the highest levels in history.[43] In such major cities as New York and Washington, D.C., police officials reported no discernible reduction in drug sales.[44] Perhaps the most disturbing result of the drug war, however, is that the United States, with 5 percent of the world's population, now consumes more than 50 percent of cocaine production—a figure (never approached) when cocaine was legal in the United States.[45]

The Netherlands again provides a useful basis for comparison. Arnold Trebach's monumental study of drug usage around the world reveals that drug usage in the Netherlands declined dramatically after marijuana use was decriminalized in 1976.[46] Teen marijuana use dropped by a staggering 33 percent after legalization.[47] By 1985, only one-half of one percent of

Dutch high school students used marijuana, compared to more than five percent in the United States.[48] Although the Netherlands is known for having liberal drug laws, a recent study concluded that the Netherlands had "the lowest number of addicts in Europe and the lowest proportion of AIDS patients (3 percent) who are intravenous drug users."[49] A policy of heroin maintenance in Great Britain has resulted in a heroin addiction rate less than a third of that in the United States,[50] and drug-related crime is virtually nonexistent.[51]

In contrast to the United States, countries with legalized drugs have one policy view in common, namely that a small amount spent on education and treatment can have a greater effect on reducing drug addiction than a vast amount spent on arrest, incarceration, military mobilizations, and wiretaps. Indeed, the money spent on enforcing drug laws can increase, rather than reduce the rate of addiction.

In the United States, a study by James Ostrowski revealed that when marijuana use was legalized in Alaska, use by high school seniors declined to 4 percent compared to a 6.3 percent rate in other states where such drug use was illegal (and punishable by up to life in prison without parole).[52] According to William Chambliss' monumental study of drug laws in the United States, "Use of marijuana actually declines after legalization."[53]

Opponents of legalization rarely consider the possibility that drug use might actually decline as a result of decriminalization. Often, no amount of data, studies, or experience from other countries can convince the proponents of legalization otherwise. The theory, of course, is that the lure of drugs is so overwhelming that if they were legalized, citizens from all walks of life who never before used drugs would leap at the chance. Various reasons explain why this does not occur, not the least of which is simple common sense. Indeed, as discussed in chapter 3 of this book, drug use in the United States became a serious problem only when it was criminalized, just as abortion in Romania became pandemic when so brutally suppressed by Ceausescu.

It is true that some surveys reveal a possible small degree of curiosity usage immediately after decriminalization, which almost certainly would not exist had the drug not been previously criminalized. A study conducted by the National Commission on Marijuana and Drug Abuse in 1972 revealed that 3 percent of adults who did not use drugs indicated that they might try the drug if it were decriminalized.[54] Another study revealed that 4 percent might try cocaine.[55] If one were to assume the worst possible scenario, that 4 percent of Americans would try and become addicted to drugs if legalized, this would increase annual drug-use deaths to 3,703, still less than 1 percent of the 550,000 deaths caused by alcohol and tobacco use. However, this figure would be curtailed by the thousands of lives saved by the availability of uncontaminated supplies, clean needles, and fewer drug-related crimes and murders. Nevertheless, proponents of continued enforcement of the harshest drug laws propound that even an extreme 1 percent increase in addicts is hardly an indication of the national disaster that would result from decriminalization. Yet, studies conducted in countries with legalized drugs reveal that legalization is much more likely to result in lower levels of drug use and far lower levels of drug abuse.

Milton Friedman, winner of the Nobel Prize in economics, has explained why legalization often results in reduced usage. As his study on the question reveals, the very fact that a drug is illegal makes it attractive as a "forbidden fruit."[56] This alone might explain why marijuana usage among high school students in Alaska was so much lower than in other states where marijuana was illegal.

A study by Walter Block has offered a similar explanation as to why drug use declines after a drug is legalized. According to his study, the very illegality of a drug "increases its attractions to so many people. If taking heroin were perceived merely to be stupid...instead of dangerous, because illegal, fewer would take it."[57] He concludes that criminalization only plays into the hands of the criminal element: "Better to ruin their business by deflating the profit balloon than by acting in a way (prohibition) which only supports them."[58] Other explanations, however, carry equal importance.

A perverse effect of U.S. drug enforcement policies is that even modest enforcement victories serve to intensify the drug problem. For example, after spending billions of dollars on the drug war, federal enforcement agencies claimed as the fruits of victory that up to 5 percent of drug imports had been intercepted. What those enforcers did not realize, however, was even this small "victory" did nothing except raise the price of the prohibited drugs, increase the profit margin for drug dealers, and send an economic signal to drug producers to increase production (which, of course, is exactly what happened). As Walter Block has observed, "Every time a battle is won in the [drug war], paradoxically, the enemy is strengthened, not weakened. [Interdiction] only succeeds in raising the profit motives attendant upon production. Thus, the more vigorous and successful the activities of the Drug Enforcement Administration, the greater the strength of the illicit drug industry."[59]

A study by Steven Wisotsky has revealed the relationship between the illegality of a drug and its price.[60] The study cites the price in 1981 for an ounce of pharmaceutical cocaine hydrochloride produced by a major U.S. pharmaceutical company as being about $1.80 per gram.[61] That same year, the Drug Enforcement Administration estimated a street price for cocaine of more than $55,000 per kilogram. Taking into account differences in purity, the study concluded that the criminal law had succeeded in "taxing cocaine about $800 per gram, or about $22,350 per ounce...thereby making the illegal [production of cocaine] extraordinarily profitable. "It has been estimated that the total premium over actual cost of production exceeds $72 billion annually—almost all of which goes to support and promote criminal activity instead of to education and drug treatment programs."[62]

Higher prices also have another effect—on the user. Instead of only having to burglarize two homes a week to earn enough money to support a habit, an addict might have to burglarize six homes a week to earn enough to pay the higher price for the drug. A study by the Drug Abuse Council revealed that for every 10 percent increase in the price of heroin, crime increased by 2.87 percent.[63] In Washington, D.C., the murder rate doubled after police began to step up drug law enforcement. [64] Thus, even a modest "victory" claimed by those conducting the drug war has the direct result of increasing crime—a result felt by every American, rich or poor.

The costly drug enforcement "victory" has four major consequences: (1) it increases profit to the drug dealer and helps support the lavish tax-free lifestyle of the privileged few; (2) it diverts $72 billion in potential taxes away from the government (which could be used for education and drug treatment programs) to organized crime where it is sure to be used for a variety of criminal purposes; (3) it increases the economic incentives of drug producers to increase drug production; and, (4) it instigates the addict to increase the number of violent and property crimes committed to support a habit. An analysis of Federal Bureau of Investigation statistics reveals that addicts deprived of their drug commit more than four million crimes a year, steal $7.5 billion in property. They commit 1,600 murders in order to earn the money to pay the high drug prices created by prohibition.[65]

Criminalization apologists prefer to ignore these real and documented consequences. Instead, they seek to justify the billions of dollars spent on the drug war by expressing the forlorn hope that if prices rise, perhaps fewer people will want to use them. The problem with such a simplistic rationale for this wasteful expenditure of taxpayers' billions is that drugs are not toothbrushes. An economist would explain that the demand for drugs is inelastic. People do not go bargain hunting when contemplating drug use. They do not say, "I really want to use drugs, but the price is a little too high today, so I guess I won't." In any case, a first-time user may be offered the drug for free. An addict does not give up the addiction because drug prices increase, but instead will simply commit more crimes to support the habit. In short, the apologist's rationale is either deliberately specious or it reveals a tragic misunderstanding of the true causes of drug addiction.

THE CAUSES OF DRUG ADDICTION

Both advocates and opponents of drug legalization are apt to begin their argument with a statement as to the evils of drug use and the adverse effects of addictive drugs on the human body. Certainly, the deaths of 3,562 people from drug abuse supports the view that drug abuse is harmful. Opponents rely on the harmful effects of drugs to justify criminalization and enforcement even at extravagant human and social cost. However, many advocates of legalization also rely on the fact that drugs are harmful to justify their view that drugs should be legalized, pointing out that criminalization has historically resulted in higher rates of addiction. It also diverts scarce societal resources away from education and treatment programs, which have proven far more effective than criminalization in reducing rates of addiction. These advocates may also point out the inconsistency in laws that support and even subsidize tobacco and alcohol use, which lead to the deaths of more than 100 times as many people as drugs kill.

Most advocates of legalization, however, have several reasons for not resting their cases primarily on the assumption that legalization will reduce rates of addiction. First, this point fails to persuade opponents of legalization. As has been seen, no amount of data, empirical, historical, or comparative can persuade an opponent who clings to cherished preconceptions about the effects of harsh laws and enforcement on rates of drug use. To be fair to such opponents, it should also be noted that not all studies unambiguously support the view that legalization would result in reduced levels of drug abuse. An example is the study discussed above that suggested at least some curiosity use of drugs after legalization by first-time users.

Most legalization advocates rely primarily on an evaluation of societal priorities. They concede that although illicit drugs are harmful and may cause deaths, tobacco and alcohol are more harmful and cause more deaths and yet are legal. Legalization advocates also point out that the costs of criminalization (increased drug-related crime, diversion of valuable resources to organized crime, monopolization of scarce prison resources and early release of violent offenders, corruption of government) vastly exceed any possible benefit in terms of possibly keeping 3,562 people from voluntarily jeopardizing their health. This is clearly the advocate's strongest argument in favor of decriminalization and will be the primary focus of the remaining chapters in this book.

Advocates of legalization often use less than persuasive arguments, and in fact may undermine the more persuasive line of argument regarding societal priorities. They often argue that such drugs as marijuana, cocaine, and heroin are not in fact harmful. Aside from the fact that such an argument will never persuade opponents of legalization, many of whom believe that private drug use is the moral equivalent of first-degree murder, it detracts from the force of the argument based on societal priorities. Most advocates of drug legalization also favor the continued legalization of tobacco and alcohol and are content to note the much higher number of deaths resulting from tobacco and alcohol use than from drug use. Advocates extrapolate from that glaring discrepancy that drugs should be legalized for the same reasons that tobacco and alcohol are legalized.

Nevertheless, a discussion of the harmful effect of drugs is useful in understanding the causes of addiction (which in turn are relevant to evaluating the effectiveness of enforcement programs) and for that reason are reviewed briefly here.

MARIJUANA

Those who claim that drug use is harmless make their strongest case with marijuana. Andrew Weil, who conducted the first modern studies on marijuana use, states that marijuana is an "active placebo"[66] that produces "trivial effects."[67] Other more recent studies have revealed that though it is used for a variety of purposes ranging from stimulation to relaxation, marijuana tends to have "whatever effects a user wants."[68] A study of the effects of marijuana on driving revealed the commission of the same number of driving errors by those who had heavily smoked marijuana as by those who had not taken the drug. The experimenter who conducted the study remarked that "this result is puzzling because of the elaborate efforts made in this study to maximize marijuana intoxication."[69]

Indeed, the lack of evidence of toxicity has frustrated attempts to calculate a lethal dose. The best that experimenters have managed is to extrapolate from animal experiments that "a person might die after eating 24 ounces all at once."[70] Unfortunately for advocates of criminalization, however, it appears that more people have died from drinking too many glasses of water at once than from ingesting too much marijuana.[71]

The 1986 Drug Abuse Warning Network reported that traces of marijuana were implicated in 12 fatalities.[72] However, this did not mean that marijuana was responsible for the deaths, but only that traces were found. In any case, aspirin traces were implicated in a greater number of deaths than marijuana. A study conducted by researchers Steven Duke and Albert Gross concluded flatly that "no death from a marijuana overdose has ever been established."[73]

Such experimental evidence hardly justifies laws imposing life imprisonment on marijuana users, but legalization opponents have attempted to justify criminalization on grounds that it might provide a transition to more harmful drugs. Although no reliable evidence has supported this contention, even if true it would prove little because studies have shown that tobacco and alcohol are the classic gateway drugs to more harmful drugs.[74] One early study even concluded that coffee drinking leads to opium use,[75] while another has concluded that tobacco use leads to opium smoking. Whatever the merit of such studies, however, the *Wootton Report* issued by the British government concluded that "marijuana found no progression to heroin in any country."[76]

None of these studies and evidence has had any noticeable effect on governmental authorities. In 1987, more than 400,000 Americans were arrested for possessing marijuana, clogging the court system, causing the release of thousands of violent offenders, and making a virtual mockery of the integrity of the U.S. justice system.

In any case, it has already been noted that alcohol was a major factor in 23,987 traffic deaths (about half the total traffic fatalities), more than half of the murders and rapes, 62 percent of assaults, and 30 percent of suicides. If policymakers can justify life imprisonment without parole for marijuana use, one shudders to think what punishment they would impose were marijuana to prove a factor in as many crimes as alcohol.

COCAINE

Opponents of drug legalization often buttress their arguments by conjuring up the probable national disaster if cocaine were legal. However, we need not speculate as to how the legalization of cocaine would affect society; we have an actual historical comparison available. Before 1914, cocaine and opiates were completely legal in almost all jurisdictions of the United States[77] and available over the counter at pharmacies, general stores, and grocery stores.[78] Indeed, it could be ordered through mail-order houses.[79] Cocaine was widely distributed and consumed in soft drinks, cough syrups, and the like. Indeed, the public attitude toward cocaine resembled that of tobacco today. Although it was recognized that some people might become addicted, people did not lose their jobs or lose their children because they were addicted to cocaine.

Several studies have revealed why cocaine accessibility prior to 1914 did not create societal problems. At low dosages, studies reveal that users cannot tell the difference between cocaine and a placebo.[80] Another study of typical cocaine users revealed a cocaine user who used cocaine daily for fifty-five years. She would switch to aspirin when her cocaine supply ran short.[81] At consumption levels of two grams per week, one comprehensive study revealed "no organic, mental, or social deterioration," and that "persons can sniff or smoke crack without becoming addicted and without losing social productivity."[82]

Besides consensus that cocaine addiction is not pharmacological,[83] the American Psychiatric Association in 1987 claimed to have found evidence of "cocaine dependence" based on psychological criteria that did not include criteria of physical dependence.[84] Others have claimed to find a "physiological" dependence on cocaine in the sense that a person becomes temporarily sick when drug use ceases, but recovers when drug use is resumed. As researcher Richard Miller has pointed out, however, "by such a definition a diabetes sufferer is addicted to insulin, an asthma sufferer is addicted to theophylline, (and) a headache sufferer is addicted to aspirin."[85]

It requires a great leap of logic, however, to conclude that a person who needs aspirin to avoid headaches is an "addict," or that such an "aspirin addict" is a threat to society if he doesn't get his "fix." One might, however, argue that a person with a terrible headache might be more likely to perform an antisocial act.

Readers of the Sherlock Holmes mysteries may recall the fabled detective's cocaine use. A study of cocaine users in Canada revealed that the typical cocaine user used the drug in much the same way as Sherlock Holmes. That is, he "rarely kept a supply of the drug, normally bought only 1 to 3 grams in a single purchase, made no more than four purchases per year, and took a dose less than once a month."[86] A study conducted in the early 1980s at a California clinic gave cocaine to 200 volunteers. Not a single one became an addict."[87]

While it is certainly true that cocaine users can become psychologically addicted, the degree of potential addiction pales when compared to that of cigarettes. While a survey of cocaine users revealed that 3.8 percent had tried to give it up but failed, a survey of tobacco users revealed that 18 percent had tried to quit but failed.

Given the results of such studies on cocaine, it is understandable that cocaine use was not a problem prior to its criminalization in 1914. Criminalization, however, changed everything. One reason for that change can be found in a phenomenon that also occurred during the period of alcohol prohibition.

Prior to alcohol prohibition, most alcohol consumption in the United States was of the milder forms of alcohol, such as beer and wine. After criminalization, however, bootleggers discovered, in comparison to such harder and more concentrated liquors as whiskey and bourbon, that beer and wine were too bulky, difficult to store clandestinely, and transport. Bootlegging wine and beer yielded insufficient profits to justify the risks of illegal distribution. As a result, national alcohol consumption patterns soon shifted to hard liquor. Not surprisingly, alcohol poisoning among consumers also rose dramatically with no government regulatory body to oversee and prevent the abasement and contamination of the hard liquor supply.[88]

A similar phenomenon occurred after the criminalization of cocaine, which had been based less on scientific considerations than on political ones. In considering grounds for criminalization, Congress in 1910 took into account testimony that "colored people seem to have a weakness for [cocaine].... They would just as soon rape a woman as anything else," and that "'Jew peddlers" were exploiting African Americans by selling them cocaine.[89] Congressman Hamilton Wright urged criminalization of cocaine on the grounds that it turned African Americans into rapists of white women.[90]

Criminalization based on such a rationale inevitably changed the public view of cocaine. As with alcohol under prohibition, cocaine soon became

adulterated and altered into more concentrated and dangerous forms. By
the 1980s, such adulterated and concentrated forms as "crack" were finding their way into the inner cities. But it took a much shorter time for criminalization to perform its deadly work of creating a problem where none
had existed before. In the 1920s Congressman Richard Hobson declared
that "ten years ago, [before criminalization] the narcotic drug addiction
problem was a minor medical problem. Today, it is a major national problem, constituting the chief factor menacing public health."[91]

While it is true the unregulated abuse of cocaine today results in four
deaths per 100,000 users[92] (compared to 650 per 100,000 tobacco users), the
most deadly consequences flow directly from its criminalization. It has
already been noted, for example, that more than 4 million crimes a year,
including more than 1,600 murders, are committed by drug dealers and
users who are denied any legal means of obtaining their drug. But other
social consequences of criminalization are equally tragic. At a time when
African Americans continue their struggle for economic opportunities, 90
percent of those actually prosecuted for drug-related offenses are African
Americans.[93] The devastating impact this has on the families, social fabric,
and economic opportunities of African Americans is so enormous, it is
almost impossible to measure. These tragic consequences of cocaine criminalization provide an excellent reason why even tobacco, which has
much higher death and addiction rates than cocaine, should also remain
legal.

An interesting case study of the effects of prohibiting tobacco is provided by the experiment of a Vermont prison that in 1992 attempted to
prohibit tobacco use by inmates. Prison authorities have more power and
control than could ever be exerted over citizens at liberty. Yet, in the prison
where cigarette prohibition was introduced, a black market in cigarettes
emerged virtually overnight in which the price of a cigarette rose to 2,000
percent of its market value. So desperate were tobacco addicts to get their
"fix," that incidents of violence and disruptive behavior skyrocketed, and
prisoners began to exchange drugs and sex for tobacco. In November
1992, Vermont wisely rescinded its tobacco prohibition policy.[94]

Similar effects were observed in Europe after World War II. Cigarettes
were so scarce that "nicotine addicts reduced themselves to depravity.
They became liars and thieves, bargained treasured possessions, traded
away food, though they were already underfed, [and]...women smokers
resorted to prostitution."[95]

The many cultural changes in society over time make it impossible to
form precise comparisons of drug use rates before and after criminalization. One critic perhaps put it best when he observed:

We do not know how many people used drugs in that era; estimates vary wildly.
Perhaps the number was small; if so, free access did not lead to widespread use.
Perhaps the number was large; if so, the nation nonetheless prospered and normal

family life continued. We do know that no drug houses blighted neighborhoods, no drug gangs had street corner shoot-outs, "drug-related" crime did not exist, and people lived ordinary middle class lives while consuming drugs avidly. We are talking about twentieth-century America, just before World War I, a country with great urban centers suffering from most problems known today and even from some that have since ended. Our own history proves that we have nothing to fear from legalizing drugs, and much to gain.[96]

In short, perhaps no other action by government has had such a devastating effect on its own people than the criminalization of drugs, particularly cocaine.

HEROIN

Like cocaine, opiates were legal in the United States until the early twentieth century. The first anti-opium laws were passed in California as an anti-Chinese measure based on the rationale that such laws were necessary to prevent the seduction of white women in opium dens. Just as the criminalization of liquor during prohibition resulted in increased production and consumption of hard liquor (as a percentage of total consumption), so the criminalization of opium, and the congressional ban on its import in 1909 led to the creation of a domestic heroin industry.[97] Before the criminalization of opium, hundreds of over-the-counter remedies (such as Mrs. Winslow's Soothing Syrup) contained psychoactive drugs. Many Americans consumed these drugs without apparent disaster to the republic.

The millions of users of mild opiates did so without being associated with the crime, disease, murder, and violence associated with its use since criminalization. Even among those who eventually became dependent on opium, most opium users led normal and productive lives, just as many users of alcohol do today. Indeed, doctors considered alcohol so much more destructive than opium, that they often prescribed opium as treatment for alcoholism.[98]

Although legalization opponents have attempted to resurrect the caricature of dazed and shiftless society dropouts lounging around smoke-filled opium dens, the perception before criminalization was different. Indeed, labor leader Samuel Gompers led the movement toward criminalization on grounds that the use of "opium gave the Chinese immigrant workers an unfair advantage in the labor market. The Chinese were said to be able to work longer and harder because of the drug."[99]

By 1906, when doctors began to realize that opium could also be addictive (though not as addictive as tobacco or as destructive as alcohol), they began to moderate the number of prescriptions they wrote for patients. In that same year, the government passed one of the few constructive statutes in the long tragic history of drug control. The Federal Pure Food and Drug Act required that any over-the-counter drug products disclose how much cocaine and opium they contained. The result was one of the most dramatic reductions in opium and cocaine use in the history of the Republic.[100] Had government at that point continued in the direction of education and treatment rather than criminalization, drug use would almost certainly have diminished, perhaps to the point where only the stupid and foolhardy would have continued to use them. With no attraction for organized crime, the nation's subsequent tragic history of crime, violence, and self-defeating expenditures of the national treasure might have been avoided.

Tobacco provides a useful comparison in assessing the effectiveness of education programs. Prior to 1922, only thirty-four states permitted the smoking of tobacco.[101] All the remaining states provided for criminal sanctions for smoking a cigarette. Opponents of legalization of cigarettes argued vigorously (as opponents to drug legalization do today) that legalization might result in more people smoking cigarettes. In the case of tobacco, despite its greater health dangers, states rejected the criminalization approach, and by 1922, all states had legalized the smoking of cigarettes. An education program, begun in earnest in the mid-1960s with the *Surgeon General's Report*, has succeeded in reducing tobacco smoking far more than criminalization has inhibited drug use. Between 1965 and 1987, for example, numbers of male smokers declined 36 percent and adult smoker numbers dropped by 28 percent.[102] Smoking has now been banned on all domestic airline flights and in many public places and provides substantial revenue to the government in the form of taxes.

As with cocaine and marijuana and liquor in prohibition, criminalization of opium served to channel consumption to the more concentrated and virulent derivatives of opium, such as heroin. Even heroin use does not involve physical dependence, but, without heroin, addicts do "get sick but soon get better and recover. Heroin users never have an organic need for the substance; that is why some drug abuse treatments seek abstinence, because heroin users have no physical need for the drug."[103]

Although legalization opponents fear that drug use will increase if drugs are legalized, research reveals that "opiates have less appeal than many antidrug zealots claim. Experimenters who give heroin and morphine injections to subjects report that hardly anyone finds the effects desirable; and almost everyone expresses indifference or dislike."[104] In order to reach a state of physical resonance, many users become nauseated after taking an intoxicating dose. As one observer of addicts observed, "Learning the joys of nausea takes fortitude."[105]

One study reported a double-blind test of twenty nonaddicted volunteers. Less than half of volunteers given an opiate experienced any kind of euphoria, and most volunteers reported the experience as distinctly unpleasant. Indeed, the "pleasure score" of those given heroin was lower than those given a placebo.[106] The great majority of medical students who have tried heroin report that they "found it difficult to understand why anyone would ever become addicted."[107] A study by McAuliffe of 150 postoperative patients given an opiate revealed that only fourteen experienced a euphoric effect, and of these eleven indicated that the "euphoria" came primarily from the relief of postoperative pain.[108]

Contrary to the popular notion that heroin addicts are dysfunctional, "British physician addicts have been allowed to continue their medical practices and treat patients."[109] In the United States, a noted doctor was known to have taken opium derivative for sixty-two years without noticeable impairment of physical or mental abilities.

In 1971, the general counsel for the District of Columbia Police Department discovered that more than 100 police officers had been taking heroin for extended periods of time. The officers were discovered, however, not because of poor work performance, but only after urine samples were taken.[110] Another study reports the case of an engineer for the New York Central railroad who never missed a run during twenty years of morphine use.[111]

None of these studies suggests that heroin use is desirable, and doctors no longer recommend opium to cure garden-variety physical ailments. Just as a diabetic needs insulin to keep from becoming ill, a heroin addict needs an opiate to avoid sickness. However, like its more destructive alcohol cousin and more addictive tobacco cousin, heroin use is best discouraged thorough a comprehensive education and treatment program. The most effective source of funds for such programs could come from a tax on its use. Under present policy, all such potential revenues are instead channeled toward drug kingpins and organized crime. What funds remain are directed primarily toward the drug war, every victory in which serves to increase the profits flowing to organized crime and drug producers.

DRUG USE IN CONTEMPORARY SOCIETY

Once the effects of drugs are understood, the causes of addiction can also be better understood. The typical heroin user is not a successful doctor, lawyer, or businessperson, but rather one who has no meaningful focus in life. Geoffrey Pearson's study of social deprivation concluded that:

(D)rugs offer to people meaningful structures around which to organize their lives in an eventful and challenging way. In the absence of competing routines and structures of meaning and identity, such as might be supplied by work commitments, we can then say it will not only be more difficult to 'come off' and 'stay off' heroin by breaking out of its routines and replacing them with alternative patterns of daily activity. It will also be more likely that a novice user will establish a pattern of habitual heroin use in the first place. Heroin is not instantly addictive, and it is necessary to work quite hard at becoming a heroin addict: that is to say, the drug will need to have been taken regularly on a daily basis for some length of time before the onset of dependence.[112]

Although a nonaddict might find it difficult to imagine why anyone would "work quite hard" to become a drug addict, understanding the causes of addiction requires understanding the role criminalization has played in the creation of a drug culture. In some South American countries, an underclass neglected by corrupt and inefficient government has found champions of their cause among the drug lords. It should not be surprising to learn that in the United States, a disproportionate number of users are economically deprived and underprivileged African Americans. In economically depressed areas, drug dealers cater to their customers in the inner cities—areas where refrigerator and mutual fund salespeople are unlikely to tread. Drug dealing provides a means of making a living for those without the education or economic opportunities to make a satisfactory living in any other way. The profession of drug dealing would not exist in the absence of criminalization. Inner city drug dealing would pay less than flipping hamburgers at McDonalds, a job many inner city residents reject in favor of illicit drug dealing, which can earn them thousands of dollars in a week. In short, illegal drugs provide the societal "structure" for which little alternative is provided. Society's tragic "solution" is to promote and foster this drug culture through criminalization. In short, criminalization provides a financial and social "bonus" to those in society willing to use violence to earn a living.

THE VICTIMLESS CRIME

Under the strictest definition, there is no such thing as a victimless crime. For example, many of the economic laws in the Soviet Union (before its collapse) made it a crime for any person to sell a good to another for a profit. Soviet bureaucrats denied that such a crime was without a victim. They would explain that the purchaser was the "victim" of the seller, who exploited his labor and took advantage of him. The degree of exploitation manifested itself in the amount of profit. The fact that the buyer was a willing participant acting in his own perceived best interest made no difference in defining the crime. The government had decided the buyer was a victim and would brook no protest otherwise, even by the buyer.

In the same way, a Massachusetts law forbidding a husband and wife from having intercourse in any way other than a supine position was not considered a victimless crime by those applying the strictest definition. Under their definition, the victims of such a crime were the participants, who were ruining themselves morally by engaging in such conduct. Today, Georgia has a similar statute that provides for twenty years' imprisonment for the act of having oral sex with one's spouse.[113]

The crime of using contraceptives in Connecticut was in many state legislators' opinions not a victimless crime because available contraceptives were thought to encourage promiscuity by taking away the "punishment" of having a child. The victims were the perpetrators who degraded themselves by using the contraceptive with their spouse in the privacy of their home. As in the case of the Soviet view of the crime of selling a good, the government of Connecticut did not consider consent in using contraception a relevant factor in determining whether the crime had a victim.

A more liberal definition of a victimless crime will include acts violating such laws as those prohibiting race car driving, trapeze acrobatics, coal mining, and skydiving. While such activities are entirely consensual, they nevertheless involve a real danger to the person who participates in them. The theory of those who criminalize such activities is that the victim is the participant who endangers himself by engaging in such activities.

A better definition of the victimless crime focuses on the nature of the consensual activity proscribed and addresses the issue of harm to others than those engaged in the consensual activity. For example, skydiving off a building in lower downtown Manhattan might be prohibited on grounds of grave potential harm to someone other than the skydiver (such as pedestrians on the street). Skydiving in the desert might also be regulated by the imposition of certain safety requirements. Ultimately, however, the consensual act of skydiving would not be absolutely prohibited if it posed no threat to anyone other than the skydiver.

Under the definition proposed, tobacco and alcohol use are considered consensual and victimless activities. This is not to say that use should not be regulated. Strong evidence indicates that passive tobacco smoke has serious adverse health consequences on innocent bystanders. However, this can be dealt with by prohibiting smoking on planes and public transportation, and in public buildings and the like. The fact remains, however, that the vast majority of the 400,000 annual smoking-death victims are those who, knowing the dangers, choose to engage in tobacco use.

Alcohol use presents a weaker case for legalization. When alcohol is a major factor in more than 50 percent of murders and 62 percent of assaults committed in the United States, it is more difficult to rationalize legalization on grounds of a lack of victims. However, even these tragic figures, combined with the harm done to alcohol abusers themselves, do not support a case for outright prohibition. As the following chapter reveals, the costs to society during the prohibition era vastly outweighed the modest benefits of reduced alcohol consumption.

The weakest case of all for criminalization, of course, is drug use. The harm to the user, while it exists, is minimal compared to the harm done to users of tobacco and alcohol. The harm to third parties is the consequence of criminalization itself: the crimes committed by addicts seeking money to buy their drugs and the violence committed by drug dealers. In short, drug use provides the classic example of a victimless crime, with the possible exception of consensual contraception and sexual acts between spouses.

It remains now to apply this definition of victimless crimes to the two other topics of this book, prostitution and gambling. First, however, two final consequences of the criminalization of the victimless crime are considered.

INVASIONS OF PRIVACY

By definition, the victimless crime lacks a complainant. In the classic case of a crime involving a victim, such as robbery or assault, the existence of the crime is brought to the attention of the authorities by a complainant. A victimless crime, however, is not so easily discovered. The authorities must actively seek evidence of the crime's existence despite the lack of any complainant who alleges harm.

A variety of methods are employed to discover the existence of the victimless crime, ranging from confidential informants, covert surveillance, and wiretaps, to searches of private homes. In extreme invasions of privacy, a high-powered telescope might be used to peer into a home to find evidence that a husband and wife are engaging in oral sex.

In a case of a man arrested in a Denver suburb in 1980, the police made peepholes in the ceiling of the public restroom in a local mall in order to observe possible drug transactions. Surveillance that involved peering at hundreds of law-abiding citizens in various states of undress using the toilets in the supposed privacy of locked stalls was apparently considered a small price to pay for the opportunity to observe a possible drug transaction. The police force's hard work finally paid off, however, when they saw and arrested a man for masturbating in the privacy of his locked toilet stall.[114] The surveillance, of course, was justified on grounds that it occurred in a public place.

As demonstrated by this occurrence, drug apprehension measures are not limited to those actually involved in drug transactions. Existing civil penalties permit the seizure of any property on which drugs have been used, regardless of whether the property owner is aware of any drug transactions. Under such laws, the owner who rents an automobile or boat to another who then uses drugs in that automobile or boat is subject to property seizure without compensation. This is true even though the owner had no knowledge that the renter would use drugs on his or her property.

It is unfortunate that criminalization advocates have been so successful in convincing the voters that drug use should be suppressed at all costs, that those same voters have been willing to suffer the kinds of privacy invasions permitted under current law.

HEALTH CONSEQUENCES AND AIDS

One common mode of transmission of the acquired immune deficiency syndrome (AIDS) virus is through shared drug injection needles contaminated with infected blood. As of 1992, about a third of AIDS cases in the United States resulted from shared needles.[115] More than half of the AIDS cases that resulted from heterosexual contact involved sex with an injection drug user.[116] Because drug use is criminalized in the United States, only 10 to 20 percent of injection drug users are in treatment at any given time.[117] Of those not in treatment, 78 percent share drug injection equipment with another intravenous user, including 20 percent who shared needles with total strangers.[118]

Thus, a heterosexual person who never uses drugs can acquire the AIDS virus by simply having sex with a person who once was an injection drug user. Also, drug-using mothers transmit the virus to their innocent children.

The threat of transmitting such a deadly virus as AIDS to the general population of heterosexuals who do not use drugs might be enough to trigger a rethinking of America's tragic drug criminalization laws. If drugs were legalized, drug users would have no fear of seeking treatment or obtaining sterilized needles, and the spread of AIDS to the general population could be greatly inhibited if not prevented completely.

Such a prediction fails to take into account policymakers' "no price is too high" philosophy. A 1990 congressional study reported why proposals for needle distribution have been consistently rejected: "(P)roviding injection equipment sends the wrong message, since abstinence from drug use is inconsistent with the exchange of needles." Not even the deaths of thousands of innocent children have been enough to soften the hearts of policymakers determined to prohibit at all costs the possession of drug injection equipment.

Currently, forty-eight states and the District of Columbia have laws based on a DEA model law prohibiting the possession of drug injection equipment.[119] The results of such laws have been tragic indeed. Because possession of injection equipment is illegal, addicts rarely carry them. As Feldman and Biernacki have reported, "The illegality of possessing hypodermic syringes...accounts for the unpredictable supply of hypodermic syringes, the chronic fear of arrest, and the necessity of constructing social arrangements that involve needle sharing."[120] One drug user confided to a researcher, "One thing you will not catch is someone just walking around carrying a needle. You'll catch them with dope before you'll catch them with a needle."[121]

A survey of twenty-four injectors revealed that twenty-three did not carry syringes because of the fear of arrest.[122] A study by Booth and Koester has revealed that injected drug users "frequently found themselves in situations where they used whatever syringe was available."[123] In addition, they found that "sharing the cost of drugs and users' desire to prepare drugs as quickly as possible encourage the sharing of cookers, even when each user has their own syringe."[124]

Because of the long incubation periods for the transmission of AIDS, it is not yet possible to compare transmission rates in countries with needle exchange programs to that in the United States. However, a 1989 evaluation of a needle exchange program, begun in 1984 in the Netherlands, revealed that "the incidence of hepatitis B infection declined steadily from 49 per 100,000 users in 1984 to 9 per 100,000 in 1989."[125]

The results of criminalizing drugs have been similar to the observed results of criminalizing prostitution and gambling. It is to those that we now turn.

PROSTITUTION

A 1985 opinion survey conducted by the United States Department of Justice ranked prostitution 174th in severity out of 204 crimes ranging from first-degree murder to school truancy (the offense ranked 175th was "a store owner knowingly puts large eggs in containers marked 'extra large'").[126]

More than a half million women work as prostitutes in the United States.[127] One study estimates that 12 to 20 percent of women have engaged in prostitution at some point in their lives. A recent study estimated that 75 percent of men have patronized a prostitute at least once.[128] It is estimated that more than 338 million acts of prostitution occur annually.[129]

Most other countries in the world do not criminalize prostitution, and many actively regulate and tax it under the auspices of the law.[130] In the United States, prostitution is legal only in certain counties of Nevada. In those counties of Nevada where prostitution is legalized, regulated, and taxed, the rate of AIDS among prostitutes is the lowest in the United States.[131] Revenues from prostitution support public services rather than pimps, hustlers, and organized crime.

A visiting Martian advised of these facts might be surprised to learn how municipal and state governments in the United States have decided to allocate scarce law enforcement resources. A study of major cities in the United States revealed that "police arrested twice as many people for prostitution as they did for all homicides, rapes, robberies, and assaults combined."[132] Murderers, rapists, and other violent offenders are receiving early release to accommodate accused prostitutes, who occupy more than 30 percent of all scarce female prison space. During a period when sixteen major city governments were expending more than $100 million of municipal funds to arrest prostitutes, more than 90 percent of perpetrators

of murder, rape, robbery, and assault evaded police detection and prosecution.[133]

High rates of violent crime appear to have little effect on the of most
American cities' decisions to allocate a disproportionate share of law
enforcement resources toward the suppression of prostitution. The cost to
the taxpayer of processing, arresting, and incarcerating each prostitution
suspect ranges from $877 per arrest in Boston, to $2,000 per arrest in New
York City.[134] With more than 100,000 prostitution arrests per year, their
financial cost alone to society is indeed staggering.[135] Consider too that
this figure excludes $150 billion in annual tax revenues lost by states and
municipalities due to the criminalization of prostitution.[136] One early
1990s study concluded that the "average American pays $800 in taxes to
pursue [those engaged in prostitution]. On the other hand, if these activities were decriminalized and taxed, we could wipe out the national debt—
that's the $4 trillion debt, not the meager $226 billion deficit—in 20
years."[137]

If criminalizing prostitution cost deficit-ridden governments only $4
trillion in potential revenues, the consequences would not be so tragic.
Unfortunately, however, the social costs of criminalization far exceed the
financial costs. The same $4 trillion lost to governments that could fund
social services, child care, and the like, instead funds the criminal activities of pimps and organizations whose crimes in other areas of society
wreak untold misery and suffering on innocent citizens. This, however, is
only the beginning.

A study by Carole Campbell of the California State University Department of Sociology, reveals that the rate of human immunodeficiency virus
(HIV) seroprevalence among female prostitutes in the United States
ranges from 0 percent in certain counties of Nevada where prostitution is
legalized to 48 percent in regions where prostitution is most zealously
suppressed.[138] The reason for such differences in the HIV rate is readily
ascertained.

Prostitution has been decriminalized in eleven of seventeen counties in
Nevada.[139] The Nevada Board of Health requires that prostitutes in state-
licensed brothels be tested weekly for venereal diseases and monthly for
the HIV virus.[140] Regulations require condom use. Prostitutes receive formal training in screening customers for sexually transmitted diseases.
Should any question arise, a consultant is available for a second opinion.
Any customer who is accepted is required to wash his genitals with warm
water and an antiseptic solution.

Because the prostitute is fully protected by the law, she can reject any
customer and enforce the rule requiring condom use. Unlike states where
prostitution is criminalized, crimes of violence on prostitutes are almost
nonexistent. Incidence of prostitutes "rolling" customers is almost unheard
of. Most brothels are located near a sheriff's station. State regulations also

require that each licensed brothel maintain a place for the storage of hygienic supplies and prophylactic devices. Solicitation outside the brothel is strictly prohibited and enforced. Indeed, unlike cities and towns in other states where prostitution is criminalized, towns near the legalized brothels report almost no problems with streetwalkers or solicitation.

There are, of course, no pimps in the legalized brothel and no incidents of forced prostitution. Indeed, regulations prohibit a brothel from hiring any male for any purpose other than maintenance or repair of the facility.[141] Prostitutes pay a predetermined fee to the brothel owner for room and board. The costs of HIV antibody tests are also deducted from the paychecks of brothel employees.

License fees are an important source of income in the counties where the brothels are legal. Wages are reported and taxes paid on all earnings. Brothels pay license fees of up to $100,000 to the county.[142] The revenues support a variety of social services unavailable in similarly situated counties that persist in criminalizing prostitution.

We can contrast conditions in the Nevada counties with legal prostitution to conditions where prostitution is suppressed. In Seattle, for example, a survey of prostitutes revealed that 76 percent had been beaten or assaulted by either their pimps or their customers.[143] Such crimes most often go unreported, of course, because a prostitute who reported such a crime would have to admit her crime of prostitution to the police. Similarly, crimes committed by pimps often go unreported because the prostitute relies on the pimp for protection.

One of the most severe consequences of criminalization is police corruption. Enforcement of prostitution is almost entirely discretionary. Most police officers soon know the identity of local prostitutes and can choose to arrest them at almost anytime. Prostitutes are almost completely at their mercy. A formal analysis by the Department of Social and Health Services of Olympia, Washington, has revealed that 20 percent of prostitutes who reported injuries in the Seattle area were injured by the police.[144] Such power over prostitutes creates a temptation many police officers fail to resist, even to the point of extorting sexual services from prostitutes.

In fact, legalizing prostitution would no more constitute condoning the practice than legalizing smoking, drinking, adultery, overeating, inadequate exercise, or jilting lovers. In fact, by persisting in policies of criminalization of prostitution, policymakers not only ensure the continued domination of prostitution by criminal elements, but also deprive society of billions of dollars of potential revenues that instead support crime. The hypocrisy of such laws is manifested not only by the widespread corruption that criminalization breeds, but also by the tactics law enforcement uses to ferret out acts of prostitution.

Comparable to illegal drug transactions, no complainant exists to a consensual act of prostitution. When arrests prove an insufficient diversion to street solicitation, enforcement agencies, instead of tracking down violent criminals, often resort to "sting" operations to ferret out possible acts of prostitution between consenting adults. In a Washington case, police authorized a female snitch to engage in "22 acts of prostitution over a three-week period and to supervise other women while taking part in prostitute recruitment activities in order to gather evidence."[145] In a California sting operation, a motel manager testified that a vice squad officer had "come to the defendant's motel approximately ten times during a two-month period, importuning her each time to find a girl for him, and that she repeatedly told him she did not have any girls and to stop bothering her." When she finally decided to get the officer off her back by sending him to see someone at another hotel, she was arrested for promoting prostitution.[146]

The consequences would be less tragic were the costs of criminalizing prostitution limited to the billions of dollars in wasted enforcement costs and lost tax revenues and the incalculable amount of support provided to crime. Instead, each year, thousands of innocent people die from AIDS, the eradication of which criminalized prostitution makes extremely difficult, if not impossible. As is the case with consensual use of drugs, no "price is too high" to enable self-serving policymakers to pat themselves on the back for refusing to "condone" prostitution.

GAMBLING

[Lotteries are] a tax on the willing.

Thomas Jefferson[147]

In early 1993, thirty-three states and the District of Columbia sponsored official lotteries.[148] Twelve states, including South Dakota and Colorado, have legalized casino gambling.[149] Fifty-two Indian tribes in 17 states operate casinos.[150] Forty-seven states sponsor some form of gambling.[151]

In Nevada, which first legalized casino gambling in 1931, the gambling industry accounts for 60 percent of all jobs and pays for more than half of taxes.[152] As a result, the state's only income tax is a voluntary one—paid for by willing gamblers. Low corporate taxes, made possible by gambling revenues, have fostered the fastest growing economy in the United States.[153]

In the earliest days of the Republic, state-sponsored gambling financed everything from the revolutionary army to the most prestigious universities, including Harvard, Dartmouth, and Princeton.[154] However, a series of lottery scandals in the late 1800s triggered a wave of antigambling hysteria, so that by 1962 no state operated a lottery.

In the United States criminalization of gambling proved a boon to the burgeoning organization of crime during the early 1900s.[155] Prohibition

gave organized crime another big boost.[156] When the Twenty-first Amendment finally ended prohibition, organized crime faced the real possibility
of its own extinction. Indeed, had prohibition's repeal ex-tended to gambling, prostitution, and drugs, organized crime would almost certainly
have met an ignominious end.

But it was not to be—and the continued criminalization of gambling
played a crucial role in organized crime's resurrection. By the 1950s gambling was its big business. A 1952 study by the American Bar Association
reported that "illegal gambling has been the principal source of profits
and backbone of organized crime during the twenty years since the repeal
of Prohibition and up to the present time."[157]

The California Special Crime Study Commission reported that "in California, as in most other states of the Union, the principal profits of organized crime are realized from illegal gambling, prostitution, the narcotics
trade [and a variety of lesser rackets]."[158] A 1969 study reported that illegal gambling grossed more than $20 billion, of which "$2 billion per year
finds its way directly and indirectly into the hands of corrupt public officials and law enforcers."[159]

Although the criminalization of gambling costs local government billions of dollars in lost tax revenues, the diversion of those same billions to
organized crime costs society much more, as did the billions diverted
toward corruption of public officials. Indeed, the social and human costs
of criminalized gambling are virtually incalculable.

Within thirteen years after the criminalization of alcohol use, John Stuart Mill's prediction (that "wrong opinions and practices gradually yield
to fact and argument") was vindicated. Such a yielding to "fact and argument" took many more years in the legalization of contraception and has
yet to occur in the legalization of drugs. It is not surprising, therefore, that
it has taken almost a century to legalize gambling on a broad basis and
thereby deprive organized crime of a major profit base as well as earn
much needed revenues for social services.

As with opposition to drug and alcohol legalization, moral hypocrisy
continues to play a large role in opposition to legalized gambling. For
example, the governor of Connecticut stridently opposed gambling in his
state on moral grounds—until, that is, Connecticut Native Americans took
advantage of a Supreme Court ruling on Indian rights of sovereignty[160]
and offered the state a $100-million gambling revenue-sharing deal.[161]

The answer to moralist opposition to gambling is essentially the same as
to moralist opposition to the legalized alcohol and drugs: Such activities
should be legal not because they are good but because they are bad—and
criminalization deprives government of the very resources needed to fund
programs proven effective in inhibiting them. For example, no amount of
criminalization or heavy-handed enforcement could significantly reduce
the level of tobacco consumption, but an education and information pro-

gram on the dangers of smoking reduced smoking by 36 percent between 1965 and 1987.

Unfortunately, the history of decriminalization in the United States reveals a tendency toward "all or nothing" policies. One of the most distinct advantages of legalization is that it releases law enforcement resources to focus on the more narrow aspects of regulating particular types of usage. For example, the repeal of prohibition might have been accompanied by extremely strict laws on drinking and driving, and enforcement resources released by repeal might have been directed toward the enforcement of such laws. In Finland, for example, most people consume alcohol, but consumption is heavily taxed. Few citizens risk drinking and driving, which is considered extremely serious and is severely penalized (mandatory incarceration in camps above the Arctic Circle). In the United States, by contrast, first-time drunk drivers often receive nothing more than a fine.

Although U.S. tobacco consumption has been greatly reduced by education and antitobacco campaigns, a well-financed tobacco lobby has succeeded in procuring legislated tobacco subsidies and in limiting tobacco taxes to levels far below that which would trigger a black market. As a result, the government forfeits potential tax revenues that could further promote education and antismoking campaigns. More important, higher taxes would give those on the verge of quitting an extra financial incentive to give up a habit far more deadly than drugs.

Hypocrisy is not limited to the opponents of legalization. Opponents to higher tobacco taxes claim that higher tobacco taxes would constitute a regressive tax on the poor. (In other words, higher taxes would only inhibit the poor from smoking themselves to death, while the rich would suffer no such financial inhibition. Thus, only the lives of the poor would be saved by higher tobacco taxes). Only tobacco tax opponents could argue that such taxes hurt the poor.

Relatively low tobacco taxes in the United States have succeeded in destroying a Canadian policy of inhibiting smoking thorough imposition of high taxes. Canada was finally forced to rescind its high cigarette taxes after the smuggling of cheap American cigarettes from the United States undercut its tobacco taxation program.

Policymakers' "all or nothing" mentality has carried over into legalized gambling. One of the most important goals of legalization should be to deprive organized crime of its profits. We should instead divert money that would be spent on gambling in any case (either legal or illegal) to the public coffers for socially useful purposes. Such a goal is perverted, however, when states attempt to encourage gambling by those who would otherwise have no inclination to do so.

Many states that permit legalized gambling also permit the advertising and promotion of such gambling. Typical of such promotion is that of a giant Illinois lottery billboard in a ghetto of Chicago that teased: "This Could Be Your Ticket Out."[162] In some states, lottery operators deliberately time their advertisements to coincide with the dates on which social security checks reach low-income recipients.[163] Radio and television advertisements target working-class people.[164]

Such promotion conveys a message that "gambling is not a vice but a normal form of entertainment."[165] This message is not only inconsistent with the rationale for legalization; it is diametrically opposed to it. In a perverse way, it also provides ammunition to those who oppose legalization in the first place.

The fact is that legalizing personal vices is justified by a considered weighing of the costs and consequences of criminalization. Tobacco and alcohol have not been legalized because government encourages or even condones their use. Indeed, they have been legalized because the government has, by expensive trial and error, determined that their use can be more effectively inhibited by legalization, education, and rehabilitation. Government, too, can find better uses for the proceeds than organized crime can. Indeed, creation of a police state is too high a price to pay to enforce absolute prohibition of what is essentially consensual conduct. In short, legalization is a policy based on a reasoned and responsible consideration of societal priorities.

A legitimate theory of legalization therefore requires a concomitant policy of education, treatment, and discouragement of use. Most important, a policy of legalization requires a forthright acknowledgment that the activity legalized is still considered a "vice," and that government is committed to using every means of persuasion and education to inhibit it.

Thus, legalizing alcohol and tobacco should have included not only a ban on promotion and advertising[166] (as belatedly addressed television and radio advertising), but also a more extensive antiuse campaign funded by higher taxes on consumption. Today, both liquor and cigarette taxes in the United States are far below those of many foreign countries. Higher such taxes in the United States could fund far more extensive pubic service antismoking and antidrinking advertisements in both the air and print media. For example, one of the most effective antismoking advertisements (and one that most enraged the smoking lobby) portrayed glamorous young movie actress Brooke Shields with cigarettes sticking out of her ears, implying that she did not find smoking "cool," nor would she date someone who smoked. Indeed, evidence revealed that the ad had such a devastating effect in reducing tobacco use by young people that lobbying groups eventually succeeded in having the ad taken off the air.

A ban on promotion and advertising should accompany any future legalization of drugs. Government should make clear that legalizing use should not be confused with condoning or encouraging its use. Taxes earned on drug sales should be devoted toward funding education and treatment centers. Today, the wealthy can detoxify at a Betty Ford–style clinic. Poorer addicts are showered with billions in incarceration and prosecution expenses, but provided little in terms of treatment and education.

Legalized gambling should include not only a ban on promotion and advertising, but also a vigorous education campaign. Just as cigarette manufacturers are required to warn cigarette users of the dangers of risks of smoking, lotteries and casinos should be required to advise all their customers of the economic stupidity of their wagers. Although most lotteries do require that the lottery ticket state the actual odds on the back of the ticket, the print is usually so small that it can be read only with a magnifying glass. A short warning along the lines of "You should be aware that you are, over the long term, betting one dollar for the chance of winning 50 cents"[167] might be appropriate. Instead of posting the portraits of jackpot winners, casinos might be required instead to post the names of cooperating losers along with the amounts they had lost. If casinos balked, the state has the ultimate negotiating tool of the power to criminalize gambling. Any casino that disliked the regulations could simply decline to enter the gambling business.

Indeed, one reason why significant illegal gambling still exists in the United States is that legal gambling enterprises persist in trying to fleece and mislead their customers. A favorite ploy of almost all lotteries insults the intelligence of all but the most ignorant of lottery customers: advertising a huge jackpot payable only in installments over twenty or thirty years. In fact, of course, the present cash value of such jackpot "annuities" is only a small fraction of the advertised jackpot advertised. Illegal numbers operations almost always pay off in a lump sum in the actual amount advertised.

The typical legalized state lottery keeps a "rake" of more than 50 percent of the amounts wagered.[168] As Scarne has noted, "[S]tate run lotteries have not hurt the illegal numbers games, for a very good reason: the numbers racket pays better odds than the state lotteries do."[169] Most illegal numbers rackets retain no more than 30 to 40 percent of wagers.[170] Indeed, if a gambling enterprise in Las Vegas attempted to keep a rake as unconscionable as that of the typical state lottery, the owners would probably be run out of town on a rail. By contrast, horseracing retains only 19 percent of wagers,[171] slot machines 3 to 11 percent, sports bookmakers 4.5 percent, and casino table games about 3 percent.

For such reasons, in many states legalizing gambling has had only a limited effect on illegal gambling. Governments have gone from prohibiting gambling altogether to actively promoting gambling and extracting the greatest possible rake from players. Such governments in fact cause far greater harm than the illegal gambling they purport to replace.

A responsible gaming policy must include not only an education and treatment program for compulsive gamblers and those who can least afford it but also strict prohibitions against promotion and advertising. Those who wish to gamble in states that forbid gambling have no trouble finding outlets for their illegal gambling activities. Because the purpose of legalization is to provide an outlet for those who will gamble in any case, legal gambling should prohibit promotion or advertising.

Opponents of legalized gambling point to the fact that gambling's losers often are those least able to afford it. While this is undoubtedly true, such an argument fails to take into account the fact that many of the same people who lose money in a legal gambling establishment would also lose money in an illegal one. The difference is that in the case of legalized gambling, the player has a legal recourse against fraud and extortion. Likewise, a legalized gambling operation will have a legal recourse against a cheating player, whereas violence may be the only recourse for an illegal gambling operation.

Legalization opponents also sometimes argue that legalized gambling attracts undesirable elements of society. In fact, however, this has not proven to be the case. As one critic has noted, "the claim that casinos attract unsavory characters as compared to families has no merit. Can anyone prove that the millions of vacationers and conventioneers—consisting of professional people, blue collar workers, and their families—who have frequented Las Vegas, Reno, Lake Tahoe, the Bahamas, and Atlantic City, are undesirable visitors?"[172]

Despite evidence that legalized gambling has siphoned off billions of dollars from organized crime, legalization opponents persist in their claim that legalized gambling attracts organized crime. It is true, of course, that in the early days of legalized gambling, when Las Vegas had one sheriff and virtually no state regulation, organized crime became involved in Las Vegas casinos. Today, however, legalized gambling is closely regulated, particularly in Las Vegas and Atlantic City. Gambling license applicants are subject to the most rigorous background checks of any industry in the United States.

Notwithstanding claims by those who have an ax to grind (such as Atlantic City casino owner Donald Trump), the recent expansion of gaming to Indian reservations has been remarkably free of organized crime influence. Although legitimate concerns arose about mob influence in the early 1980s,[173] by 1992 the Justice Department reported that it found "no widespread or successful effort by organized crime to infiltrate Indian gaming operations."[174]

Indeed, gambling profits on reservations, which exceeded $400 million in 1992, have financed community, health, and education programs for impoverished tribal communities.[175] In 1982, for example, 70 percent of the members of the Shakopee Mdewakanton Sioux (Dakota) community were on welfare. Two of every three families lived in squalid trailers. Ten years later, after the infusion of millions of dollars of gambling profits, children of tribal members were guaranteed a free college education and liberal trust fund payments for their development and job training.[176]

In 1985, the Bureau of Indian Affairs reported a 39 percent unemployment rate among American Indians and a 45 percent poverty rate.[177] The government's response was to cut Bureau of Indian Affairs spending by 75 percent between 1977 and 1990.[178] In 1991, however, Indian gambling profits were eleven times greater than the money spent by the Bureau of Indian Affairs.[179]

Critics were quick to criticize the legalization of gambling in Atlantic City when it did not immediately result in the elimination of urban blight. Today, however, casino tax revenues have significant impact on community development. The Northeast Inlet area of Atlantic City provides a useful illustration. Before gambling was legalized, the Inlet was a war-torn area populated by drug dealers, and arson fires burned nightly. By 1992, however, the Casino Reinvestment Development Authority was pumping more than $100 million of casino tax revenues into the demolition of burned-out and boarded-up houses and the construction of the Harbor Point development of "blue-trimmed, cottage-style homes." More than 20 percent of these homes have been set aside for low- and moderate-income residents. An additional half-billion dollars is earmarked for future community development in the Inlet.

The legalization of gambling represents government recognition of the human instinct for risk taking. Some people manifest this instinct by investment in risky penny stocks, real estate ventures, or pork bellies. For others, risk taking is a recreational activity. In the long term, this instinct can no more be suppressed than the profit motive communist governments attempted to suppress. Ultimately, policymakers must make the difficult decision as to whether gambling profits will fund further illegal activities or promote the public good.

Thus, the challenge of legalized gambling is twofold: first, to channel the profits of gambling away from organized crime to the public coffers where it can help promote the public good; second, to educate consumers as to the risks and dangers of gambling. This can be accomplished only when legalization includes strict regulation of promotion and advertising of gambling activities and the creation of fair gambling activities that can realistically divert revenues from illegally conducted activities.

NOTES

1. John Stuart Mill, *Utilitarianism, On Liberty, and Representative Government* (New York: Dutton, 1910), pp. 102–28, cited in David Schultz, "Rethinking Drug Criminalization Policies," 25 *Tex. Tech. L. Rev.* 152, 1993.

2. Center for Disease Control, *A Call for Action: Surgeon General's Report, Reducing Tobacco Use* (CDC, April 11, 2001), http://www.cdc.gov/tobacco/sgr/sgr_2000/factsheets/factsheet_callforaction.html.

3. Number of deaths and age-adjusted death rates per 100,000 population for categories of alcohol-related (A-R) mortality, United States and States, 1979–96, National Institute on Alcohol Abuse and Alcoholism, http://www.niaaa.nih.gov/databases/armort01.txt, last accessed Feb. 12, 2001, citing Alcohol Epidemiologic Data System, F. Saadatmand, F. S. Stinson, B. F. Grant, and M. C. Dufour, *Surveillance Report #52: Liver Mortality in the United States, 1970–96* (Rockville, Md.: National Institute on Alcohol Abuse and Alcoholism, Division of Biometry and Epidemiology, December 1999).

4. National Highway Traffic Safety Administration, U.S. Department of Transportation, *Traffic Safety Facts 2000: Alcohol,* DOT HS 809 323 (2000).

5. Kurt L. Schmoke, "An Argument In Favor of Decriminalization," 18 *Hofstra L. Rev.* 501, 1990.

6. James Ostrowski, Thinking About Drug Legalization, *Cato Institute Policy Analysis,* No. 121, May 1989, p. 25, cited in Doug Bandow, War on Drugs or War on America, 3 *Stan. L. & Pol'y Rev.* 242, Fall 1991.

7. See *Harmelin* v. *Michigan,* 501 U.S. 957, 1991 (upholding sentence of life imprisonment without parole for possession of less than 1 1/2 pounds of cocaine).

8. Bandow, *supra* note 6, p. 250.

9. Rex Greene, Toward a Policy of Mercy: Addiction in the 1990s, 3 *Stan. L. & Pol'y Rev.* 227, Fall 1991.

10. Peter Reuter, Hawks Ascendant: The Punitive Trend of American Drug Policy, *Daedalus,* Vol. 121, Summer 1992, pp. 33–34.

11. *Harmelin, supra* note 7.

12. Steve France, The Drug War: Should We Fight or Switch?, *American Bar Association Journal,* Vol. 121, February 1990, p. 5.

13. *Id.*

14. Steven Jonas, Solving the Drug Problem: A Public Health Approach to the Reduction of the Use and Abuse of Both Legal and Illegal Recreational Drugs, 18 *Hofstra L. Rev.* 758, 1990.

15. *Id.*

16. Steven Wisotsky, Exposing the War on Cocaine: The Futility and Destructiveness of Prohibition, 1983 *Wis. L. Rev.* 1384, 1983.

17. Senator Morris Sheppard, quoted in Ethan A. Nadelmann, Yes, *American Heritage,* February/March 1993, p. 48.

18. Bandow, *supra* note 6, p. 244.

19. Tariff Act of 1930 §305, 19 U.S.C.A § 1305; see also *U.S.* v. *One Book Entitled "Contraception," by Marie C. Stopes,* 51 F.2d. 525 (1931), book on contraception held not "drug, medicine, or article for prevention of contraception."

20. See, e.g., McKinney's Education Law § 6811, NY EDUC § 6811(8), which made it a crime to "sell, give away, or advertise . . . any articles for the prevention of conception."

21. *Griswold* v. *Connecticut,* 381 U.S. 479 (1965).

22. *Eisenstadt* v. *Baird,* 405 U.S. 438 (1972).

23. 18 U.S.C. § 1461; 19 U.S.C. § 1462.

24. Emily Taft Douglas, *Margaret Sanger, Pioneer of the Future* (Garrett Park, Md.: Garrett Park Press, 1975), p. 44.

25. Cited by Chief Justice Warner Burger of the Supreme Court in *Bowers* v. *Hardwick*, 478 U.S. 186 (1986).

26. *Id.*

27. Steven B. Duke and Albert C. Gross, *America's Longest War: Rethinking Our Tragic Crusade Against Drugs* (New York: G. P. Putnam's Sons, 1993), reviewed by Randy E. Barnett, 103 *Yale L.J.* 2593, 1994.

28. See John A. Powell and Eileen B. Hershenov, Hostage to the Drug War: The National Purse, the Constitution and the Black Community, 24 *U.C. Davis L. Rev.* 557, 1991. The cost of incarcerating one million people is $16 billion.

29. *Id.*

30. *Harmelin, supra* note 7.

31. Barnett, *supra* note 27, p. 2594.

32. A. Jones, *Cruel Sacrifice* (New York: Windsor Publishing., 1994), p. 137.

33. *Id.*, p. 317.

34. *Id.*, p. 353.

35. *Harmelin, supra* note 7.

36. Off With Their Heads? Thoughts From the Drug Czar, *Washington Post*, June 20, 1989, p. A1.

37. Edward M. Brecher, and editors of *Consumer Reports, Licit and Illicit Drugs: The Consumer Union Reports on Narcotics, Stimulants, Depressants, Inhalants, Hallucinogens, and Marijuana—Including Caffeine, Nicotine and Alcohol* (Boston: Little, Brown, 1972), pp. 419–20, cited in Richard Lawrence Miller, *The Case for Legalizing Drugs* (Westport, Conn.: Praeger, 1991), p. 69.

38. *Id.*

39. *Id.*

40. Karen Breslau, Overplanned Parenthood: Ceausescu's Cruel Law, *Newsweek*, January 22, 1990, p. 35.

41. Paul Barrett, Strategic Muddle: Federal War on Drugs Is Scattershot Affair, With Dubious Progress, *Wall St. Journal*, August 10, 1988, p. A1, cited in Bandow, *supra* note 6, p. 243.

42. *Id.*, p. 39.

43. Douglas Jehl, U.S. Estimate of World Cocaine Output Up 94%, *Los Angeles Times*, March 2, 1990, p. A12.

44. Robert Reinhold, Police Hard Pressed in Drug War, Are Turning to Preventive Efforts, *New York Times*, December 28, 1989, p. A1, cited in *Id.* p. 244.

45. Jonas, *supra* note 14, p. 779.

46. Arnold Trebach, *The Great Drug War* (New York: Macmillan, 1987), cited in Clifford F. Thies and Charles A. Register, Decriminalization of Marijuana and the Demand for Alcohol, Marijuana, and Cocaine, *Social Science Journal*, Vol. 30, 1993, p. 389.

47. Ethan A. Nadelmann, Drug Prohibition in the U.S.: Costs, Consequences, and Alternatives, *Science*, Vol. 245, 1989, p. 944.

48. Trebach, *supra* note 46, p. 105.

49. Thies and Register, *supra* note 46, p. 254.

50. Trebach, *supra* note 46, p. 305–306.

51. *Id.*

52. Ostrowski, *supra* note 6, p. 3.

53. *Id.*

54. Thies and Register, *supra* note 46, p. 389.

55. *Id.*

56. *Id.*

57. Walter Block, Drug Prohibition: A Legal and Economic Analysis, *Journal of Business Ethics,* Vol. 12, 1993, p. 696.

58. *Id.*, p. 697.

59. *Id.*, p. 696.

60. Wisotsky, *supra* note 16, p. 1325.

61. A price of $80 is cited in Wisotsky, *supra* note 16.

62. Ostrowski, *supra* note 6, p. 15.

63. L. Silverman N. Sprull, and D. Levine, *Urban Crime and Drug Availability* (Public Research Institute, Center for Naval Analysis, PRI 75–1, 1975), p. 13.

64. Bandow, *supra* note 6, p. 250.

65. Schultz, *supra* note 1, p. 4.

66. Andrew T. Weil, Norman Zinberg, and Judith Nielsen, Clinical and Psychological Effects of Marijuana in Man, *Science,* Vol. 12, 1968, pp. 1234–42, cited in Miller, *supra* note 37, p. 18.

67. *Id.*

68. Duke and Gross, *supra* note 27.

69. Lawrence R. Sutton, The Effects of Alcohol, Marijuana, and Their Combination on Driving Ability, *Journal of Studies on Alcohol,* 1983, p. 442, cited in Miller, *supra* 37, p. 18.

70. Erich Goode, *Drugs in American Society* (New York: Alfred Knopf, 1972), p. 59, cited in Miller, *supra* note 37, p. 19.

71. National Institute of Drug Abuse, DAWN (1984), p. 52, cited in Erich Goode, *supra* note 70.

72. *Id.*

73. Duke and Gross, *supra* note 27, p. 51.

74. Earl Rowell and Robert Rowell, *On the Trail of Marijuana: The Weed of Madness* (Mountain View, Calif.: Pacific Press Publishing, 1939), pp. 72–74.

75. Charles Touns, The Injury of Tobacco and Its Relation to Other Drug Habits, *Century,* Vol. 83, 1912, p. 770.

76. *The Controller of Her Britannic Majesty's Stationery Office for Cannabis,* Report by the Advisory, Committee on Drug Dependence, 1968, pp. 12–13.

77. One rare exception to legalization was an 1875 San Francisco ordinance closing opium dens on grounds that they attracted "white women," cited in Miller, *supra* note 37, p. 188.

78. Ronald Hamowy, Introduction: Illicit Drugs and Government, in Robert J. Michaels, *Dealing with Drugs: Consequences of Government Control* (Ronald Hamowy, ed., Pacific Studies in Public Policy, Lanham, Md.: Lexington Books, 1987), p. 9.

79. Patricia G. Erickson, et al., *The Steel Drug: Cocaine in Perspective* (Lanham, Md.: Lexington Books, 1987), cited in Miller, *supra* note 37, pp. 136–137.

80. *Id.*, p. 76.

81. *Id.*, pp. 10–11.

82. See Nora V. Demleitner, Organized Crime and Prohibition: What Difference Does Legalization Make? 15 *Whittier L. Rev.* 613, 1994.

83. Frank Ganin and Herbert Kleber, Abstinence Symptomatology and Psychiatric Diagnosis in Cocaine Abusers: Clinical Observations, *Archives of General Psychiatry,* 1983, p. 43, cited in Miller, *supra* note 37, p. 12.

84. *Diagnostic and Statistical Manual of Mental Disorders* (Washington, D.C.: American Psychiatric Association, 3rd ed., 1987), cited in *Id.* pp. 12–13.

85. *Id.*, p. 15.

86. Craig Van Dyke and Robert Byck, Cocaine, *Scientific American,* 1982, p. 246, cited in *Id.*, p. 139.

87. R. Brown and R. Middlefell, Fifty-Five Years of Cocaine Dependence, *British Journal of Addiction,* 1989, p. 946, cited in *Id.* p. 27.

88. *Id.*

89. *Id.*

90. *Id.*, pp. 12–13.

91. Hamilton Wright, *Report on the International Opium Commission and on the Opium Problem as Seen Within the United States and its Possessions.* In Opium Problem. Message from the president of the United States, 61 Cong., 2 sess., 1910, S. Doc. No. 61–377 1910, cited in *Id.* pp. 89–92.

92. David Musto and Manuel Ramos, A Follow-Up Study of the New Haven Morphine Maintenance Clinic of 1920. *New England Journal of Medicine,* Vol. 304, 1981, pp. 1075–76, cited in *Id.* p. 32.

93. Powell and Hershenov, *supra* note 28, p. 568.

94. Brecher *supra* note 37, p. 277.

95. Barnett, *supra* note 27, p. 2600.

96. Miller, *supra* note 37, p. 133.

97. Nadelmann, *supra* note 47, p. 45.

98. *Id.*

99. *Id.*, p. 46.

100. Brecher, *supra* note 37, p. 231.

101. See Bruce Alexander, Robert Coambs, and Patricia Hardaway, The Effect of Housing and Gender on Morphine Self-Administration in Rats, *Psychopharmacology,* Vol. 58, 1978, pp. 175–178, cited in Miller, *supra* note 37, p. 4.

102. Jonas, *supra* note 14, p. 777.

103. Miller, *supra* note 37, p. 4.

104. *Id.*

105. *Id.*

106. Henry K. Beecher, *Movement of Subjective Responses: Quantitative Effects of Drugs* (New York: Oxford University Press, 1959), pp. 321–41.

107. Louis Lasagna, John M. Von Felsinger, and Henry K. Beecher, Drug Induced Mood Changes in Man: Observations on Chronically Ill Patients and Post Addicts, *Journal of the American Medical Association,* Vol. 157, March 19, 1955, p. 1017, cited in John Kaplan, *The Hardest Drug* (Chicago: University of Chicago Press, 1983), p. 118.

108. William McAuliffe, A Second Look at First Effects: The Subjective Effects of Opiates on Non-Addicts, *Journal of Drug Issues,* Vol. 5, Fall 1975, p. 383, cited in *Id.* p. 119.

109. Miller, *supra* note 37, p. 4.

110. *Id.*

111. *Id.*

112. *Id.*

113. Ga. Code Ann. § 16–6-2 (a) (1984), provides: "A person commits the offense of sodomy when he or she performs or submits to any sexual act involving the sex organs of one person and the mouth or anus of another."

114. Case of a client represented by a student lawyer in the student's law clinic of the University of Denver College of Law Clinical Program (1980).

115. Jon Liebman and Nina Mulia, *An Office Based AIDS Prevention Program for High Risk Drug Users in Drugs and Society* (New York: Haworth Press, 1993), pp. 205–207.

116. *Id.*

117. *The Effectiveness of Drug Abuse Treatment: Implications for Controlling, AIDS/HIV Infection* (Congress of the U.S. Office of Technology Assessment, Sept. 1990), p. 2.

118. *Id.*

119. Robert Booth, Steven Koester, Charles Reichardt, J. Thomas Brewster, *Quantitative and Qualitative Methods to Assess Behavioral Change Among Injection Drug Users in Drugs and Society* (New York: Haworth Press, 1993), pp. 161–171.

120. H. Feldman and P. Biernacki, Contributors, *The Ethnography of Needle Sharing Among Intravenous Drug Users and the Implications for Public Policies and Intervention Strategies,* in J. Batties and R. W. Pickens, et. al., *National and International Perspectives, Needle Sharing Among Intravenous Drug Users* (Wash. D.C.: National Institute on Drug Abuse, Monograph 80), cited in *Id.* p. 175.

121. *Id.*

122. *Id.*, p. 176.

123. *Id.*, p. 178.

124. *Id.*

125. Congressional Report on Drugs and AIDS, *supra* note 117, p. 111.

126. Jerry Taylor, Laws Lax for 'Oldest Profession,' *Boston Globe,* Feb. 27, 1988, p. 21.

127. Vorenberg and Vorenberg, The Biggest Pimp of All: Prostitution and Some Facts of Life, *Atlantic Monthly,* January 1977, p. 28.

128. Ross Wetzsteon, Why Nice Guys Buy Sex, *Mademoiselle,* Vol. 90, November 1984, pp. 196–197.

129. John F. Decker, *Prostitution: Regulation and Control* (Publications of Criminal Law Education and Research Center, New York University, Vol. 13, Fred B. Rothman & Co., 1979), p. 94.

130. Moira Griffin, Wives, Hookers, and the Law, *Student Lawyer,* Vol. 10, January 1982, p. 21.

131. Julie Pearl, The Highest Paying Customers: America's Cities and the Costs of Prostitution Control, 38 *Hastings L.J.,* 769, April, 1987.

132. *Id.*, p. 769.

133. *Id.*

134. Marvin M. Moore, The Case for Legitimizing the Call Girl, 5 *Cooley L. Rev.* 337, May 1988.

135. Joe Urschel, If We're Going to Tax Sin, Go Whole Hog, *U.S.A Today,* September 28, 1993, p. A10.

136. *Id.*

137. *Id.*

138. Carole A. Campbell, Prostitution, AIDS, and Preventive Health Behavior, *Social Science Medicine,* Vol. 32, 1991, p. 1368.

139. *Id.,* p. 1370.

140. *Id.,* p. 1371.

141. Decker, *supra* note 129, p. 91.

142. Helen Reynolds, *The Economics of Prostitution* (Springfield, Ill.: Charles C. Thomas, 1986).

143. Barbara Milman, New Rules for the Oldest Profession: Should We Change Our Prostitution Laws? 3 *Harv. Women's L.J.,* 1, September 1980.

144. A. James, Prostitution and Addiction: An Interdisciplinary Approach, *Addictive Diseases: International Journal,* Vol. 2, 1976, p. 607, cited in *Id.* p. 23.

145. *State* v. *Putman,* 639 P.2d. 858 (1982).

146. *People* v. *West,* 139 Cal. App. 2d. Supp. 923 (1956).

147. Thomas Jefferson quoted in Mark Jaffe, Lottery Frenzy Expands, *Philadelphia Inquirer,* July 31, 1983, p. G1.

148. Ronald J. Rychlak, Lotteries, Revenues, and Social Costs: A Historical Examination of State-Sponsored Gambling, 34 *B.C.L. Rev.* 11, December 1992.

149. George F. Will, Gambling With Our Character, *Washington Post,* Feb. 7, 1993, p. C7.

150. *Id.*

151. *Id.*

152. *Id.*

153. William Thompson, Gambling: A Controlled Substance, *Pittsburgh Post-Gazette,* August 14, 1994, p. E1.

154. Will, *supra* note 149, p. C7.

155. U.S.A.: Las Vegas Remakes Itself, *Economist,* March 26, 1994, p. A31.

156. Morris Ploscoe, et. al., *Organized Crime and Law Enforcement: The Reports, Research Studies and Model Statutes and Commentaries,* American Bar Association on Organized Crime (American Bar Association, New York: Grosby Press, 1952).

157. *Id.* Part I, p. 273.

158. Cited at *Id.*

159. Rufus King, *Gambling and Organized Crime* (Washington, D.C.: Public Affairs Press, 1969), p. 10.

160. *Id.*

161. Chris Reidy, Gambling Has Become the Nice Vice, *Boston Globe,* Jan. 17, 1993, p. 69.

162. Will, *supra* note 149, p. C7.

163. Rychlak, *supra* note 148, p. 22.

164. *Id.*

165. Ricardo Chavira, The Rise of Teenage Gambling, *Time,* February 25, 1991, p. 78, cited in *Id.* p. 18.

166. Some First Amendment constitutional questions would, of course, be raised by a ban on advertising in the print media. This author, however, as a professor of constitutional law, contends that if a government has the power to ban a product absolutely, it has the lesser included power to ban it partially by restrictions on advertising and promotion.

167. This phrase suggested by Rychlak, *supra* note 148, p. 22.

168. John Scarne, *Scarne's New Complete Guide to Gambling* (Simon & Schuster, 1986), p. 175, cited in *Id.* p. 81.

169. John Scarne and Clayton Rawson, *Scarne on Dice* (Military Service Publishing, 1945), pp. 201–218.

170. *Id.*

171. See Philip J. Cook and Charles T. Clotfelter, *Selling Hope: State Lotteries in America* (National Bureau of Economic Research Bill, Harvard University Press, 1991), p. 239, cited in Rychlak, *supra* note 148, p. 158.

172. Leonard Robbins, Casino Gambling, *Miami Herald,* July 19, 1986, p. A23.

173. For a discussion of mob influence during the early 1980s, See James Popkin, Gambling With the Mob? *U.S. News & World Report,* August 23, 1993, p. 30.

174. Leah L. Lorber, State Rights, Tribal Sovereignty, and the "White Man's Firewater": State Prohibition of Gambling on New Indian Lands, 69 *Ind. L.J.,* 255, 1993.

175. *Id.,* p. 109.

176. *Id.,* p. 258.

177. *Id.,* p. 256.

178. *Id.*

179. *Id.* Chapter 2.

CHAPTER 2

The Lessons of Prohibition

Policy is formed by preconceptions and long implanted biases. When information is relayed to policymakers, they respond in terms of what is already in their heads and consequently make policy less to fit the facts than to fit the baggage that has accumulated since childhood.

Barbara Tuchman

If a law is wrong, its rigid enforcement is the surest guaranty of its repeal.[1]

Herbert Hoover

Perhaps no other experience in American life draws a closer parallel to the prohibition of drugs, prostitution, and gambling than the prohibition of alcohol by the Eighteenth Amendment of the Constitution. America's great experiment, prohibition, raised fundamental questions about how law is created, and the role of values and cultural traditions in the lawmaking process of a democratic society.

The lessons of prohibition were learned only after years of upheaval, violence, suffering, and corruption. Even so, lessons learned often are forgotten by the next generation. It is history's important role to remind succeeding generations of those lessons so that they can be learned in a way less expensive than hard experience.

Most members of the present generation cannot remember a time when drugs were legal in the United States. They therefore lack the advantageous ability to compare personal experience in a society in which drugs are legal with one in which they are criminalized. The repealers of the Eighteenth Amendment could make a comparison, however, and this direct comparison made repeal inevitable. Policymakers today must rely on history books to make their comparisons. Such comparisons, like sound bites, make a far less vivid impact than actual experience.

When Barbara Tuchman observed that "Policy is formed by preconceptions," she might also have added that policies are far easier to discard than preconceptions. In the case of national prohibition, an overwhelming majority in Congress and in forty-five of the forty-eight states had an almost ideological preconception about the role of law in society. It was a preconception that law could be a substitute for social reform; that the basis of law should extend beyond protecting citizens from unwanted and harmful conduct of others, to protecting citizens from the consequences of their own behavior. (Of course, what was good for a person in the minority was to be determined by those in the majority.) Thus, laws against using contraceptive devices or engaging in consensual sexual acts with one's spouse were based on the notion that the "perpetrators" of such acts were their own victims.

For example, during the Spanish Inquisition, perpetrators of heresy were thrown into prison or tortured into recanting on the theory that they were being "saved" from the consequences of their own heretical acts or thoughts. Thus, heresy was not a "victimless crime" at all. The perpetrator was her own victim. In the case of the Inquisition, policymakers decided that those committing heretical acts were dooming themselves to everlasting damnation. (It was beside the point that those who committed heresy might have different beliefs as to what constituted moral thoughts or conduct.)

Such a preconception made simple the process of creating law. First, find evidence that a certain type of behavior is contrary to the moral beliefs of the majority. Second, determine that such behavior has an adverse effect on the perpetrator. And third, criminalize that conduct as a means of protecting the perpetrator-victim. Conspicuously absent from such a process is the requirement that the perpetrator and the victim be different persons.

Preconceptions, like ideology, almost always fall hard. For example, the collapse of the worldwide communist movement in the early 1990s was a shattering experience for many intellectuals who had formed preconceptions about the role of self-interest and the relationship between power, equality, and justice. That a system founded on self-interest and selfishness could better provide for the common good than one founded on principles of egalitarianism required a drastic rethinking of preconceptions.

Twenty years after the Civil War, Jefferson Davis refused to discard his preconceptions about the morality of slavery, and not until 1994 did the last state ratify the Thirteenth Amendment abolishing slavery.

The failure of Prohibition also required a drastic rethinking of preconceptions. For the better part of the prohibition years, such rethinking was resisted. A politician responsible for a constitutional amendment as radical as the Eighteenth Amendment would find admitting error almost unthinkable. Drastic efforts were made to conceal the mounting evidence of failure. Political commentator Walter Lippmann wrote in 1931 in *Vanity Fair*, referring to the whitewashing Wickersham Commission on Prohibition, "everything possible was done to conceal the truth from the public generally.... What was done was to evade a direct and explicit official confession that federal prohibition is a hopeless failure."[2]

The accumulating evidence was indeed staggering. For example, the average annual consumption of spirits doubled from 101 million gallons in 1919 at the beginning of prohibition to 204 million gallons in 1926, at the height of prohibition[3] (see Figure 1.1). Death rates per 100,000 people from alcoholism and alcohol poisoning skyrocketed from a rate of 1.4 in 1919 to 4.1 in 1926. Meanwhile the number of prisoners serving long-term sentences tripled between 1921 and 1931. By 1930, more than a third of the nation's scarce prison space, for those serving long-term sentences, was allocated to those convicted of prohibition offenses. Indeed, there were more prisoners serving long-term prison sentences for prohibition offenses in federal institutions in 1931 than there were prisoners serving long-term sentences for every type of offense, including murder, in 1921.[4]

A report to the Wickersham Prohibition Commission in 1929 revealed that "crime had increased by 50% as a result of Prohibition." Another report revealed that the "increase in juvenile delinquency is the direct result of a disrespect for law bolstered in the homes of these delinquents

Figure 2.1
Total Production of Alcohol in the United States, 1919–1926

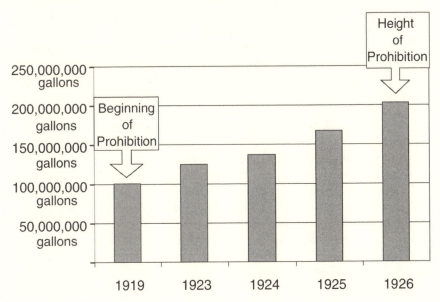

by the parents in the disrespect for the law of prohibition for liquor and the consequent fear and contempt for the righteous sheriff or policeman."[5]

John Marshall Gest of the Orphans Court of Philadelphia reported that "the deplorable conditions...are in great measure attributable to the Eighteenth Amendment...which [has] produced greater demoralization in politics, morality, and society than any laws that were ever enacted."[6]

Social commentators began to note the hypocrisy of politicians who defied the prohibition laws in private, while professing support for prohibition in public. (In this regard, it may be recalled that in the current era of drug criminalization, the president, vice president, and Speaker of the House have confessed to using drugs.)

But just as today policymakers resist rethinking drug and prostitution laws, so the policymakers of the 1930s stuck their heads in the sand. Those advocating repeal of prohibition were reviled as insensitive to the deadly effects of alcohol on society. The whole notion of repeal was derided as absurd. Senator Morris Sheppard of Texas confidently asserted, "There is as much chance of repealing the Eighteenth Amendment as there is for a hummingbird to fly to the planet Mars with the Washington Monument tied to its tail."[7] Representative James M. Beck of Pennsylvania observed, "No general revolt against the enforcement of a law has ever been known in our history."[8]

Just as today, policymakers had great difficulty in distinguishing between the issues of whether a substance or behavior is harmful and what method would be most effective in inhibiting it. The advocates of Prohibition repeal did not, any more than the advocates of drug criminalization today, argue that the use of the criminalized substance was harmless. The same alcohol that in 1986 was the major factor in more than 50 percent of all homicides, 52 percent of rapes, 62 percent of assaults, and 30 percent of suicides, was no less harmful in 1919.[9] But just as policymakers today find it difficult to accept that drug use declines with legalization, so the policymakers of the 1920s tried to ignore the rise in alcohol use during prohibition. The figures just had to be wrong, or fraudulent, or distorted. They could not accept that their extreme law enforcement efforts, the invasions of traditionally expected civil liberties, and the incarceration of thousands of otherwise law-abiding citizens, had done nothing more than increase alcohol use, cause a skyrocketing in deaths by alcohol poisoning, the corruption of governmental officials, and a dramatic rise in crime.

Rethinking preconceptions is perhaps the policymaker's most difficult task. Such a rethinking usually requires an overwhelming tide of events, and the process can be delayed for many years by refusal to face the evidence until it is so great that it simply cannot be ignored. The policymakers of today who steadfastly ignore the mounting evidence of drug criminalization are no more guilty than their predecessors who blindly imposed prohibition of alcohol.

Another likely result of prohibition has been little discussed since its repeal, namely its contribution as one of the causes of the Great Depression. Prohibition denied the government more than a third of its revenues, which had to be made up by taxes extracted from cash-strapped producers in the general economy. By 1929, the cumulative effects of this diversion of funds to nonproductive uses had taken a deadly toll on the economy. As historian Sean Cashman has noted, "Wealth...was now diverted to gangsters and corrupt public officials."[10]

Matthew Woll, vice president of the American Federation of Labor, observed in 1931, "Certain great employers supported prohibition so that the workers might be more efficient to produce, to produce, to produce. Well, we have produced and six million are unemployed. And prohibition has produced too. It has produced the illicit still, the rumrunner, the speakeasy, the racketeer, graft, corruption, disrespect for the law, crime."[11]

Will Rogers made a similar point when he observed, "What does prohibition amount to, if your neighbor's children are not eating? It's food, it's not drink is our problem now. We were so afraid the poor people might drink, now we fixed it so they can't eat.... The working classes didn't bring this on, it was the big boys that thought the financial drink was going to last forever."[12]

Prohibition had only one redeeming aspect. The economic injuries suffered by farmers, although extensive, were not as extensive as they could have been; their grain crops were still used in the production of illegal alcohol.

Today, the criminalization of drugs deprives the government of untold billions in tax dollars that, as they were during prohibition, are diverted toward nonproductive criminal uses. While it is impossible to precisely determine the economic effects of criminalized drug use and prostitution, the economic effects of government loss of billions of dollars can be nothing less than staggering when government programs such as social security and Medicare compete for scarce dollars from a deficit-ridden treasury.

UNDERSTANDING THE CAUSES OF PROHIBITION

Americans today find it difficult to understand how prohibition could possibly have happened. Perhaps no political agenda is more difficult to achieve than a constitutional amendment. Even such a relatively uncontroversial proposed constitutional amendment as the Equal Rights Amendment for women failed to muster ratification support among the necessary number of states. And yet, in a democratic society in which a true consensus on much of anything is notoriously difficult to achieve, the Eighteenth Amendment prohibiting consumption of any alcoholic beverages, including wine and beer, passed by the one of the most overwhelming majorities in American political history. In 1917 it was approved 65–20 in the Senate, 246–95 in the House, and was ratified by forty-five of the forty-eight states within twenty-five months. (Only thirty-six states were needed for ratification.) By way of comparison, the Twenty-seventh Amendment regarding congressional compensation took more than 200 years to be ratified by the requisite number of states.[13]

When the Volstead Act, the enforcing legislation, was vetoed by President Woodrow Wilson for technical reasons on October 27, 1919, Congress overrode his veto by a vote of 176–5 in the House and 65–20 in the Senate.[14]

Although the consensus today for drug criminalization is not as great as the consensus was for prohibition, it is sufficient to ensure that American society suffers many of the same economic and social consequences suffered under prohibition. Just as under prohibition, policymakers will continue to ignore the mounting evidence of failure until the consequences become too severe to be ignored. Just as under prohibition, occasional voices of reason (such as those of conservative economist and Nobel Prize winner Milton Friedman, or President Reagan's secretary of state, George Shultz) will be ignored until the revulsion level finally convinces even policymakers to rethink cherished preconceptions.

In the case of prohibition, the revulsion level reached a crescendo during the presidential election campaign of 1932. The long delayed rethinking of preconceptions now produced an explosion that approached overreaction. An influential article in the *American Public Mind* written by Peter Odegard complained that "every time a crime is committed, they cry prohibition. Every time a girl or boy goes wrong, they shout prohibition. Every time a policeman or politician is accused of corruption, they scream prohibition. As a result, they are gradually building up in the public mind the impression that prohibition is a major cause of the sins of society."[15]

THE CONVERSION OF HERBERT HOOVER

For die-hard prohibitionists, perhaps the most disillusioning event was the recanting of their prohibition champion, President Herbert Hoover. In accepting the Republican nomination on June 16, 1932, President Hoover stated, "I have always sympathized with the high purpose of the Eighteenth Amendment, and I have used every power at my command to make it effective over the entire country. I have hoped it was the final solution of the evils of the liquor traffic against which our people have striven for generations." While his original intentions had been "clear and need not be misunderstood," the mounting evidence had finally changed his mind. All of the arguments for legalizing liquor that he had adamantly rejected for so long, he now accepted. Criminalizing alcohol use, he now claimed, had led to "a spread of disrespect not only for the law but for all laws, grave dangers of practical nullification of the Constitution, a degeneration in municipal government and an increase in subsidized crime and violence."[16]

Hoover's conversion, of course, came too late to save the Republican Party, which suffered one of its greatest defeats in the 1932 presidential election.

Soon after his inauguration in 1933, President Franklin D. Roosevelt began threatening higher taxes if prohibition was not repealed. His postmaster general, James Farley, declared on May 25, 1933, "unless the Eighteenth Amendment is repealed, every income taxpayer in the country will have to contribute six to ten dollars out of every $100 earned."[17]

If today, legalizing and taxing drugs resulted in a 35 percent reduction in income taxes, and ten years later the American people were informed that their income taxes would increase by 35 percent if they decided to recriminalize them, one wonders what the response might be. Would the American people be willing to have their income taxes raised by 35 percent, their prisons filled and early release given to violent offenders, while what had previously been drug tax revenues is being channeled back to organized crime?

Ironically, the state of Utah on December 5, 1933, cast the final ratifying vote for repeal in the form of the Twenty-first Amendment.[18] President Roosevelt immediately began to use repeal as a lever to persuade states to begin legalizing and taxing alcoholic beverages. He made it clear to several states that they could expect no federal financial relief unless they first began to raise revenues by taxes on alcohol.[19]

Only grudgingly did the policymakers of the 1920s rethink their preconceptions, and then only after an overwhelming tide of events that included the suffering and hardships of millions of innocent people. It was no easier for them than it would be for today's policymakers to rethink their preconceptions about criminalizing drugs.

Today, the question remains: how did prohibition happen? In seeking the answer, we can learn much about the role of preconceptions and long-implanted biases in the process of creating law in society. Much that we learn is useful in the current debate over legalizing drugs, prostitution, and gambling.

THE ORIGINS OF PROHIBITION

The American temperance movement can be traced to a widely reported sermon against the sins of drunkenness delivered in 1673 by the Reverend Increase Matter of New England. Ministers of such religious denominations as the Methodists, Presbyterians, and Congregationalists followed this call with their own intemperance sermons. Many church leaders, such as Methodist minister John Wesley in 1789, demanded total abstinence from alcohol from all members of their church congregation.

Because such calls for voluntary abstinence had only limited effect among churchgoers and were widely disregarded by those outside the church, they were soon followed by demands for enforced laws.

As early as 1685, the Society of Friends demanded at their yearly meeting that a law be passed making it illegal to sell liquor to Indians. In 1783, the Dunkard Brethren declared that all those who disobeyed a prohibition on drinking alcohol should be excommunicated from church.

Early efforts to use laws to inhibit alcohol consumption met with limited success. In 1784, noted Doctor Benjamin Rush, an instrumental figure in promulgation of the Declaration of Independence, published a paper outlining the harm caused by the consumption of alcohol. This paper, directed only toward consumption of distilled spirits and not beer or light wine, was adopted and approved by the War Board of the Continental Congress. On March 25, 1776, there followed orders to Continental army officers to prevent the visiting of bars known then as "tippling houses" by American soldiers. The sale of spirits to soldiers was prohibited by act of the Continental Congress on September 20. Two years later, the Continental Congress passed resolutions calling upon each colony to prohibit the distilling of alcohol. Several did so, including Pennsylvania, which took strong measures against distilling in 1779.

In 1785, Rush published his famous article on the harmful physical effects of alcohol, "An Inquiry into the Effects of Ardent Spirits Upon the Human Body and Mind."[20] Other physicians and surgeons soon took up the temperance cause from the medical perspective, with the result that the New York College of Physicians in 1790 presented to the U.S. Senate a comprehensive document setting forth the adverse physical consequences of alcohol consumption and urging that action be taken to curb the use of alcohol.

Many leaders of this period encouraged the passage of laws to prohibit the consumption of alcohol, but others urged a more realistic and practical approach. Alexander Hamilton, for example, foresaw the potential harm and tragedies of alcohol prohibition and urged instead inhibition by high taxes for which the government could then find productive uses. In 1791, Congress adopted Hamilton's approach by passing the Revenue Act that would bring the federal government an estimated annual income of $826,000—A sum desperately needed to pay off war debts. Although subsequent sessions of Congress raised or lowered the tax amount, resistance to these liquor taxes soon prompted Congress to repeal the act. In 1802, Congress shifted emphasis to prohibition of liquor to Indians, authorizing President Jefferson to take all necessary measures to prevent such sales. In 1805, future president William Henry Harrison, governor of the Northwest Territory, pushed through legislation prohibiting the sale of liquor to Indians residing within a forty-mile radius of the town of Vincennes.

THE AMERICAN TEMPERANCE SOCIETY

The first attempt to organize a temperance movement came in 1789. Two hundred farmers in Litchfield, Connecticut, met to create an association "to discourage the use of spirituous liquors." Although this first attempt at organization was considered fanatical in its time, Litchfield was to become the center of the New England temperance reform movement, initiated in 1810 by church leaders.

Other temperance societies soon sprang up, including the "Billy Clark" society formed in 1808 (also known as the Union Temperance Society), and the Massachusetts Society for the Suppression of Intemperance, organized in 1813.

No society spread nationwide, however, until the American Temperance Society. Known also as the American Society for the Promotion of Temperance and later as the American Temperance Union, they held their first national temperance convention in Philadelphia in 1833.

By the 1850s the temperance movement had evolved into a political action group. In 1853, the Reverend John Marsh, secretary of the American Temperance Union, declared,

> We ask at the hand of our civil legislatures a prohibitory law which we can not get except at the hands of political action. It is, therefore, to me absurd to renounce or reject all pretensions to mingle in politics. We mean to carry it to the polls and to carry the polls in our favor....We have up to this time been timid before politicians. We have said "We did not mean you." We say now, "We do mean you and will put you down if you do not give us what we ask." These are our sentiments.[21]

Political action had some successes during this period, as such states as Illinois, Rhode Island, Maine, and Massachusetts, adopted statewide prohibition, while others, such as Louisiana, adopted a local option law. In 1852, Abraham Lincoln joined the Sons of Temperance in Springfield, Illinois. Reaction to such laws was sometimes fierce, however. In Illinois and Mainein 1855, the militia had to be called out to quell protests against alcohol prohibition.

Political action soon led to the formation of the Prohibition Party in Mansfield, Ohio, on July 24, 1869. The party first ran a national presidential ticket in 1872, and by 1892 was polling more than a quarter million votes in the national presidential election.

During the late 1800s, other reform movements such as the Women's Crusade of 1873, and the Woman's Christian Temperance Union were organized in support of prohibition. This latter organization was successful in securing "scientific temperance instruction" in the public schools. A second wave of state prohibition laws initiated during this period involved additional states such as Kansas and North Dakota. Many states later repealed their prohibition laws, however, so that by the end of 1890, only six states had statewide prohibition laws or constitutional prohibition amendments.

The decade of the 1890s proved a low point in the prohibition movement. Not only did many states repeal their prohibition laws, but those that retained them found the laws all but impossible to enforce. As a result, the alcohol industry began a period of expansion and growth. In reaction to such developments, the Anti-Saloon League was formed in 1893 in Oberlin, Ohio, and local leagues were soon established around the country.

THE PROGRESSIVE MOVEMENT

The Progressive movement, which arose between the election of Theodore Roosevelt in 1901 and the repudiation of President Wilson in 1919, was essentially a movement to reclaim democracy after a period of industrial consolidation, the growth of big business, and the creation of a discontented urban underclass. Although the Progressive movement promoted a wide variety of legal and political reforms, prohibition was considered progressive reform.[22]

Understanding prohibition requires an understanding of the political and social climate in which it was created. In the first decade of the 1900s, prohibition was seen as a means of eliminating alcohol consumption, thought to impair human reasoning and to undermine religion and government. It was based not only on the teachings of science , but also on the democratic principle of curbing a plutocracy, the most corrupting of which was the liquor industry.

The Progressive movement also had a recognizable religious component. Protestant denominations in particular saw alcohol consumption as undermining Christianity's most powerful incentive to self-discipline and social morality. The result was wretched homes, pauperism, crime, disease and vice, and a general lowering of the moral tone of society. Catholic reformers perceived alcohol consumption as destroying human decency and honor. Religious reformers used many of the same arguments against liquor as drug opponents use today—namely that liquor use leads to further evils.

These reformers were probably on the weakest ground, however, when they attempted to invoke biblical scriptures to support their demand for prohibition. Such reliance soon triggered a vigorous theological debate on whether the Greek and Hebrew words for wine should be properly translated as "unfermented grape juice." If the suggested vision of Jesus and his disciples at the Last Supper drinking something akin to Welch's grape juice was not enough to arouse the snickers of the wine industry, other readers of the Bible suggested that perhaps Ephesians 5:18 should be changed to read: "And be ye not drunk with unfermented grape juice."

Other members of the Progressive movement emphasized the dangers alcohol posed for representative democracy. If the lower classes were permitted to continue drinking, they would become both corrupted and impoverished and would eventually sell their votes to those who would confiscate and redistribute property and abolish liberty and free government.

Although several Catholic organizations formed prohibitionist societies (such as the Catholic Prohibition League of America), most Catholics resisted the prohibition movement, especially after some prohibition laws refused to exempt even the use of sacramental wine for communion services.[23] Most Jewish organizations also resisted prohibition, the Reform Wing of American Judaism denouncing it in 1914 as a fanatical movement.[24]

SCIENTIFIC CONTRIBUTIONS

By 1900, prohibition advocates had amassed a formidable mass of scientific literature to buttress their demand for prohibition. As early as 1866, Dr. Benjamin Watson had reported his scientific findings that alcohol, far from warming the body, actually caused the body to rapidly cool by causing the blood vessels to dilate and allow more blood to reach the body's surface, creating only the illusion of warmth. He also concluded that, in spite of popular perception, alcohol acted as a depressant rather than a stimulant.

In 1892, Professor Emil Kraepelin of the University of Heidelberg reported that alcohol functioned as a narcotic drug. It depressed both the brain and the nervous system and diminished a person's ability to function and perform physical tasks.[25] Other studies revealed that alcohol depressed the heart and interfered with digestion.

In 1896, the Massachusetts Bureau of Labor Statistics reported that more than one-fifth of all mental diseases were directly caused by alcohol use. A study by the American Medico-Psychological Association reported that 24 percent of mental diseases were caused by alcohol, and that alcohol was the sole cause of insanity in more than 14 percent of cases. Alcohol was also linked to cirrhosis of the liver, Bright's disease, heart disease, and chronic catarrhal inflammation of the stomach, and the lowering of resistance to a host of other serious diseases.[26]

Years before modern science linked alcohol consumption to birth defects, alcohol before prohibition was linked to no less than four classes of mental retardation in children, including epilepsy and those referred to as imbecility, idiocy, and feeble-mindedness. A 1908 issue of McClure's Magazine reported a study revealing that 5 percent of all cases of imbecility, and 20 percent of cases of epilepsy (more than 160,000) were caused by parental alcohol use. A study of fifty-seven children produced by alcohol-consuming parents revealed that 82 percent suffered defects, including deformation, idiocy, and epilepsy. Only 10 percent were found to be normal.[27]

To those who insisted that alcohol was harmless if taken in "moderation," studies were cited that alcohol, even when taken in small quantities, was an addictive poison. A national 1914 meeting of neurologists and psychiatrists declared alcohol a "definite poison to the brain and other tissue" and the cause of many severe mental and physical defects. In 1918, the American Medical Association declared itself as opposed to the use of alcohol on grounds of its medical harm, its president declaring that the AMA would "welcome national prohibition."[28]

School textbooks of the period stated, "Alcohol is a colorless liquid poison," inferring that alcohol is always a poison and always harmful to the human body. A contributor to *Cosmopolitan* magazine in 1908 declared that alcohol is "poison pure and simple," and that it should be "subjected to legislation like other drugs...such as arsenic, strychnine, etc."[29]

Dr. Henry Smith Williams, a prominent scientist, declared in 1908 that even "moderate" drinking was a severe health hazard:

You are tangibly threatening the physical structure of your stomach, your liver, your kidneys, your heart, your blood-vessels, your nerves, your brain. You are entailing upon your descendants unborn a bond of incalculable misery...As a mere business proposition, is your glass of beer, or your glass of wine worth such a price?[30]

Statistical reports seemed to confirm the scientific literature. A study of insurers between 1866 and 1910 conducted by a national life insurance company revealed that even moderate drinkers had a 37 percent higher mortality rate than nondrinkers, and that the mortality rate for drinkers between the ages of thirty-five and forty was a staggering 83 percent higher. *The American Underwriter* reported that alcohol was a significant factor in 7.7 percent of all deaths.[31] A joint study reported in the *Atlantic Monthly* by the Actuarial Society of America and the Medical Directors' Association, which represented more than forty-three insurance companies in North America, showed that even moderate drinkers (those who drank less than two beers a day) had a mortality rate 18 percent greater than nondrinkers. Drinkers who only occasionally drank to excess (e.g., on New Year's Eve) had a 74 percent higher mortality rate, and heavier drinkers had an 86 percent higher mortality rate from diabetes, cirrhosis, and pneumonia, and a suicide rate twice that of the average.[32]

A study of the returns of thirty-three charity organization societies, published in the "Economic Aspects of the Liquor Problem," found that more than a quarter of all cases of poverty were traceable to alcohol.[33] The Massachusetts Bureau of Labor Statistics reported in 1895 that 39 percent of their poverty cases were directly caused by alcohol.[34]

In 1914, the *Literary Digest* published a study of 13,402 convicted criminals in twelve states that concluded that alcohol was a significant contributing factor in half of all crimes, and the primary cause in a third of all crimes.[35] Modern studies have reached similar conclusions (see chapter 1). Convicted criminals were convinced that the percentage was even higher. In 1914, 1,008 out of 1,478 prisoners in the Philadelphia Penitentiary signed a petition to the Pennsylvania legislature demanding the passage of a prohibition law on grounds that alcohol caused more than 70 percent of all crimes.[36]

THE COALITION OF PROHIBITION INTERESTS

By 1915, an unlikely coalition of powerful interest groups united to press for national prohibition. Business groups became convinced that the $2 billion spent on liquor could be diverted toward more productive consumer goods, thus raising the standard of living for all. Companies that stood to benefit most directly from prohibition, such as Welch's Grape Juice and Coca-Cola, were at the forefront.

A study of the effects of prohibition in several states concluded that wherever prohibition laws were enacted, increases occurred in bank deposits, trade, and business activity. World War I increased concerns about national survival and caused many people to support prohibition as a means of increasing military efficiency.

At a time when business and labor could agree on little, union leaders supported business in pushing for prohibition, stating their belief that liquor dulled the workingman's "class consciousness" and rendered him incapable of fighting vigorously for better pay and working conditions.

Supporters of the Progressive movement shrugged off concerns about the loss of government revenues that prohibition might cause, noting that the $340 million in liquor tax revenues only made the government more beholden to the liquor industry.

Southern politicians determined to perpetuate a system of racial segregation believed that liquor might encourage racial protests and violence. A not uncommon perception was that a barroom would precipitate a race war. Indeed, many racial violence incidents involved alcohol use.

Others expressed concern that liquor played a major role in the rape of white women. *Collier's* magazine published a 1908 article suggesting that the liquor industry's practice of selling liquor bottles with labels of naked white women inflamed sexual passions of African Americans: "The primitive Negro field hand, a web of strong, sudden impulses, good and bad...sits in the road at the height of his debauch, looking at that obscene picture of a white woman on the label, drinking in the invitation which it carries. And then comes—opportunity. There follows the hideous episode of the rope or the stake."[37]

THE EIGHTEENTH AMENDMENT

The Eighteenth Amendment to the Constitution was the culmination of a process of a gradual but relentless national prohibition strategy. The process began in 1901 when Congress passed the Anti-Canteen Law, and continued with a 1908 ban on shipping liquor through the mails; the Webb-Kenyon Act of 1913 prohibiting interstate shipment of liquor to prohibiting states; the Lever Food and Fuel Control Act of 1917 forbidding use of food products in liquor production; the War Prohibition Act of 1918 prohibiting sale of beer and wine; and finally the National Prohibition Act of 1919 (more popularly known as the Volstead Act), which provided for enforcement of the War Prohibition Act and defined an intoxicating liquor as any beverage containing more than 0.5 percent alcohol.

The Eighteenth Amendment provided that the "manufacture, sale, or transportation of intoxicating liquors within, the importation thereof into, or the exportation thereof from the United States and all territory subject to the jurisdiction thereof for beverage purposes is hereby prohibited." It further provided that "the Congress and the several States shall have concurrent power to enforce this article by appropriate legislation."

THE PROHIBITION EXPERIENCE

In 1919, the American people secured their demands with one of the most overwhelming electoral majorities ever recorded in the history of the Republic namely, total prohibition of the sale and consumption of alcoholic beverages. A mere fourteen years later, the American people demanded and received, again by overwhelming popular support, total rejection of the prohibitionist agenda. What began as a policy permanently codified in the Constitution became the only constitutional amendment to be repealed. The unprecedented shift in law reveals more than a view of American life in the 1920s. Prohibition's failure may say much about the ability of law to regulate behavior in a free society.

Public desire and ability to evade dry laws was actually apparent before national prohibition was enacted. Americans have never allowed the law to stand between them and their drink. In the mid-1800s, Portland, Maine, outlawed the selling of alcohol. Saloonkeepers, complying with the strict letter of the law, did not sell alcohol but did sell soda crackers for a nickel each, with which they served a free drink. Others charged admission to see a "blind pig," the viewing of which entitled one to a free tumbler of rum. The blind pig was the nineteenth-century version of the speakeasy.[38]

By 1914, 74 percent of the United States by area and 47 percent by population was dry.[39] However, these laws were most commonly evaded by importing alcohol from wet states. Because Congress has exclusive power to regulate interstate commerce, dry states were powerless to prevent this circumvention of their laws.[40] Congress then passed the Webb-Kenyon law, forbidding shipments of liquor where they would be consumed in violation of state law.[41] But still the laws were circumvented. Even under Webb-Kenyon, "liquor forces poured their liquor into dry states and communities; . . . it became perfectly clear to the people that the liquor problem could only be solved by an amendment to the Constitution of the United States that would outlaw the liquor traffic in every foot of American soil. . . ."[42]

It is interesting that prohibitionists believed that a national dry law would succeed where state dry laws had failed. State laws were violated internally, for instance, by "blind pig" establishments and externally by importing alcohol from wet states. Importation occurred even in the face of the Webb-Kenyon law making it illegal. A national dry law could, of course, be circumvented in the same way: by surreptitious production within the borders or by importing across the borders from countries where alcohol was legal. There was little reason to believe that the Volstead Act would be successful in containing these violations. As the seventeenth-century philosopher Baruch Spinoza said, "Men of leisure are never deficient in the ingenuity needed to enable them to outwit laws formed to regulate things which are almost forbidden." This is an apt description of the failure of national prohibition. The law was effectively impotent against those who wanted to buy and sell alcohol for their own benefit.

The Volstead Act, the federal law designed to enforce prohibition, contained major loopholes. It allowed the use of alcohol for medicinal and sacramental purposes, and it did not "prohibit the purchase and sale of warehouse receipts covering distilled spirits on deposit in government bonded warehouses."[43]

Those seeking relief from the dry law first exploited the Volstead loopholes. Doctors, for instance, could prescribe whiskey, beer, and wine for medicinal purposes. When Volstead first went into effect, "Thousands of Americans complained of ailments which could be relieved only by copious draughts of these beverages."[44] It was certainly inevitable that the public would tempt their doctors into writing unnecessary prescriptions with a bribe. According to one estimate, doctors were paid $40 million in graft to write the fraudulent prescriptions.[45] In 1920, 15,000 doctors and 5,700 pharmacists applied for medicinal use permits.[46] In 1921, more than eight million gallons of alcohol were prescribed, a twenty-fold increase over the pre-prohibition era.[47] By 1929, the 100,000 permitted doctors were writing

prescriptions at a rate of eleven million per year.[48] In Chicago, it was estimated that one-half of the half million whiskey prescriptions were fraudulent.[49]

Of course, some found it convenient to eliminate the doctors as mid-
dlemen altogether. Huge numbers of counterfeit prescription forms and
forged doctor signatures emerged. In 1920, prohibition agents in Chicago
counted 300,000 forged prescriptions. In New York in 1922, agents uncovered a counterfeit ring in which bootleggers had forged the names of
most of the doctors in the New York telephone directory.[50] The prescriptions were filled at drug houses or by retail druggists. Eager to participate
in the source of newfound wealth, bootleggers set up shop as druggists
and received government permits to fill prescriptions. Prior to prohibition, 400 drug houses filled the demand for medicinal alcohol; by the late
1920s, there were 3,300 such firms.[51] When the Willis-Campbell law was
enacted to address these problems, the primary effect was to increase the
price of the prescription. The doctor received two dollars for the prescription, the druggist from three to six dollars for the half pint.[52] Fore-
telling the demise of prohibition, enforcing the law simply made it more
profitable to break it.

The alcohol sold by druggists had been accumulated and warehoused
by the government prior to the commencement of prohibition. Estimates
of these supplies in 1920 range from forty million to seventy million gallons.[53] The supplies were stored by the government but still owned by the
distillers, who were prohibited from disposing of them.[54] Distilleries continued to operate to replenish the whiskey used for medicinal purposes,
brandy used to fortify sacramental wines, and rum used to treat tobacco
products.[55] A major exception of the Volstead Act was that it did not prohibit the sale of stored distilled spirits in government warehouses.[56] Under
Volstead and existing notions of property rights, nothing prevented the
sale of the warehoused alcohol, only that it could not be moved.[57]

George Remus, a Chicago attorney, understood the enormously lucrative potential under this section of Volstead. He eventually bought more
than a dozen distilleries in Kentucky, Missouri, and Ohio, thereby taking
rights to the stored supplies owned by those distilleries.[58] Under the
medicinal permit system, he then accepted prescriptions.[59] Because he
was not transporting the alcohol, he was perfectly legal under Volstead; he
was selling liquor on permit under government control.[60] But by controlling manufacture and sale, he saw "excellent discretionary opportunities
in bookkeeping, distribution, and other business methods."[61]

Remus understood that immediate access to huge quantities of alcohol
required a larger scale distribution system. He bootlegged his supplies by
rail and truck throughout the Midwest and to New York and Philadelphia.
He would leave enough liquor in the warehouse to satisfy government
inspectors.[62] After a few years of operation, he had built a $50-million-a-

year business employing 3,000 people.[63] His personal take was $5 million over a five-year period. In one eleven-month span, he deposited $2.8 million in one Cincinnati bank.[64] For his short but profitable life in crime, Remus served five short jail sentences and paid $11,000 in fines.[65]

Remus was the largest, but not the only, bootlegger of warehoused alcohol. Enormous quantities of stored liquor passed through the illicit distribution system. By 1925, legal controls on medicinal liquor had been tightened. The number of permits had been reduced to 446. The alcohol was consolidated into thirty-seven warehouses. By 1930, legal withdrawals from the warehouses had been reduced to about 1.5 million gallons. By the time the controls were instituted, however, as much as two-thirds of the original seventy million gallons stored before the onset of prohibition had been siphoned off.

Wine was something of a favored drink under prohibition. Volstead contained an "apple-cider" provision that allowed "home fermentation of fruit juices."[66] This exception was exploited by every household that enjoyed wine; in these homes, "the cellar, garage, or a closet usually held a keg of grape juice quietly obeying the call of nature...." [67] Under this exception, consumption of wine rose by two-thirds under prohibition. By 1930, 100 million[68] gallons of wine were produced. From 1920 to 1926, sales of grapes doubled. In California, the acreage devoted to growing grapes grew from 97,000 acres in 1919 to more than 680,000 in 1926.[69] Andrew Volstead was nicknamed "the patron saint of the San Joaquin Valley."

The exception for sacramental wine was, of course, also exploited for monetary gain. The exception was an allowance to Jewish families who could have up to five gallons of wine a year. The wine was purchased by rabbis who must have a government-issued permit and must present a list of their congregation members. Government, however, neglected to oversee who could become a rabbi. Permits were rarely checked, and anyone convincingly presenting themselves as a rabbi could buy wine. The congregation lists were often simply names copied from a telephone book. One woman actually made a business out of providing fraudulent lists to fake rabbis to buy the wine.

Big cities swarmed with fake rabbis busily diverting wine to bootleggers. Many opened wine stores; they were supposed to sell only to members of their own congregation and to Jews certified by other rabbis. Actually, they sold to everyone.[70] According to one estimate, the demand for sacramental wines increased by 800,000 gallons during the first two years of prohibition.[71] One prohibition proponent fumed that the sacramental wine use was converted into sacrilegious use.[72]

Beer was not a favored drink under prohibition, but it was probably the easiest beverage to make under Volstead. The law prohibited the production of "cereal beverage" with an alcohol content greater than one-half of one percent.[73] It was supposed that "near beer" with alcohol content less than this percent would replace the consumption of real beer. However, near beer production required brewing real beer and drawing off the alcohol. "A perfectly legal process was dependent on a first stage that was illegal, and that the government had to accept."[74] The manufacturers were required to ship the alcohol to government warehouses, but much was diverted to bootleggers.[75] Real beer could also be made by the mixture of two perfectly legal products: yeast and wort.[76] The brewer might further put the alcohol back in the keg or ignore the second step altogether. General Andrew, the prohibition commissioner, said in 1930, "If a brewer is disposed to violate the law, it is just a question of putting a hose in a high-powered beer tank and filling near-beer kegs with high-powered beer and running it out as near beer. So it is a rather difficult thing to get at."[77]

The number of brewer permits issued rendered government oversight of near-beer production and alcohol transport to warehouses minimal.[78] As a result, "[t]here was nothing to compel the brewer to lower the alcoholic content of his beer except his conscience."[79]

The public did not take to near beer. In 1914, American breweries produced more than two billion gallons of real beer. In 1926, the total production of near beer was 150 million gallons, just 7 percent of the erstwhile production of real beer.[80] It was obvious, especially to the large breweries attempting to adhere to the law, that the nation was quenching its thirst with real beer. A spokesman for Anheuser-Busch, the world's largest brewery, wrote as follows:

Through the corporation's own traveling representatives, and its 2,000 wholesale dealers, it learned that the entire country was being flooded with products prohibited by the prohibition law. A considerable number of smaller breweries changed hands, for considerations of a fraction of their original value, and the new owners found it easy to make arrangements for their illegal operation in partnership with politicians—on a profit-sharing basis, of course. This soon grew to such enormous proportions that the sale of lawful cereal beverages was practically killed.[81]

Real beer was so difficult to control that it became a virtually open violation of the Volstead Act. One commentator said, "Really enormous amounts of beer were diverted to bootleggers...trucks loaded with beer traveling the streets in broad daylight were a common sight in many large cities."[82] Beer drinkers did not have to depend on black-market beer suppliers, though. Anyone could produce beer in a covert and virtually undetectable manner with wort. Wort production increased to six times the amount produced before prohibition.[83]

The amount of alcohol distributed and consumed through Volstead's loopholes was undeniably a significant quantity. However, those sources of the illicit good were a small trickle compared to the flood of illicit booze smuggled from other countries. Protecting against smuggling was difficult, given the sheer size of territory to be patrolled: 12,000 miles of coast-line, 3,700 miles of land border and 3,000 miles of lake and river front.[84] The Canadian border presented a particularly daunting task for enforce-ment agents. Between the countries passed 400 good or fair roads, 150 passable roads, and 100 known trails. The Great Lakes, Lake Champlain, and the Detroit and St. Lawrence rivers also provided access for smug-glers.[85] The terrain of northern New York provided ideal cover for smug-glers as well as numerous towns too small for customs stations.[86] Simple proximity also contributed to the ease of smuggling. One enterprising farmer lived close enough to the border that he could load up his horses with bottles in Canada and trust them to find their way home.[87] Detroit offered the most propitious access to the American market because "The waterway...was narrow, dotted with islands, and equipped with plenty of small docks and landing places....In summer a boat would speed across in just a few minutes, and in winter it was possible to drive trucks right across the ice."[88]

The amounts smuggled from Canada cannot be specified with accuracy. However, it is certain even the minimum amounts smuggled were enor-mous. In the first half of 1920, 900,000 cases of alcohol were imported into Canadian border towns. The amount of liquor imported into Ontario alone rose from 9 gallons per capita to 102 gallons per capita with the onset of prohibition.[89] Canadian imports of liquor from Britain alone multiplied by six between 1918 and 1922.[90] Just eleven days after prohibition went into effect, the customs director told Congress that large quantities were cross-ing the border and infinitesimal amounts were being intercepted.[91] Plug-ging the leaks along the border was no more successful as prohibition proceeded. In 1928, the Department of Justice said smuggling had increased by 75 percent since 1925.[92] Smugglers employed all means of travel. In 1928, an estimated $15 million of alcoholic beverages were com-ing across in rail cars annually.[93] Rail was a particularly efficacious means of smuggling; large quantities of the product could be brought across. Three cars seized in 1927 alone carried $200,000 of alcohol.[94] In April 1930, sixty-two planes loaded with liquor took off from Canada for landing fields in the United States.[95] In the mid-1920s, an estimated 800 rum boats operated in the Great Lakes, with equal numbers on Lake Champlain and the rivers.[96] Overnight tourists and small-time smugglers would return to the United States with bottles in baby carriages, hot water bottles, or the toes of oversize shoes.[97] The most definitive evidence of inability to stop the illicit traffic occurred in 1927, when Canada agreed to notify the United States when boats carrying alcohol cleared Canadian customs headed for the United States. In the year ending March 1928, Canadian records indi-cated that boats loaded with 3.4 million gallons of liquor headed for U.S. shores. Of this quantity, prohibition agents seized less than 5 percent.[98] Given the ingenuity and doggedness of the smuggling campaign, rumors of an underground alcohol pipeline or electric torpedoes filled with whiskey crossing the lakes seemed not so far-fetched.[99]

Detroit was the primary point of exchange with Canada. It is estimated that 75 percent of alcohol from Canada came in through the "Detroit-Windsor funnel."[100] The *New York Times* reported that in one week in May 1927, 40,000 cases of liquor landed in Detroit.[101] The *Detroit News* said in 1928 that at least $35 million worth of alcohol came to the city annually.[102] It was estimated that the value of all aspects of the illicit trade in Detroit, including smuggling, manufacturing, and distribution, totaled $215 million, employed 50,000 people, and was the second largest industry behind automobile manufacturing.[103] Nor was Detroit "the only point through which liquor is smuggled, and Canada is not the only county from which liquor comes."[104]

At the beginning of prohibition, Larry Fay was a thirty-one-year-old independent cabdriver making twenty-five dollars a week. One day, he found himself walking the streets of Montreal, having just been paid by his passenger to make the 385-mile trip. He noticed that high-quality whiskey was selling for ten dollars a case. Although not a drinker himself, he was certain the selling price in New York City would be much higher. He purchased two cases and drove back to the city. Upon arrival, he quickly converted his $20 investment into $160. He was on his way back to Montreal.[105]

The price differentials more than justified the trip. While the return on whiskey was highest, one could buy a case of beer for five dollars and sell it in New York for twenty-five dollars. A carload of twenty-five cases would thus net $600. A bottle of rye would cost four dollars in Canada and sell for twelve dollars in New York. The selling price of champagne would quintuple the amount of the investment. A smuggler could make two trips a week in the summer and one in the winter.[106]

Within nine months, Larry Fay owned several cabs and trucks, all of which were put to service in his new operation.[107] He considered the business unsavory and a little risky, but the profits were irresistible to an Irish immigrant with an impoverished upbringing.[108] In 1922 alone, he earned a half million dollars. By 1923, he owned a fleet of hundreds of cabs that were famous throughout New York City.[109] Always seeking respectability, Fay invested his significant earnings into a string of New York's most opulent nightclubs. Within a few years, prohibition had propelled him from a $25-a-week job to the heights of the New York social elite.

Smuggling also occurred along the Mexican border, albeit on a much smaller scale. Of course, the smaller magnitude of traffic meant less enforcement and less risk to the smugglers. During the initial years of prohibition, only thirty-five agents were assigned to patrol the entire length of the southern border.[110] Smugglers could bring alcohol across with a minimum of trickery. Women would traverse the bridge between Juárez and El

Paso "wearing voluminous skirts and bulging in all directions because of the goat bladders and stomachs filled with mescal and tequila and tied about their waists."[111] Some simply pushed the barrels across the Rio Grande or floated them across in rafts.[112] Although the border was never an important source of supply, it was unquestionably a feasible source and waiting to be exploited should the market require.

Although smuggling from Canada was highly effective and profitable, it lacked the sheer excitement and romance of smuggling from overseas. Some rumrunners, in fact, saw themselves as swashbucklers ruling the high seas.[113] Most, however, considered it a means of delivering liquor to the paying public. The actual amount of alcohol smuggled must be estimated by indirect means. Compared to pre-prohibition years, the West Indies increased the importation of British alcohol by five times. Prior to prohibition, the Bahamas and Bermuda both imported about 1,000 gallons yearly; by 1922, the figures were 386,000 and 40,000 gallons, respectively.[114] The profits made were at least as large as those generated from the Canadian trade: an $8 case of Scotch or cognac could be sold for $65 in the large cities of the American Atlantic coast.[115] The size of the boats employed in the endeavor grew larger as prohibition progressed. The initial boats were small cutters and schooners, capable of carrying between 1,000 and 3,000 cases of booze.[116] Later, as the organized syndicates moved in, they employed huge boats capable of transporting enormous quantities of liquor. For instance, the Norwegian steamer *Sagafjord*, boarded by the Coast Guard, had 43,000 cases on board.[117]

In the beginning stages of prohibition, the Coast Guard faced the greatest enforcement challenge. The rumrunners could essentially operate with impunity by staying outside the three-mile territorial limit. Although U.S. registered vessels were subject to seizure outside this limit, simply registering the ship with a different country circumvented this problem.[118] The boats would be "immune from U.S. authorities, and waited for the well-informed to come to him."[119] Thus was born the famous "rum row," a line of ships, stretching the length of the Atlantic coast and the Gulf of Mexico, and outside the reach of American law.[120] In 1922, Prohibition Commissioner Roy Haynes estimated that hundreds of these ships were anchored off the Atlantic coast, with as many as sixty off New Jersey alone.[121] The rumrunners also enjoyed the logistic advantage of proximity to their markets: the heaviest concentration of ethnic groups most likely to drink alcohol—Germans, Irish, and Italians—were located in the major urban cities of New York, Boston, and New Jersey.[122] Given that the actual smugglers were beyond their reach, enforcement authorities were reduced to attempting to interdict the innumerable small, fast craft that actually brought the product ashore.

A boatman by the name of Bill McCoy is credited with developing the rum row concept. He had been an experienced skipper working out of the family boatyard in Jacksonville, Florida. He was approached by a prosperous-looking man who, a few months before, had been a struggling independent fisherman. The man proposed to pay McCoy $100 a day to captain the man's schooner to Nassau and then to Atlantic City. McCoy turned the offer down because it sparked grander ideas of selling his fleet of small boats and buying a large one to smuggle the loads himself.[123] He bought a ninety-foot fishing schooner called the *Henry L. Marshall*.[124]

McCoy's first stroke of genius was understanding that transporting alcohol in wooden cases took too much space. He devised a way of transporting the bottles in burlap bags, doubling his ship's capacity to 3,000 cases.[125] McCoy quickly generated a large bank account; by 1921, he had the means to purchase the *Arethusa,* with a capacity of 5,000 cases, and lease the *Henry L. Marshall* to other smugglers for $15,000 per trip. Not wanting to take the risk of landing this much cargo on shore, he would leave the ship at the three-mile limit while he went ashore to drum up business. McCoy could clear more than $50,000 per trip using this technique.[126]

McCoy was the victim of his own success. By October 1922 his rum row concept had inspired numerous imitators. His profits were down, and purchases of more ships brought him near bankruptcy. His final innovation may have been his most profitable and enduring. While most of the boats sold poor or highly diluted product, he cut out a market niche by selling the highest quality rye. Customers seeking this product were referred to his boat where they could purchase "The real McCoy."[127] Aided by his famous appellation, McCoy became the nation's best-known rum-runner and generated huge revenues. One voyage in January 1923 garnered $127,000. His two boats were each generating $100,000 per trip. Later that year, unbeknownst to McCoy, the three-mile territorial limit was extended to twelve miles. After a high-speed chase during which he was fired upon by the government cutter *Seneca,* McCoy finally yielded to the law.[128]

Off-coast smuggling enterprises may best reflect the thrust and parry between law enforcement officers and lawbreakers. Although rumrunners had their way in the early years, in 1924, Congress gave some help to the Coast Guard: $13 million to restore twenty World War I naval destroyers. By 1928, the Coast Guard put 3 cruisers, 25 destroyers, 243 patrol boats and 11,000 officers into the prohibition effort.[129] Throughout the 1920s, half of the Coast Guard budget, about $15 million per year, was devoted to enforcing prohibition.[130] An agreement with Great Britain allowed the Coast Guard to search all British ships within one hour's running distance from the coast.[131] Other countries agreed to extend the territorial limit to twelve miles.[132]

For every step law enforcement took, the smugglers seemed to take a counter step. Whatever boats the Coast Guard would use, the smugglers would design their boats a touch faster.[133] To combat the twelve-mile limit, the smugglers would not simply wait at a spot for their customers. Rather, a large mother ship would rendezvous with several small, fast boats to make the exchange before detection by the Coast Guard.[134] Or one slow, expendable boat carrying a minimal load would create a diversion so that several faster boats with sizable cargoes could escape.[135] In the event a boat was boarded, the cargo might be cleverly hidden. In the case of the ship *Alice*, the bottles were stored in 22-foot compartments built onto the outside of the ship's hull.[136]

If all else failed, smugglers were prepared to fight. Both sides were usually heavily armed. In one colorful episode in July 1924, a Coast Guard cutter pursued two speedboats along Coney Island beach before 100,000 beach spectators. The smugglers fired submachine guns, and the cutter responded by firing three-inch shells until the speedboats were out of range.[137] By 1929, eighteen rumrunners and eight Coast Guardsmen were killed in these shootouts.[138] Some of the battles, though not deadly, were vicious. During one incident, the combatants, having exhausted their supply of bullets, resorted to heaving potatoes at each other.

The exertions of the prohibition forces seemed to have little effect on the ability of rumrunners to deliver their goods. Perhaps the real effect was to make the rumrunners bigger, smarter, and more sophisticated. When Bill McCoy finished his fifteen-month jail sentence, he declined the opportunity to run alcohol again. The syndicates had taken over the operation and had turned it from a free and adventurous sport into a "cold, ruthless, efficient business...."[139] Despite the expense of equipping the Coast Guard, Admiral Bullard testified in front of Congress that "Smuggling is now carried on almost exclusively by large, highly organized international syndicates."[140] Radio communication was critical. As many as 100 radio stations on the Atlantic coast guided the ships.[141] Bullard estimated that ninety-one rumrunning vessels continued to operate on the Atlantic coast, forty-seven in the Gulf of Mexico, and thirty-three in the Pacific.[142] Ultimately, restricting the amount of alcohol coming from overseas became unfeasible. Even a moderate degree of success with smuggling along the coasts would have required a two-ocean naval blockade.[143]

HEALTH EFFECTS OF PROHIBITION

Industrial alcohol was the most hazardous circumvention of Volstead. Certain industries, the chemical industry in particular, require huge amounts of alcohol as a purifying agent. One large rayon plant, for example, would require two million gallons of alcohol yearly.[144] Under a 1906 act called the Tax Free Industrial and Denatured Alcohol Act, industrial alcohol was not subject to the same tax as beverage alcohol. However, in order to ensure that such alcohol would not be consumed, Congress required that it be "denatured," that is, poisoned to make it undrinkable and unpalatable.[145] The most common denaturant was methanol, thereby rendering the substance wood alcohol.[146] Other possible ingredients included kerosene, gasoline, formaldehyde, bichloride of mercury, mercuric acid, or benzene.[147] While the production and distribution of pure and specially denatured alcohol (used for cosmetics, soaps, etc.) were controlled by a permit system, completely denatured alcohol was not permitted.[148]

Production of denatured alcohol was essentially uncontrolled. Not coincidentally, when prohibition went into effect, production shot up. In 1910, seven million gallons were made. In 1920, the figure was twenty-eight million gallons, in 1923 almost sixty million gallons.[149] It was, of course, illegal to divert denatured alcohol for consumption purposes. However, under law, prohibition agents were limited to checking only one transfer of ownership of the substance. Thus, a manufacturer would produce the alcohol, sell it to a dummy corporation, known as a cover house, show the agent the receipt, and the investigation would be complete.[150] The amount actually diverted for bootlegging purposes was a matter of some dispute. James Doran, chief chemist of the Prohibition Unit, estimated that, over the course of a year, twelve to fifteen million gallons were diverted. U.S. District Attorney Emory Buckner put the figure at closer to sixty million gallons.[151] Perhaps the estimate best revealing the magnitude of diversion was given by Major Mills, prohibition administrator of the Second Federal District. He said that in 1925, sixteen denaturing plants in New York City alone diverted ten million gallons.[152]

The apparent assumption was that no one would drink poisoned, unpalatable alcohol. This is probably a valid assumption when legal, safe alcohol is available. Under prohibition, however, the assumption proved to be literally sickening. The bootleggers, of course, did their best to make the product at least palatable:

The government and bootleggers waged battles over industrial alcohol, as the government would denature and the bootleggers would attempt to re-distill the booze. To prevent this sort of re-distilling the government tried various formulas for making industrial alcohol strictly industrial. They put in stuff that gave it a sickening smell. But the bootleggers hired smart chemists and learned how to get rid of that. The government made the poison more poisonous. And the bootleggers fixed that. The government even put in kerosene that could not be distilled out and it was distilled out. Finally, the government made alcohol muddy-looking and guaranteed against bootlegging. And the bootleggers fixed that, too.[153]

Although the bootleggers made the product at least minimally palatable, they could not make it innocuous. Removing some of the denaturants, especially wood alcohol, required special apparatus unavailable to most bootleggers.[154] Poisons were pervasive in the alcohol on the market. A test of 480,000 gallons of confiscated booze showed that 98 percent contained poisons.[155] Government pursuit of this policy took its toll in the most dramatic way. In 1920, the national death toll from poisoned liquor was 1,064. In 1925, it was 4,154. On New Year's Day, 1927, forty-one people died in New York City alone.[156]

Government policy of purposefully poisoning alcohol was an initial cause of the public's rejection of prohibition. The reaction intensified when Wayne Wheeler of the Anti-Saloon League justified the use of denaturants as a deterrent and accused those who continued to drink of suicide.[157] Ironically, the temperance movement had justified prohibition on the grounds that alcohol itself was "a deadly form of poison."[158] Most people believed death an excessive punishment for violating prohibition.[159] Increasingly, the public held the government and prohibition proponents responsible for the deaths.[160] Dr. Nicolas Butler, president of Columbia University, called the use of denaturants "legalized murder."[161] Or, as Will Rogers said, "Government used to murder by the bullet only. Now, it's by the quart."[162]

The most ubiquitous form of alcohol production, of course, was moonshining. Huge distilleries and breweries were replaced by many thousands of small stills across the country. This dispersed production was undoubtedly the most difficult to control. Prohibition Commissioner General Andrews said, "When we cut off one source of supply, moonshine wells up to fill the gap." The general further estimated that moonshining accounted for eight times more alcohol than government warehouses.[163] The government's Wickersham Commission concluded that seventy million gallons of alcohol were moonshined annually from corn sugar alone.[164] These small stills were perhaps the most economical method of illicit production. A commercial still, set up for $500, would pay for itself in four days.[165] A gallon of moonshine cost fifty cents to make and sold for at least twelve dollars.[166]

Government seizures of stills occurred at an astounding rate. From 1921 to 1925, 696,933 stills were seized; General Andrews nevertheless estimated that this was only one of every ten stills in operation.[167] Moonshining was such "an enduring presence" among certain groups, especially "French, Italian, and Slavic ethnicity, [that] Prohibition may have seemed something of a mystery; few people could understand how pietists could take it seriously."[168] One commentator concluded: "There were illegal stills, home breweries, and bathtub gin mills by the hundreds of thousands which presented a challenge so unnerving it could be neither defined nor contained."[169]

Forcing production underground and outside of the view of the law had other unintended consequences. One effect of all kinds of prohibition is to make the prohibited product smaller, less bulky, and easier to transport.[170] In the case of alcohol, beer production fell and production rose of concentrated and potent hard liquor that was "more readily marketable and easier to smuggle."[171] Prohibition was at least one significant factor in the shift in consumption from beer to hard liquor.[172] Beer constituted 90 percent of all alcohol consumption before prohibition.[173] New York Representative Fiorello La Guardia suggested that, in his opinion, prohibition had resulted in America having the highest percentage of whiskey drinkers in the world.[174]

Moonshiners usually made their product in the home. Of course, this is the most dangerous environment in which to conduct this business. Tenement manufacture was a particular danger. Explosions and fires in the crowded conditions were common: "Children in the home are taught to 'tend still' as they once tended bobbins in the mill. It is a new form of child labor of a most dangerous sort."[175] Further, without government regulation, moonshiners conducted their business with little emphasis on hygiene.[176] Government agents often seized stills with rats, cats, cockroaches, and decayed meat in the fermenting vats.[177] Thousands of stills also used lead coils instead of copper, and traces of lead were found in the liquor.[178]

Virtually all distilled alcohol that reached the bootlegger's hands would be "cut," the distilled alcohol was diluted and raw alcohol added to raise the proof.[179] This would increase the quantity of whiskey, for instance, from one case to three to five cases.[180] However, ingredients such as iodine, sulfuric acid, and creosote were used to approximate the necessary color and "kick" of the authentic liquor.[181] Such ingredients were even added to the already poisoned industrial alcohol.[182] Some notoriously dangerous brands of alcohol floated throughout the market. Yack Yack bourbon in Chicago contained iodine; Soda Pop Moon in Philadelphia contained poisonous isopropyl alcohol. Panther whiskey used esters and fuel oil. Jackass brandy caused internal bleeding.[183] In the summer of 1930, a brand called Jamaica Ginger induced 15,000 cases of temporary paralysis nationwide.[184] Hundreds of these people died,[185] and none were known to completely recover.[186]

The most persistent objective of the American temperance movement was the elimination of the saloon. In this regard, the forces of prohibition may have suffered their worst defeat. Speakeasies, different in name but the same in function, prospered as always. They arose in whatever location their customers would support. Fiorello La Guardia testified to Congress in 1926, "We now have delicatessen stores, pool rooms, drug stores, millinery shops, private parlors, and fifty-seven other varieties of speakeasies selling liquor and flourishing."[187] Most estimates indicate more speakeasies during prohibition than saloons before enactment. In 1917, an estimated 150,000 saloons operated nationwide and 10,000 additional stores sold liquor for consumption off the premises. A prohibition director of New York estimated 225,000 speakeasies nationwide by 1929, and Police Commissioner Whalen of New York estimated 32,000 establishments in that city alone.[188] A further estimate, made by a prohibition agent, was that New York City had more than 100,000 speakeasies.[189] Judge Talley of New York testified to Congress in 1926 that three speakeasies had arisen for every saloon that had disappeared.[190]

Like production, forcing alcohol consumption underground, gave the experience a tinge of anarchy. By operating without the law, speakeasies operated without any controls. As Judge Talley observed: "They are a terrible menace as they have brought the sale of liquor into tenement and dwelling houses, and within the purview of children.... Terrible fights are common in them, provoked by the raw liquor they sell and unavoidable absence of police supervision."[191]

The diversity of consumers was increasing, as well. Women now drank in public for the first time. Moral and social restraints had disappeared, and legal controls, such as the New Orleans law prohibiting a woman from going into a saloon, became inoperative.[192] For the same reasons, and because Volstead had given liquor "an augmented burden of illicit connotations," rebellious youths now frequented speakeasies, too.[193]

PROHIBITION AND CRIME

One justification for national prohibition was that alcohol caused crime. Prohibition, almost by definition, however, added immeasurably to the numbers of crimes committed. By criminalizing a victimless, consensual, and everyday act, "almost the entire country engaged in illicit behavior."[194] This included those who advocated or were responsible for enforcing the law. In San Francisco, a jury on a prohibition case drank the evidence and found the defendant not guilty.[195] In the mid-1920s, prohibition agents owned and ran their own speakeasy in Manhattan for nine months; when discovered, they claimed they were "investigating."[196] One man, both a congressman and strong advocate of dry laws, was discovered smuggling nine trunks of alcohol from Canada when one of the trunks started dripping brandy.[197] In 1920, a still was discovered on the property of Senator Morris Sheppard himself, the author of the Eighteenth Amendment. The still was producing 130 gallons a day.[198]

But not all alcohol-related crimes were victimless. Robert Croul, a former police commissioner, argued that crimes of violence associated with drinking had increased under prohibition.[199]

Organized crime was the most destructive result of prohibition. Some have argued that prohibition was necessary in order that criminals would organize themselves into large, businesslike entities. This is firstly true, because the law created huge profits for the criminal entrepreneur who was willing to supply the prohibited good. The best-organized entity can satisfy all of the demand in the market, thereby realizing monopoly profit: "The monopoly nature of the market increases the profit potential of organized crime. It is precisely the large profit margin which renders organized crime lucrative and increases the threat to community values, such as the work ethic."[200] Secondly, the supply of alcohol required the conglomeration of numerous functions. The "empire" must consist of "breweries, distilleries, bottling plants, truck drivers, places to sell it (speakeasies), waiters, cooks, jazz musicians, to entertain...."[201] In this sense, organized crime resembles a vertically integrated business enterprise. Like a legitimate business, organized crime becomes self-perpetuating and independent of the individuals in it,[202] and Johnny Torrio, mastermind of the Chicago crime organization, could retire and Al Capone ascend to the position.[203]

The resilience of organized crime is demonstrated by Chicago enforcement efforts. Spasms of enforcement and arrests of crime organization members were ultimately futile. In 1921, the Chicago police undertook a campaign to break the syndicate. In one day, they made 500 arrests and closed several hundred speakeasies. Within a month, the syndicate returned to full strength. In 1923, Mayor Dever also undertook to enforce the dry laws. In three days, 700 arrests were made; within a few weeks the speakeasies were open again. Despite his best efforts throughout his term, Mayor Dever never controlled the mob.[204] Through it all, profits flowed unhindered to the gang elite. By 1926, Capone's annual income was approaching $100 million.[205]

Organized criminals during prohibition were, of course, not above using violence to protect their monopoly. In Chicago alone, rival gang factions killed 500 men over a five-year period, 300 of these in 1926 and 1927.[206] One journalist commented that in some weeks, "The outline of a day's news read like a war communiqué."[207] Chicago's gang warfare culminated in the St. Valentine's Day massacre. Al Capone's men deceived seven members of a rival gang into believing they were prohibition agents. The rivals were disarmed and shot in cold blood.[208]

The gangs also relied on their ability to corrupt elected officials and police to protect their market. The corruption of police was widespread in large cities. In congressional testimony, Mayor Dever estimated that up to 60 percent of his police force "was actually in the liquor business."[209] In Philadelphia, fifteen policemen were dismissed when their combined bank accounts totaled more than $800,000.[210] Representative La Guardia estimated graft payments of $7.50 to $12 a case by the time liquor reached the consumer.[211] Graft also reached federal agents. Of the 18,000 agents employed during prohibition, 1,608 were dismissed for bribery, corruption, extortion, embezzlement, or filing false reports.[212] Major Mills described the relationship between the politicians and agents in his district: "Three quarters of the 2,500 dry agents are ward dealers and sycophants named by the politicians. And the politicians, whether professionally wet or professionally dry, want prohibition because they regard prohibition as they regard postmastership—a reservoir of jobs for henchmen and of favors for friends.... Prohibition is the new pork barrel."[213]

Payoffs to government officials were made possible by "large profit margins in the supply of illicit goods...."[214] Ultimately, corruption of public officials, gangsterism, and racketeering proved the "most persuasive indictment of prohibition.... [I]t led to a breakdown of law and order with the connivance of those in authority."[215]

The net effect of prohibition seems impossible to discern. The statistics varied so widely on numbers of drinkers, amount of alcohol consumed, and deaths caused that "it is a bit difficult to believe they dealt with the same subject."[216] However, some arguments can probably be discarded and some broad conclusions drawn. One conclusion to discard is based on a study by the renowned professor of economics, Irving Fisher of Yale. Fisher found that in 1928 the average price of a bootleg quart of beer was $.80, gin was $5.90, and whiskey was $7.00, at a time when the average family income was $2,600.[217] These prices would dictate that alcohol was too expensive for the average wage earner; therefore, the high prices under prohibition meant that "a good deal less is spent on liquor by the masses...."[218]

However, the average price tells us little about the affordability of alcohol. It is almost certainly true that the rich were paying significantly more for high quality, unadulterated alcohol; everyone else would then be paying lower than average prices. Probably even the poorest Americans could afford the alcohol that was most cut, most poisoned, and most dangerous. Surely it was not the rich dying from Jamaica Ginger. As one commentator has said, "[T]he rich drank openly and well; the poor drank secretly and badly."[219] Scholar Dr. Alain Locke argued that blacks in particular suffered disproportionately: "[T]he Negro has borne in several ways the unjust brunt of the conditions produced by our present system of administration of the Eighteenth Amendment. Negro districts, both rural and urban, are regarded as the logical 'dumps' for the worst and most harmful of the substitute concoctions; Negroes are enlisted in the most dangerous phases of the liquor traffic—the disposal to the retail customer."[220]

If only the rich were drinking, it is hard to see why prohibition would have failed. The law was undone by the drinking masses. Although this class was unable to thwart the enactment of prohibition, wage earners were still strong enough to ensure its ultimate failure.[221]

Another conclusion to be drawn is that legislation is ineffective in regulating drinking habits. Some commentators have argued that prohibition is not responsible for the increase in drinking among women and youth in the 1920s. Rather, this phenomenon sprang from the rejection of social convention and liberated attitudes toward women's drinking.[222] But this argument in defense of prohibition is self-defeating. It demonstrates that much behavior is a function of underlying social and cultural conditions and does not necessarily conform itself to legislative edicts. With regard to alcohol, Prohibition took on the impossible task of regulating an ingrained habit: "So these are the reasons why we drink: because it is the custom of our race, because we have the habit, to drown our sorrows, to help our work, to improve our health, to be smart and do as those higher up do, to spur us to pleasure—or, just because we like the taste."[223]

Perhaps most importantly, the law was ignored as an infringement on personal liberty.[224] The *Machinists Monthly Journal* predicted this effect as early as 1904: "Prohibition never yet prohibited. People cannot be made good by law, and every effort to make people do something under compulsion which they did not wish to do has proven a failure."[225] The upshot was summarized by Massachusetts senator Henry Cabot Lodge in the debate on the Eighteenth Amendment: "Where large masses of people would consider it even meritorious—at least quite venial—to evade and break the law, the law would inevitably be broken and in a large and effective way."[226]

ENFORCEMENT EFFORTS

Perhaps it can be said of prohibition what author Gore Vidal once said of Christianity: "We don't know if it works; it's never been tried."[227] Certainly, a main argument of prohibition proponents was that ineffective enforcement doomed the effort from the beginning. One of the most glaring deficiencies of Volstead was the intention that enforcement be shared among state, local, and federal governments. In perhaps an unprecedented example of an unfunded mandate, the states were intended to be the primary enforcers of the law.[228] The first prohibition commissioner, John Kramer, asked that county, state, and city officials be zealous in enforcing the law, and that the federal government had the secondary role of acting "to ensure that the ban was obeyed."[229] Unfortunately for the drys, many states failed to enact any legislation at all that would trigger enforcement at the state level.[230] Those states with laws lacked the necessary resources to make them effective. By 1926, states were spending less than $700,000 on enforcement, one-eighth as much as was spent on the collective departments of fish and game.[231] Only eighteen states spent any money on enforcement, and three states—Missouri, Nevada, and Utah—put less than $1,000 each to the cause.[232] In Illinois, where Volstead was notoriously violated, only twelve of the state's fifty-three most populous counties actively attempted to enforce the law.[233] The concurrent enforcement scheme provided "an excellent excuse to states to abdicate their law enforcement responsibilities."[234]

But the drys had much to complain about on the federal level as well. In 1922, the Prohibition Bureau was allocated less than seven million dollars and 3,000 employees.[235] The Prohibition agents were widely thought to be ill equipped for the task. A grand jury investigating a liquor raid stated, "The agents are not men of the type and intelligence and character necessary for the job."[236] The National Civil Service League charged that the agents were either incompetent and untrained or venal and dishonest.[237] The average yearly pay of the agents was a relatively paltry $2,000.[238] Congress, for the most part, was unwilling to allocate to the Prohibition Bureau the resources necessary for a reasonable enforcement effort. Emory Buckner, U.S. district attorney for the Southern District of New York, requested 1,500 agents, with salaries sufficient to resist corruption, for his district alone. R. C. Meerick, Prohibition administrator on the East Coast, suggested that nationwide enforcement would require twelve thousand agents and $50 million.[239] But by 1929, the Prohibition Bureau still numbered only 4,129 employees and Congress improved an increase in the budget of less than $2 million. Senator Carraway of Arkansas wondered aloud that Americans wanted prohibition, but whether "it was for themselves or their neighbors, he could not say."[240]

This argument, however, obscures the massive level of enforcement undertaken on behalf on the prohibition cause. The expenditures devoted to federal government law enforcement grew five times between 1920 and 1930, significantly more than any other function of the government.[241] The amount of money allocated to the Prohibition Unit, before 1928, and the Prohibition Bureau, after 1928, grew from $2 million in 1920 to a peak of more than $13 million in 1930.[242] When the amounts allocated to the Department of Justice, Coast Guard, and Customs are factored in, the total amount expended on Prohibition enforcement was more than $40 million.[243] This is a significant fund compared to a total size of federal government budget of $3.6 billion.

The resources expended equated to a huge number of arrests, trials, and imprisonments. In the San Francisco federal courts, raids on bootleggers produced fifty new cases a day. More than 5,000 cases awaited trial. One trial by jury would take a full day. Emory Buckner noted that giving a trial by jury on all prohibition cases would require eighty-five additional courts in the Southern District of New York alone.[244] Prisons were also filled to capacity. After two years of prohibition, 130,000 violators had been sentenced and imprisoned.[245] By 1929, more than 500,000 violators had been arrested.[246] In 1923, federal district attorneys were spending 44 percent of all their time working on prohibition cases.[247]

President Hoover believed the law must either be vigorously enforced or repealed. He chose the former, requiring the construction of six new prisons. In 1930, more than one-third of all prisoners serving long sentences in federal prisons had been convicted under Volstead.[248] In the 1929–1930 fiscal years, Hoover's policies resulted in the arrest of more than 68,000 people and the confiscation of 8,633 vehicles and 64 boats.[249] In

1932, 80,000 state and federal prohibition convictions were recorded. [250] In surveying the total effort to enforce the prohibition laws, the Wickersham Commission said in 1931 that "[T]here has been more sustained presence to enforce this law than on the whole has been true of any other federal statute....No other federal law has had such elaborate state and federal enforcing machinery behind it."[251]

The mounting frustration at prohibition's futility led to ever-harsher penalties for violators. This policy was strongly endorsed by anti-alcohol pietists. The Reverend Mark Matthews said the law "ought to be enforced if every street in America had to run red with blood and every cobblestone had to be made of a human skull."[252] Official policy never rose quite to the minister's zeal, but Clarence Darrow was surely correct when he said that the drys, "are constantly asking for new laws to still further limit the rights of the individual and compel men to conform more and more of the narrow views of the class of men and women who have always believed that anything that they believe is not good for the people should be forbidden by stern criminal statutes;...neither liberty nor property is safe from the paralyzing hands of the majority who makes the law." [253]

Proving Darrow's point, in 1929, Congress passed the Jones Act, increasing maximum penalties under Volstead from six months in jail and a $1,000 fine to five years and a $10,000 fine.[254] Not only did violation of Volstead become a felony, but buying a drink, or knowledge of a bootlegger or speakeasy without disclosing this knowledge to the authorities was also a felony.[255] An almost "incalculable number of felonies" was thus created.[256] Jones greatly exacerbated all of the problems associated with enforcing the dry mandate. It further blurred the line "between acceptable and criminal behavior," multiplied the chaos in the judicial and prison systems, and gave many good reason to wonder whether America was in the midst of a crime wave or social rebellion.[257] Former prohibition advocate William Randolph Hearst argued that the Jones Act was "the most menacing piece of repressive legislation that has stained the statute books of this republic since the Alien and Sedition laws."[258]

Even constitutional guarantees began to give way under the weight of the prohibition failure. When the Eighteenth Amendment came into conflict with constitutional rights, the Supreme Court usually ruled that the Constitution must yield. In 1922, the Court held that it was not a violation of the Fifth Amendment right against double jeopardy to prosecute the same offense under both state and federal law.[259] Search and seizure protections under the Fourth Amendment were significantly eroded. In the case of *Carroll v. United States,* a car that made no indication that it carried liquor was stopped and searched by police without a warrant. The search subsequently revealed dozens of bottles of whiskey behind the driver's seat.[260] The court found that probable cause existed because the search took place in Grand Rapids, Michigan, an access point commonly used to smuggle alcohol into the country.[261] Upon this ground, the Supreme Court upheld the validity of the search. In dissent, Judge Andres noted the dangers of allowing officers the right to search the car prior to, and not incidental to, making the arrest. He said, "Under such circumstances, the police officer is made, in effect, prosecutor, judge, jury, and executioner."[262]

In the case of *Olmstead* v. *United States*, the Court upheld the conviction of a Seattle bootlegger based on evidence gathered over several months by wiretapping his telephone. The court ruled that wiretapping is similar to overhearing a public conversation, so no violation of the Fourth Amendment occurred.[263] The Court also held that the amendment protected only material goods such as "persons, houses, papers and effects." Because wiretapping is not a search, evidence so gathered is not excluded under the Fourth Amendment.[264] In dissent, Justice Brandeis complained that wiretapping is untenably intrusive of privacy expectations and that, in terms of empowering the police, "Writs of assistance and general warrants are but puny instruments of tyranny and oppression when compared with wiretapping."[265]

Many commentators noted the Court's proclivity to place enforcement of prohibition laws above the rights of individuals. In his famous *Olmstead* dissent, Justice Brandeis realized that the Court was compromising cherished values, specifically "the right to be left alone—the most comprehensive of rights and the right most valued by civilized men."[266] Noting that individual rights seemed to be more prone to intrusion under prohibition laws than other statutes, others suggested the existence of two constitutions: one for Prohibition, and one for all other matters.[267]

In the end, regardless of the oppressive or intrusive measures adopted, it was simply not feasible to enforce prohibition laws. The resources required would have been far too burdensome to bear. According to Emory Buckner, just to contain bootlegging and manufacturing in New York alone would have required $15 million.[268] After working a short time in Detroit, famed Prohibition agent Izzy Einstein said that to keep this single city dry would require the entire Prohibition force.[269] Prohibition commissioner Doran told Congress in 1927 that effective enforcement would cost $300 million.[270] This was almost ten times the amount of money actually allocated to enforce the law. Increasingly it was clear that enforcement would involve far more than merely monetary concerns. As one commentator said, "[T]he only way of enforcing complete prohibition would have been by imposing a police state on American society, thereby completing the subversion of democracy that prohibition had instigated."[271] In 1926, Treasury Secretary Andrew Mellon also argued against full enforcement of the law: "...were the Federal government to accept this responsibility, it must organize large police forces on the various communities, and in addition, must provide adequate judicial machinery for the disposition of the local cases: an interference by the Federal government with local government which could not be other than obnoxious to every right thinking individual."[272]

THE REPEAL MOVEMENT

As the Prohibition era aged, most people perceived that the law exacerbated problems related to alcohol. Elizabeth Tilton of Boston Associated Charities argued that without a national prohibition law they were "Bailing water out of a tub with the tap turned on; letting the drink custom and the liquor traffic run full blast while we stood limply around and picked up the wreckage,"[273] is an ironically apt description of the effects of prohibition. Prohibition could not turn off the alcohol tap: it was produced, distilled, smuggled, bootlegged, sold, and consumed at a rate that embarrassed the law. At the same time, the social wreckage from Volstead accumulated. The contradictions were legion: it aimed to reduce crime but made criminals out of untold numbers of people; it aimed to reduce alcohol-related disease but resulted in thousands of deaths from poisoned alcohol; it aimed to eliminate the saloon but created speakeasies; it aimed to reduce alcohol consumption but caused the consumption of higher-proof alcohol; it aimed to reduce the alcohol industry's influence but led to the rise of the organized crime industry. By the late 1920s, a combination of social forces started to gather momentum to release America from the grip of prohibition.

The first significant stirring of an anti-prohibition movement was the advocacy of repeal by leading social figures. These groups even included some original supporters of the dry agenda. Doctors, proving the ills of alcohol with scientific and objective findings, were one of the earliest and strongest inspirations of prohibition. They were also one of the first groups to reconsider their support. In 1921, the American Medical Association refused to confirm its 1917 resolution against alcohol. Leading health experts came out in opposition to "the intentions and consequences of prohibition." Dr. Nicholl, health commissioner of New York, attributed the increased mortality from drinking to the illicit manufacture of and consumption of poisoned alcohol that prohibition had brought about.[274] The doctors' defection was critical to the demise of prohibition for the same reasons that their support was critical to its birth.

Leading industrialists also reconsidered their initial support for the law. The Association Against the Prohibition Amendment was formed by the most prominent millionaires of the age, including the DuPonts, Harvey Firestone, John Rockefeller, and William Randolph Hearst. The wives of many of these men also formed the Women's Organization for National Prohibition Reform.[275] Although this most powerful segment of society originally supported prohibition to promote worker efficiency and safety, they had come to believe that it was "better for workers to imbibe good beer legally than bad booze illegally."[276] Others have charged that these groups actually worked to legalize alcohol so it could be taxed, thereby lowering their income tax burden.[277] If they were so motivated, their efforts were in vain. Following prohibition, tax rates fell for everyone except the top income earners.[278] Whatever the motivation, the effect on politicians and the public of the most powerful men aligned against prohibition was, by some estimates, decisive.[279]

Other prominent groups also came out against prohibition. Lawyers were increasingly vocal in opposition. In 1927, a New York group calling itself the Voluntary Committee of Lawyers proclaimed that the Eighteenth Amendment was unconstitutional and "in derogation of the liberties of the citizens."[280] City and state bar associations began to echo this sentiment. In 1930, the American Bar Association voted in favor of repeal by a two-thirds majority.[281] Newspaper articles also reflected the change in national thinking. Perhaps half the major newspapers initially supported prohibition; by the late 1920s, they were virtually unanimously opposed. In 1915, newspaper articles in support of prohibition outnumbered articles in opposition by twenty to one. By 1920, articles favored the policy by four to three. By 1930, articles favored repeal by at least two to one.[282]

President Hoover empowered the Wickersham Commission in 1929 to study the prohibition matter. The scope of the investigation was limited to the method of enforcement.[283] Although most of the eleven commissioners were thought to be advocates of the dry position when appointed, the report ultimately was not what Hoover had hoped for. Apparently, the investigation itself caused many of the appointees to reconsider their position.[284] The report went beyond a review of possible enforcement schemes to an argument about the wisdom of prohibition policy itself. Two of the members favored immediate, outright repeal of the amendment. Five members in effect recommended repeal by advocating legal sales of alcohol by a government, monopoly, and corporation. Two others, believing that prohibition was a failure, believed it should be revised and given one more chance. Only two of the eleven members believed the Eighteenth Amendment should be kept essentially as it was.[285] Although Hoover touted the report as advocating the dry position, it was hard to dismiss the argument that the report was a harsh condemnation of prohibition. Walter Lippmann called it a "direct and explicit official admission that federal prohibition is a hopeless failure."[286] Pierre DuPont of the AAPA said the report "could not have been put in better words for our purposes."[287] Although intended to buttress support for Hoover's policies, the commission actually inspired the repeal movement. For the first time, a revision of the national policy seemed possible.[288]

It is difficult to estimate the degree to which public support in favor of prohibition had eroded. It is possible that the amendment never did enjoy the support of a majority of Americans. As the Wickersham Commission noted, the National Prohibition Act was submitted and ratified during the emotionalism that inevitably follows a huge war effort. In this context, people are more willing than usual to yield their personal liberties in favor of heightened government powers. Prohibition laws came into existence "at the time best suited for their adoption and at the worst time for their enforcement."[289] More specifically, the commission identified three problems with adoption of the amendment: the ratifying legislatures had not been elected to consider the issue; many state legislatures overrepresented rural voters who typically supported dry issues; legislatures were elected when a sizable portion of the electorate was absent for military service. As a result, the adoption process exaggerated prohibitionist sentiment.[290]

Others have argued that it is inherently invalid to amend the Constitution through state legislatures. Although convention delegates reflect public opinion on the specific issue, the Eighteenth Amendment was "not ratified by the people, but by a few thousand state legislators who were duped and goaded into ratifying regardless of the will of their constituents."[291] On this ground Judge Clark, sitting on the New Jersey federal district court, ruled the Eighteenth Amendment unconstitutional in *United States* v. *Sprague.*[292]

Regardless of the degree of popular support at adoption, most people indicated disapproval of the law even in the early 1920s. In 1922, a *Literary Digest* poll of 922,000 people indicated that 61 percent wanted either modification or repeal of the law. In 1926, a poll by the Newspaper Enterprise Association, soliciting the opinion of 1.7 million people, indicated that 81 percent were dissatisfied.[293] Out of seventeen state referendums, nine indicated a desire to discontinue their state enforcement laws. Large majorities of voters in Illinois and New York appealed to Congress in 1926 to amend the Volstead Act, and voters in Nevada, Massachusetts, Rhode Island, and Illinois requested that the Eighteenth Amendment be repealed.[294]

At the time, however, it was largely believed that repeal was impossible. The smallest thirteen states, with a combined population of only five million, could thwart the desire of the vast majority of the population who desired repeal. Clarence Darrow called repeal "well-nigh inconceivable," and Walter Lippmann declared the amendment "beyond effective attack."[295] How, then, did Americans respond to a law that the majority opposed but could not remove? Well-known figures advocated open defiance of the law. This principle of nullification was articulated by Professor Hadley of Yale University: "If any considerable number of citizens who are habitually law-abiding think that some particular statute is bad enough or dangerous enough in its effects to make it worthwhile to block its enforcement, it can do so."[296] To varying degrees, Walter Lippmann, Clarence Darrow, Henry Cabot Lodge, and H. L. Mencken, among others, embraced or at least predicted nullification. Lippmann reasoned that the Constitution was "in conflict with the living needs of the nation...."[297] Surely none of the advocates of nullification were unaware of the philosophy's dangers. Tolerance of criminals undermines respect for the law and the processes that make law. With respect to prohibition, "[A] general tolerance of the bootlegger and disrespect for federal law were translated into a widespread contempt for the processes and duties of democracy."[298]

Despite all of the failures of the dry agenda, the Depression may have been necessary to kill the prohibition beast. It is possible that failures of policy and ideology do not drive changes in the law. Rather, public choice theorists suggest that pecuniary self-interest motivates change in political outcomes.[299] With regard to prohibition, taxes and duties in liquor were the main source of government revenue until 1913, when the income tax was instituted.[300] The improving economy at this time allowed the income tax to generate huge revenues for the federal government. Viewed in this light, prohibition was enacted because it was affordable: policymakers could afford to forgo revenues on alcohol sales because these were "trivial in comparison with the rapidly growing revenues derived from the individual and corporate income taxes."[301] But with the onset of the Depression, income tax revenues plummeted and Congress needed either to cut spending or find an additional source of revenue. Economist Clark Warburton estimated that the revenues lost to the federal government through prohibition ranged from $326 million to $1.7 billion by 1931.[302] One congressman revealed that, without the argument that an alcohol tax would provide needed federal funds, repeal would have been another ten years away.[303] But funds lost to the government were only one side of the coin. The money not in the treasury coffers was in the hands of gangsters. The many millions of dollars that Al Capone used to corrupt public officials and subvert the law and spread terror through the streets of Chicago could surely have been more productively used by society.

As the problems of prohibition mounted, the tide of public dissent grew to inexorable dimensions. This, in turn, transformed the political landscape. By the 1932 presidential election, both President Hoover and Democratic Party nominee Franklin Roosevelt advocated repeal. But while Hoover was seen as evasive and dissembling on the issue, Roosevelt was an unambiguous proponent that the noble experiment must end.[304] Roosevelt's victory added impetus to the repeal movement. Before the inauguration, Congress drafted seventy resolutions for repeal of the Eighteenth Amendment and fifty-six bills to amend or repeal the Volstead Act.[305]

Strategists for the repeal movement urged using, for the first time since ratification of the Constitution, state conventions to ratify the repeal amendment. Because only thirteen states could bring defeat, they feared allowing state legislatures to vote on the amendment. Instead, delegates would be elected for the specific purpose of voting on the proposal.[306] The results were overwhelmingly in favor of repeal. Of the twenty-one million voters in thirty-seven states voting for the delegates, 73 percent favored repeal.[307] A more resounding measure of Prohibition's failure is difficult to imagine. While the real level of popular support for the Eighteenth Amendment was uncertain, it was "clear that in 1933 an overwhelming majority approved the Twenty-first Amendment."[308]

Whether the noble experiment was truly noble is debatable. That it offers valuable lessons as a social experiment and government policy is indisputable. Prohibition was a test case in the government's ability to prohibit the exchange and consumption of a good in popular demand. The fact that the public still purchased the good in huge quantities triggered an irresistible dynamic: demand created a reservoir of profits for enterprising people willing to supply the good. The profits need only be large enough to overcome the risk of being caught plus any moral concerns the supplier may have. Because suppliers can rationalize their efforts as merely satisfying a legitimate want in the face of an oppressive law, moral concerns are minimal. The risk of breaking the law is reduced by two factors. First, the sheer numbers of suppliers creates unimaginable enforcement problems. Second, the profits generated can be used to entice law enforcement agents to conspire in the prohibited trade. Whenever the profits are sufficiently in excess of the inhibiting factors, suppliers will satisfy the demand.

Attacking the trade from the supply side is virtually doomed to failure. A kind of market equilibrium in the prohibited good arises. Profits will be just large enough to compensate the supplier for the cost of the good and the risk of being caught. One cost of the good is graft to law enforcement agents, thereby reducing the risk. If profits are below the equilibrium, suppliers will drop out of the market; if above, they will enter. Government enforcement changes the number of suppliers only in the short term. Even massive enforcement efforts serves only to draw others into the market. Given that the moral concerns of breaking the law are so low, the number of potential suppliers seems infinite. Viewed in this light, government enforcement of the law is always self-defeating.

But failure of a prohibition law to realize its goals is the least of its consequences. Prohibition actually aggravates the problems it is intended to solve. Given widespread supply, consumption of the prohibited good probably does not decline, but the good consumed will be more potent and toxic compared to when it was legal. The strictly monetary costs of enforcement and imprisonment are almost certainly greater than the monetary costs resulting from the legal good. Finally, the costs from a corrupt public service system and the disrespect of all laws caused by prohibition law are inestimable. These are the lessons of the prohibition era. It is wiser to learn from them than to replicate the era's mistakes.

NOTES

1. Fletcher Dobyns, *The Amazing Story of Repeal* (Chicago: Willett, Clark, 1940), p. 347.

2. Walter Lippmann, *Vanity Fair* 1930.

3. Herman Feldman, *Prohibition Its Economic and Industrial Aspects* (New York; London: D. Appleton, 1930), p. 45.

4. See generally, Feldman *supra* note 3.

5. Records of the Wickersham Commission on Law Observance and Enforcement, http://www.lexisnexis.com/academic/2upa/Aj/Wickersham Comm.htm.

6. See generally, *Judicial History of the Orphan's Division*, http:/courts. phila.gov/cpojh.htm.

7. Herbert Asbury, *The Great Illusion: An Informal History of Prohibition* (Garden City, N.Y.: Doubleday, 1950), p. 316. See also, Sidney C. Schaer, *How Alcohol Beat Last Call: Predictions From the Past That Haven't Come True...Yet*, http:// future.newsday.com/5/fbak0514.htm.

8. James M. Beck, "The Revolt Against Prohibition," Printed speech in the House of Representatives 1930 (U.S. Govt. Printing Office, 1938).

9. Doug Bandow, War on Drugs or War on America, 3 *Stan. L. & Pol'y Rev.* 242, Fall 1991.

10. Dennis Cashman, *Prohibition: The Lie of the Land* (Free Press, 1981), p. 7.

11. Testimony of Matthew Woll, National Prohibition Law Hearings, April 5 to 24, 1926, Schaffer Library of Drug Policy, http://www.druglibrary.org/ schaffer/history/e1920/senj1926/woll.htm.

12. See generally, Will Rogers, *Cowboy Philosopher on Prohibition* (1919). See also, C-Span's American Writers, http://www.americanwriters.org/works/ cowboy.asp.

13. Donald J. Boudreaux and A. C. Pritchard, The Price of Prohibition, 36 *Ariz. L. Rev.* 1, 1994.

14. See generally, John Foust, State Power to Regulate Alcohol Under the Twenty-First Amendment: The Constitutional Implications of the Twenty-First Amendment Enforcement Act, 41 *B.C. L. Rev.* 664, May 2000 (The 1919 Volstead Act was also known as the National Prohibition Act and was amended in part and repealed in part by the Liquor Law Repeal and Enforcement Act of 1935.)

15. Dobyns, *supra* note 1, p. 369.

16. Herbert Hoover, thirty-first U.S. president, acceptance speech for the presidential nomination in Chicago, Illinois. *History Channel*, http://www. historychannel.com/cgi-bin/frameit.cgi?p = http%3A//www.historychannel. com/speeches/archive/speech_129.htm.

17. James Aloysius Farley, *Jim Farley's Story: The Roosevelt Years* (Westport, Conn.: Greenwood Press, 1984).

18. Thomas M. Coffey, *The Long Thirst: Prohibition in America, 1920–1933* (New York: Norton, 1975), p. 315.

19. *Id.*

20. Benjamin Rush, *The Drunkard's Emblem, or, An Inquiry Into the Effects of Ardent Spirits Upon the Human Body and Mind: With an Account of the Means of Preventing, and of the Remedies for Curing Them* (Ambrose Henkel, 1814?).

21. Dr. John Marsh, Whole World's Temperance Convention, Speech (New York City, May 1853).

22. See generally, Gregory M. Browne, Ph.D., *The Progressive Era,* http://www.yorktownuniversity.com/documents/progressive_era.pdf.

23. Letters to E. W. J. Lindesmith on Catholic Prohibition League of America, 1903–1919, Reverend Eli Washington, John Lindesmith Papers, http://libsrve.lib.cua.edu/archive/Lindesmith/.

24. See generally, Reform Judaism (also known as Progressive Judaism), http://www.wikipedia.com/wiki/Reform+Judaism.

25. See generally, Emil Kraepelin, *One Hundred Years of Psychiatry* (New York: Philosophical Library, 1962). See also, International Kraepelin Organization, Emil Kraepelin, http://www.kraepelin.org.futuresite.register.com/.

26. See generally, American Social History Project, *Who Built America: Working People and the Nations Economy Politics Culture and Society* (New York: Pantheon Books, 1990).

27. *McClure's Magazine* (New York, London, S. S. McClure Limited, 1908).

28. See generally, *Temperance & Prohibition,* http://www.cohums.ohio state.edu/history/projects/prohibition/Medicinal_Alcohol.htm.

29. *The Cosmopolitan,* (Schlict & Field, Rochester, N.Y., 1908).

30. See generally, Dr. Henry Smith Williams, *Conference Report: To Users of Liquor* (102nd Semi-Annual Conference of the Church of Jesus Christ of Latter-Day Saints, October 1931), http://www.kingdomofzion.org/doctrines/library/lds/GC_Oct1931.txt.

31. *The American Underwriter* (Edward B. Phelps, ed., New York City).

32. *Atlantic Monthly* (Boston, Atlantic Monthly Co.). See generally, American Medical Directors Association, http://www.amda.com/.

33. John Koren, *Economic Aspects of the Liquor Problem,* An investigation made for the Committee of Fifty under the direction of Henry W. Farnam (Boston, New York: Houghton Mifflin, 1899).

34. See *American Social History Project, supra* note 26.

35. *Literary Digest* (Funk & Wagnalls, New York, 1914).

36. *Id.*

37. *Collier's* (Crowell-Collier, Springfield, Ohio, 1908).

38. Norman H. Clark, *Deliver Us From Evil: An Interpretation of American Prohibition* (New York: Norton, 1985), pp. 47–48.

39. Cashman, *supra* note 10, p.7.

40. Clark, *supra* note 38, p. 118.

41. Clark, *supra* note 38, p. 119.

42. Dobyns, *supra* note 1, p.242.

43. Coffey, *supra* note 18, p. 31.

44. Asbury, *supra* note 7, p. 219.

45. Dobyns, *supra* note 1, p. 292.

46. Cashman, *supra* note 10, p. 40.

47. Asbury, *supra* note 7, p. 219.

48. *Id.,* p. 220.

49. Cashman, *supra* note 10, p. 40.

50. Asbury, *supra* note 7, p. 220.

51. *Id.,* p. 219.

52. *Id.*

53. *Id.,* p. 216.

54. *Id.*, p. 217.
55. *Id.*, p. 218.
56. Coffey, *supra* note 18, p. 31.
57. *Id.*
58. Asbury, *supra* note 7, p. 221.
59. Coffey, *supra* note 18, p. 31.
60. Asbury, *supra* note 7, p. 221.
61. Coffey, *supra* note 18, p. 32.
62. Asbury, *supra* note 7, p. 221.
63. Coffey, *supra* note 18, p. 102.
64. Asbury, *supra* note 7, p. 220–21.
65. *Id.*, p. 222.
66. Richard F. Hamm, *Shaping the Eighteenth Amendment: Temperance Reform, Legal Culture, and the Polity, 1880–1920* (University of North Carolina Press, 1995), p. 251.
67. Asbury, *supra* note 7, p. 238.
68. Cashman, *supra* note 10, p. 38.
69. Asbury, *supra* note 7, p. 238.
70. *Id.*, pp. 230–40.
71. Clark, *supra* note 38, p. 159.
72. Dobyns, *supra* note 1, p. 297.
73. Asbury, *supra* note 7, p. 232.
74. Cashman, *supra* note 10, p. 40.
75. Asbury, *supra* note 7, p. 234.
76. *Id.*, p. 235.
77. *Id.*, p. 234.
78. *Id.*, p. 233.
79. *Id.*, p. 234.
80. Feldman, *supra* note 3, pp. 66–67.
81. *Id.*, p. 68.
82. Clark, *supra* note 38, p. 159.
83. Cashman, *supra* note 10, p. 4.
84. *Id.*, p. 29.
85. Asbury, *supra* note 7, p. 257.
86. Cashman, *supra* note 10, p. 31.
87. *Id.*
88. Detroit Historical Museum, http://www.detroithistorical.org/.
89. Cashman, *supra* note 10, p. 31.
90. *Id.*, p. 30.
91. Asbury, *supra* note 7, p. 257.
92. Cashman, *supra* note 10, p. 201.
93. Asbury, *supra* note 7, p. 258.
94. Cashman, *supra* note 10, p. 32.
95. Asbury, *supra* note 7, p. 258.
96. *Id.*, p. 259.
97. *Id.*, p. 260.
98. *Id.*, p. 259.
99. *Id.*

100. Detroit Historical Museum, *supra* note 88.

101. Feldman, *supra* note 3, p. 53.

102. Asbury, *supra* note 7, p. 260.

103. Cashman, *supra* note 10, p. 31.

104. Feldman, *supra* note 3, p. 53.

105. Coffey, *supra* note 18, pp. 21–23.

106. Cashman, *supra* note 10, p. 32.

107. Coffey, *supra* note 18, p. 53.

108. *Id.*, p. 54.

109. *Id.*, p. 122.

110. Asbury, *supra* note 7, p. 260.

111. *Id.*

112. *Id.*

113. *Id.*, pp. 246–47.

114. Cashman, *supra* note 10, p. 30.

115. Donald L. Canney, *A Rum War: The U.S. Coast Guard and Prohibition,* http://www.uscg.mil/hq/g-cp/history/h_rumwar.htm, p. 2.

116. *Id.*

117. Asbury, *supra* note 7, p. 243.

118. Canney, *supra* note 115, p. 2.

119. *Id.*

120. *Id.*

121. *Id.*, p. 4.

122. *Id.*, pp. 2–3.

123. Coffey, *supra* note 18, pp. 17–20.

124. *Id.*, p. 4.

125. *Id.*, p. 41.

126. *Id.*, pp. 57–60.

127. *Id.*, pp. 79–101.

128. *Id.*, pp. 124–28.

129. Cashman, *supra* note 10, p. 34.

130. Randall G. Holcombe, *The Growth of Federal Government in the 1920s,* CATO Journal, Vol. 16 No. 2, http://www.cato.org/pubs/journal/cj16n2–2.htm, fn 20.

131. Asbury, *supra* note 7, p. 263.

132. Coffey, *supra* note 18, p. 125.

133. Asbury, *supra* note 7, p. 243.

134. Canney, *supra* note 115, p. 9.

135. *Id.*

136. *Id.*, p. 10.

137. Asbury, *supra* note 7, p. 245.

138. *Id.*, p. 244.

139. Coffey, *supra* note 18, p. 179.

140. Cashman, *supra* note 10, p. 34.

141. *Id.*

142. *Id.*

143. Clark, *supra* note 38, p. 159.

144. Feldman, *supra* note 3, p. 47.

145. Coffey, *supra* note 18, p. 197.

146. *Id.*

147. Asbury, *supra* note 7, p. 278.

148. *Id.*, p. 223.

149. Cashman, *supra* note 10, p. 36.

150. Asbury, *supra* note 7, p. 225.

151. Cashman, *supra* note 10, p. 37.

152. Sidney J. Spaeth, The Twenty-First Amendment and State Control Over Intoxicating Liquors: Accommodating the Federal Interest, 79 *Cal. L. Rev.* 108, January 1991.

153. *Id.*, pp. 177–78.

154. Asbury, *supra* note 7, p. 280.

155. *Id.*

156. Coffey, *supra* note 18, p. 196.

157. Cashman, *supra* note 10, p. 162.

158. *Id.*, p. 39.

159. Coffey, *supra* note 18, p. 200.

160. *Id.*, p. 200.

161. *Id.*, p. 197.

162. *Id.*, p. 198.

163. Asbury, *supra* note 7, p. 227.

164. Cashman, *supra* note 10, p. 37.

165. *Id.*

166. Asbury, *supra* note 7, p. 277.

167. *Id.*, p. 232.

168. Clark, *supra* note 38, p. 165.

169. *Id.*, p. 159.

170. Nora V. Demleitner, Organized Crime and Prohibition: What Difference Does Legalization Make? 15 *Whittier L. Rev.* 613, 1994.

171. *Id.*, p. 624.

172. *Id.*, p. 634.

173. Feldman, *supra* note 3, p. 60.

174. Fiorello La Guardia, http://www.cohums.ohio-state.edu/history/projects/prohibition/laguardi.htm.

175. Martha Bensley Bruere, *Does Prohibition Work? A Study of the Operation of the Eighteenth Amendment Made by the National Federation of Settlements,* Assisted by Social Workers in Different Parts of the United States (Harper & Brothers, 1927), p. 296.

176. *Id.*

177. Asbury, *supra* note 7, p. 277.

178. *Id.*, p. 283.

179. *Id.*, p. 272.

180. *Id.*, p. 269.

181. *Id.*, pp. 272–73.

182. Asbury, *supra* note 7, p. 280.

183. Cashman, *supra* note 10, p. 38.

184. Asbury, *supra* note 7, p. 287.

185. Cashman, *supra* note 10, p. 38.

186. Asbury, *supra* note 7, p. 287.

187. La Guardia, Fiorello, *supra* note 174.

188. Cashman, *supra* note 6, p. 10.

189. Clark, *supra* note 38, pp. 164–65.

190. Cashman, *supra* note 10, p. 44.

191. *Id.*

192. Bruere, *supra* note 175, p. 278.

193. Clark, *supra* note 38, p. 151.

194. Demleitner, *supra* note 170, p. 624.

195. Peter McWilliams, *Ain't Nobody's Business If You Do: The Absurdity of Consensual Crimes in a Free Society* (Prelude Press, 1993), p.70.

196. *Id.*

197. Asbury, *supra* note 7, p. 259.

198. McWilliams, *supra* note 195, p. 70.

199. Cashman, *supra* note 10, p. 256.

200. Demleitner, *supra* note 170, p. 618.

201. McWilliams, *supra* note 195, p. 245.

202. Demleitner, *supra* note 170, p. 2.

203. Coffey, *supra* note 18, p. 155.

204. Asbury, *supra* note 7, pp. 300–01.

205. Coffey, *supra* note 18, p. 194.

206. Asbury, *supra* note 7, p. 306.

207. Demleitner, *supra* note 170, p. 625.

208. Coffey, *supra* note 18, p. 256.

209. Clark, *supra* note 38, p. 165.

210. Cashman, *supra* note 10, p. 51.

211. La Guardia, *supra* note 174.

212. Cashman, *supra* note 10, p. 47.

213. Spaeth, *supra* note 152, p. 178.

214. Demleitner, *supra* note 170, p. 619.

215. Cashman, *supra* note 10, p. 2.

216. Asbury, *supra* note 7, p. 288.

217. Clark, *supra* note 38, p. 128.

218. Feldman, *supra* note 3, p. 382.

219. Cashman, *supra* note 10, p. 152.

220. Bruere, *supra* note 175, p. 293.

221. James H. Timberlake, *Prohibition and the Progressive Movement, 1900–1920* (Harvard University Press, 1963), p. 99.

222. Clark, *supra* note 38, pp. 152–54.

223. Bruere, *supra* note 175, p. 281.

224. Cashman, *supra* note 10, p. 208.

225. Timberlake, *supra* note 221, p. 94.

226. Cashman, *supra* note 10, p. 2.

227. See generally, Gore Vidal Index, http://www.pitt.edu/~kloman/vidalframe.htm.

228. Hamm, *supra* note 66, p. 254.

229. *Id.*

230. *Id.*, p. 255.

231. Clark, *supra* note 38, p. 163.

232. Cashman, *supra* note 10, p. 50.

233. Asbury, *supra* note 7, p. 296.

234. Hamm, *supra* note 66, p. 266.

235. Clark, *supra* note 38, p. 161.

236. Spaeth, *supra* note 152, p. 179.

237. Hamm, *supra* note 66, p. 267.

238. Dobyns, *supra* note 1, p. 271.

239. *Id.*, p. 270.

240. Cashman, *supra* note 10, pp. 200–01.

241. Holcombe, *supra* note 130, p. 9.

242. *Id.*, p. 15.

243. *Id.*, p. 16.

244. Cashman, *supra* note 10, p. 155.

245. *Id.*, p. 201.

246. Clark, *supra* note 138, p. 195.

247. McWilliams, *supra* note 195, p. 73.

248. Cashman, *supra* note 10, p. 211.

249. Coffey, *supra* note 18, p. 275.

250. McWilliams, *supra* note 195, p. 73.

251. Cashman, *supra* note 10, p. 209.

252. Clark, *supra* note 38, p. 199.

253. Forrest Revere Black, *Ill-Starred Prohibition Cases: A Study in Judicial Pathology* (Boston: R. G. Badger, 1931).

254. Hamm, *supra* note 66, p. 268.

255. Clark, *supra* note 38, p. 195.

256. *Id.*

257. *Id.*, pp. 195–96.

258. *Id.*, p. 196.

259. David E. Kyvig, *Explicit and Authentic Acts: Amending the U.S. Constitution, 1776–1995* (Lawrence, Kans.: University Press of Kansas, 1996), p. 276.

260. Black, *supra* note 252, pp. 15–16.

261. *Id.*, p. 45.

262. *Id.*, p. 43.

263. Kyvig, *supra* note 258, p. 277.

264. Black, *supra* note 252, p. 80.

265. *Id.*, p. 86.

266. *Id.*, p. 87.

267. *Id.*, p. 84.

268. Cashman, *supra* note 10, p. 46.

269. Coffey, *supra* note 18, p. 156.

270. Asbury, *supra* note 7, p. 318.

271. Cashman, *supra* note 10, p. 211.

272. Spaeth, *supra* note 152, p. 176.

273. Timberlake, *supra* note 221, p. 65.

274. Cashman, *supra* note 10, pp. 153–54.

275. Clark, *supra* note 38, pp. 200–01.

276. Cashman, *supra* note 10, p. 152.

277. *Id.*, p. 153.

278. Boudreaux, *supra* note 13.

279. Dobyns, *supra* note 1, p. 17.

280. See generally, Volunteer Committee of Lawyers, Original VCL (1927–33), http://www.vcl.org/History/orig_vcl_short.htm.

281. Cashman, *supra* note 10, p. 156.

282. *Id.*, pp. 163–64.

283. *Id.*, p. 206.

284. Coffey, *supra* note 18, p. 277.

285. *Id.*, p. 278.

286. Cashman, *supra* note 10, p. 211.

287. Kyvig, *supra* note 258, p. 278.

288. *Id.*

289. Joseph Percival Pollard, *The Road to Repeal, Submission to Conventions* (New York: Brentano's, 1932), p. 182.

290. Kyvig, *supra* note 258, p. 278.

291. Pollard, *supra* note 287, p. 4.

292. *Id.*, p. 159 (this decision was short-lived and unanimously reversed by the Supreme Court).

293. Cashman, *supra* note 10, p. 157.

294. Kyvig, *supra* note 258, p. 264.

295. *Id.*, p. 262.

296. *Id.*, p. 263.

297. *Id.*

298. Demleitner, *supra* note 170, p. 626 (quoting Andrew Sinclair).

299. Boudreaux, *supra* note 13, p. 1.

300. *Id.*, p. 3.

301. *Id.*, p. 5.

302. *Id.*, p. 20

303. *Id.*, p. 7.

304. Cashman, *supra* note 10, p. 236.

305. *Id.*, p. 238.

306. Clark, *supra* note 38, p. 205.

307. Kyvig, *supra* note 258, p. 285.

308. *Id.*

CHAPTER 3

Drugs: The History of Criminalization

I. INTRODUCTION

Drug use has existed for thousands of years, but has only recently become a problem. Opium use probably dates to about 4000 B.C. in Sumeria.[1] Egypt, the Swiss lakeside cultures, Crete, Cyprus, Persia, and Greece are ancient cultures known to have used opium.[2] As early as 2700 B.C. the Chinese treated gout, constipation, and "absentmindedness" with marijuana.[3] Egyptians physicians knew of opium in 1500 B.C.[4]

Before A.D. 1800, opium was available in America in its crude form as a prescription ingredient or in nonalcoholic extracts such as laudanum or "black drop" extracts, which contain no alcohol.[5] Opium was valued for its calming effects and treated symptoms of gastrointestinal diseases such as cholera, food poisoning, and parasites.[6] Because opium has never been commercially grown to any great extent in the United States, the national supply was imported.[7] Increased trade between the Portuguese and the British East India Company increased its importation into China in the late 1800s.[8] Lack of control over this increased opium importation into China catalyzed the Opium Wars of 1840–42.[9]

In the nineteenth century, drug misuse became more prevalent when the alkaloids morphine (1805) and codeine (1832) were identified, the hypodermic needle was invented (1843), and heroin was synthesized (1898).[10] By midcentury, the coca leaf had been analyzed, and cocaine was isolated for the first time.[11] Additionally, the widespread use of narcotics for pain during the American Civil War resulted in many postwar opium addicts.[12] At this time, opium derivatives served important medical uses and could be bought easily and inexpensively in any local drugstore almost anywhere in the United States.[13]

Until the 1890s, the use of opiates was not considered an offense.[14] In 1909, the federal government made its first attempt to control opiate use.[15] In addition to the high tariff placed on opium smoking in 1909, modest tariffs were placed on the importation of opium in 1915.[16] The legal control of narcotics began in the early years of the twentieth century.[17] Marijuana was introduced from the East in 1920, and by 1937 marijuana had been outlawed for general use.[18]

II. DRUG PROHIBITION AND RACISM

The Opiates

Morphine salts were first manufactured in 1832.[19] Statistics on opium importation date from 1840 and reveal a continual increase in consumption during the rest of the century.[20] The first law against opium use resulted from an anti-Chinese crusade.[21] Between 1850 and 1890, the U.S. Chinese population grew from 4,000 to 107,000 with an overwhelming majority residing in California.[22]

The per capita importation of crude opium reached its peak in 1896.[23] This constantly expanding consumption was exacerbated by addicted Civil War veterans, a group of unknown size who may have spread addiction by recruiting other users.[24] Discoveries of silver and gold brought thousands of young men west after the Civil War.[25] Labor problems intensified following completion of the railroad in 1873, which threw thousands more Chinese people on the labor market.[26] Chinese people were working for less pay in jobs whites of the time believed rightfully belonged to them.[27] The Chinese were industrious and required less money to live on. Consequently, Chinese people were accused of driving American laborers out and monopolizing the industry.

White laborers formed coalitions in opposition of these Chinese laborers.[28] When a depression hit larger Californian industries in the 1870s, Chinese people began to take over smaller businesses formerly controlled by the white middle-class public.[29] The Chinese had found enemies in both the working and middle classes.[30] Consequently, the press began to support the campaign against Chinese people.[31] For the next fifty years, working people of California organized to promote legislation prohibiting further Asian labor immigration. [32]

Examples of exclusionary anti-Asian legislation include an 1855 state law that prohibited Chinese and Mongolians from entering the state (later declared unconstitutional), an 1870 state law providing a penalty of at least $1,000 for bringing an Asian into the state without first presenting evidence of good character, and the 1882 congressional suspension of Chinese immigration for ten years.[33]

Other Californian laws provided economic or political sanctions against Asians. In 1855, a head tax of fifty dollars per person was levied on those who employed or brought into the country "persons who could not become citizens," with Chinese people later outright denied citizenship by the California Supreme Court.[34]

After the economic depression of the 1870s, the state legislature began inquiring into the "moral" aspects of the Chinese population by creating "fact-finding" committees placing the Chinese lifestyle under a microscope.[35] The findings served to justify past prejudicial treatment and found future legislation against Chinese people.[36] Laws prohibiting gambling and lotteries were selectively enforced against Chinese people. Along with this prejudice came a fear of opium smoking as one of the ways Chinese people were supposed to undermine American society.[37] By 1900, more than 80 percent of Chinese arrests in San Francisco were for crimes against morality, such as opium use (15.95 percent) and gambling (82 percent).[38] In contrast, Chinese arrests in San Francisco for crimes against persons or property accounted for only 2.01 percent combined.[39] The California legislature was leading a moral reform crusade against Chinese people.

The first anti-opium crusade in U.S. history was directed against working-class Chinese people brought over for cheap labor and no longer needed by 1870.[40] Consequently, the anti-opium crusade was both ideological and economical.[41] Opium smoking became a special problem when white men and women in the state began to "contaminate" themselves by frequenting opium dens in Chinatown. Further, it was not the use of opium itself, but the smoking of it, a unique Chinese habit, that became the subject of much state legislation. [42]

The city of San Francisco prohibited the commingling of races in opium dens, but this statute had limited success. In 1878, the San Francisco police department made the following plea to the California State Senate Committee:

These latter places were conducted by Chinamen, and patronized by both White men and women, who visited these dens at all hours of the day and night, the habit and its deadly results becoming so extensive as to [call] for action on the part of the authorities.... The department of the police, in enforcing the law with regard to this matter, have found white women and Chinamen side by side under the effects of this drug—a humiliating sight to anyone who has anything left of manhood.[43]

The media reinforced the idea that Chinese people were responsible for all smoking among white people. The Sacramento *Union* antagonized American manhood by printing ominous descriptions of opium houses: "Upon a matting-covered couch lay a handsome white girl in silk and laces, sucking poison from the same stem which an hour before was against the repulsive lips and yellow teeth of a celestial. She was just taking

pipeful; the eyes were heavy, the will past resistance or offense. She
up lazily, but was too indifferent to replace the embroidered skirts
rounded ankles the disturbed drapery exposed."[44]

Unfortunately, the media failed to add that many such places were set
up and run by the Chinatown Guides Association as tourist shockers.[45] As
a result of this propaganda and other political pressure, in 1881, the Californian state legislature validated anti-Chinese sentiment and enacted a
law against opium smoking.

A few years after the California law, the federal government began dis-
criminating between the different uses of opium in various tax measures.[46]
It has been estimated that no more than 6 percent of the Chinese population in California engaged in the habit regularly, significantly fewer than
the whites addicted to tobacco or alcohol today.

Opium smoking was excluded in the United States in 1909.[47] However,
opium and its derivatives were permitted as major ingredients in patent
medicines.[48] Patent medicines containing opiates needed not be so labeled
in interstate commerce until the Pure Food and Drug Act of 1906.[49] Many
proprietary medicines sold at local stores or by mail order contained morphine, cocaine, laudanum, or (after 1898) heroin.[50] Hay fever remedies
commonly contained cocaine as their active ingredient.[51] Cocaine was the
stimulant in Coca-Cola until 1903.[52] Opium and cocaine were part of
American everyday life.[53]

Smoking opium alone was considered immoral or a problem, while
other opium uses were considered medical issues.[54] Smoking opium,
solely a pastime, lacked elaborate advertising campaigns, similar to those
boosting morphine and cocaine preparations, and hence lacked political
support. This double standard remained until passage of the Harrison Tax
Act in 1914, and only later did all opiate use develop into a general moral
issue.[55]

Marijuana

Marijuana prohibition began distinctly local, occurring primarily in the
states west of the Mississippi and was heavily influenced by anti-Mexican
sentiments throughout 1915–31.[56] During this period, after the passage of
the regulatory Harrison Act, most states had in fact enacted or reenacted
narcotics laws.[57] Twenty-one states also restricted the sale of marijuana as
part of their general narcotics articles.[58] For instance, one state prohibited
its use for any purpose and four states prohibited its cultivation.[59] Society's perception of the narcotic addict shifted after the passage of the Harrison Act.[60] The media portrayed narcotics addicts as the criminal "dope
fiend."[61] This fear, coupled with increases in drug-related criminal conduct following closure of the clinics, was the basis for many post-Harrison
Act narcotics statutes.[62] In 1915, Utah passed the first state statute pro-

hibiting sale or possession of marijuana.[63] By 1931, twenty-two states had enacted such legislation.[64]

Cannabis was not included in the final draft of the Harrison Act in 1914, even though it was repeatedly listed along with opiates and cocaine.[65] The pharmaceutical industry opposed its inclusion because they saw no reason why a substance used chiefly in corn plasters, veterinary medicine, and nonintoxicating medicaments should be severely restricted.[66] Aside from the Pure Food and Drug Act's labeling requirement, cannabis remained untouched by federal restraint until 1937.[67]

Lurid accounts in the media, publications of private narcotics associations, and effective separation of the addict and his problems from the medical profession all pressed legislatures into action to deal more effectively with a perceived growing narcotics problem.[68] However, the most prominent influence was racial prejudice.[69] During this time, marijuana legislation focused in the southern and western states.[70] This regionally concentrated prohibition stemmed from the drug's use primarily by Mexican Americans who were immigrating in increasing numbers to those states.[71]

Mexican Americans began to constitute a sizable minority in each western state. The Bureau of Immigration recorded the entry of 590,765 Mexicans into the United States in 1915–30.[72] More than 90 percent of these immigrants became residents in the twenty-two states west of the Mississippi.[73] Mexicans were useful in the United States as farm laborers and, as the economic boom continued, they traveled to the Midwest and the North where jobs in factories and sugar-beet fields were available.[74]

Although employers welcomed them in the twenties, Mexicans were also feared as a source of crime and deviant social behavior.[75] This fear of Mexicans emanated from federal official reports that marijuana was a cause of violence among Mexican prisoners in the southwestern states.[76] It was thought that marijuana use in the west was limited to the Mexican segment of the population.[77] Many laws were founded on pointed references to the drug's Mexican origins and inferred connections with criminal conduct inevitably generated when the Mexicans ate the "killer weed."[78] Similarly, when the New Mexico and Texas legislatures passed marijuana legislation in 1923, newspaper coverage was minimal.[79] In its only direct reference to marijuana, the *Austin Texas Statesman* stated:

The McMillan Senate Bill amended the anti-narcotic law so as to make unlawful the possession for the purpose of sale of any marijuana or other drugs. Marijuana is a Mexican herb and is said to be sold on the Texas-Mexican border.[80]

Legal and medical officers in New Orleans, believing that marijuana was a sexual stimulant that removed civilized inhibitions, published articles claiming that many of the region's crimes could be traced to its use.[81]

Consequently, sixteen of the twenty-two western states prohibited the sale or possession of marijuana before 1930.[82] The discriminatory aspects of this early marijuana legislation, suggested only obliquely by origin and apparent disinterest in Utah, New Mexico, and Texas, are directly confirmed in Montana and Colorado.[83] Montana newspapers followed the progress of the bill prohibiting marijuana use in January 1929.[84] The *Montana Standard* recorded the following:

There was fun in the House Health Committee during the week when the marihuana bill came up for consideration. Marijuana is Mexican opium, a plant used by Mexicans and cultivated for sale by Indians. "When some beet field peon takes a few rares of this stuff," explained Dr. Fred Fulsher of Mineral County, "he thinks he has just been elected president of Mexico so he starts out to execute all his political enemies. I understand that over in Butte where the Mexicans often go for the winter they stage imaginary bullfights in the 'Bower of Roses' or put tournaments for the favor of 'Spanish Rose' after a couple of whiffs of Marijuana. The Silver Bow and Yellowstone delegations both deplore these international complications." Everybody laughed and the bill was recommended for passage.[85]

That same year, a *Denver Post* story was headlined "Fiend Slayer Caught in Nebraska[;] Mexican Confesses Torture of American Baby," and subheaded "Prisoner Admits to Officer He Is Marijuana Addict."[86] This article describes a Mexican who kills his white stepdaughter because "his supply of the weed had become exhausted for several days before the killing and his nerves were unstrung."[87] Four days after the *Denver Post* printed this story, the governor signed a bill increasing penalties for sale, possession, or production of marijuana.[88] The public perception of marijuana's ethnic origins and crime-producing tendencies often went hand in hand, especially in the more volatile areas of the western states.[89]

The American Coalition was formed whose goal was to keep "America American."[90] One of the coalition's prominent members made the following statement about the connection between marijuana and Mexican people:

Marijuana, perhaps now the most insidious of narcotics, is a direct by-product of unrestricted Mexican immigration. Easily grown, it has been asserted that it has recently been planted between rows in a California penitentiary garden. Mexican peddlers have been caught distributing sample marijuana cigarettes to school children. Bills for our quota against Mexico have been blocked mysteriously in every Congress since 1924 Quota Act. Our nation has more than enough laborers.[91]

No association between marijuana and crime or violence has ever been established.[92]

The rationale behind marijuana prohibition in the eastern states was that marijuana would be used by narcotics addicts to replace prohibited drugs.[93] Commissioner Harry J. Anslinger recalled that marijuana caused few problems except in the southwestern and western states, and there the growing alarm was directed at the Mexicans.[94] These states were "the only ones then affected...we didn't see it here in the East at all at that time."[95]

In 1938–51, the federal government put forth propaganda supporting the Uniform Narcotic Drug Act that culminated in the passage of the Marijuana Tax Act.[96] The annual reports of the Federal Bureau of Narcotics during its first few years indicates that control of marijuana should be vested in state governments, finding marijuana use a minimal problem.[97] However, in 1932, the Federal Bureau of Narcotics endorsed the Uniform State Narcotic Act claiming this act would prevent marijuana use.[98] Inclusion of marijuana in the Uniform Narcotic Drug Act in 1932 and passage of the Marijuana Tax Act in 1937 marked the first nationally agreed-upon policy regarding the drug.[99]

For thirteen years after prohibition was achieved, marijuana garnered little attention. However, between the years of 1951 and 1965, marijuana was portrayed as the first steppingstone to heroin addiction. At this time, penalties for marijuana offenses paralleled increased penalties for narcotic use; soon after, all marijuana offenses were felonies in most states.[100] Marijuana use in the 1960s confronted a system of criminal prohibition that carried its own meaning emanating from a different time, "[d]ecades of classification as a narcotic, the implication of addiction, crime, and insanity has instilled in the public consciousness a fear of marijuana unjustified by the demonstrable effects of its use."[101] Modern commentary provides no indications of why marijuana was included in New York narcotics laws.[102] Numerous articles existed in the media dealing with the problems of the opiates, morphine, cocaine, and heroin, but only four major articles about marijuana.[103] Furthermore, none of the articles discussing the act after its passage refer to marijuana.[104] New York and other eastern states enacted preventive statutes prohibiting the use of marijuana in order to keep addicts from switching to it as a substitute for other drugs.[105] These statutes were passed, and marijuana use in fact increased.

The legislature received significant deference from the judicial branch, such that the argument regarding a private conduct limitation on the police power had been so discredited that it was no longer made.[106] Further, similar to the legislature, the courts relied on nonscientific materials to support the proposition that marijuana was an addictive, mind-destroying drug productive of crime and insanity.[107] In *State v. Bonoa*, the Louisiana Supreme Court held that possession of marijuana plants for any reason is prohibited because the drug's deleterious properties outweighed its uses, especially since "[t]he Marijuana plant is not one of the crops of this state."[108] The court relied on two "advisory opinions" in its decision. First, the Solis Cohen Githen's *Pharmacotheraupeutics* in its description of marijuana's effects on users states "[a]n Arab leader, fighting against the crusaders, had a bodyguard who partook of haschisch, and used to rush madly on their enemies, slaying everyone they met. The name of 'haschischin' applied to them has survived as 'assassin.'"[109] Second, a quote from Rusby, Bliss, & Ballard, *The Properties and Uses of Drugs:*

The particular narcosis of cannabis in the liberation of the imagination from all restraint....Not rarely, in [the depression] state, an irresistible impulse to the commission of criminal acts will be experienced. Occasionally an entire group of men under the influence of this drug will rush out to engage in violent or bloody deeds.[110]

The passage of the Marijuana Tax Act was based on this purported propensity toward crime.[111] Additionally, in *State* v. *Navaro,* an expert physician testified as follows:

[Marijuana] is a narcotic and acts upon the central nervous system affecting the brain, producing exhilarating effects and causing one to do things which he otherwise would not do and especially induces acts of violence; that violence is one of the symptoms of excessive use of marijuana....that the marijuana produces an "I don't care" effect. A man having used liquor and marijuana might deliberately plan a robbery and killing and carry it out and escape, and then later fail to remember anything that had occurred... ."[112]

This became the medical authority for the scientific hypothesis that marijuana use causes crime.[113]

Fifty years passed, following the start of prohibition, before the opposition to marijuana use was exposed to public debate.[114] From about 1965 to 1972, marijuana use increased. Its use expanded to the middle class, and every state reduced its penalties for offenses related to marijuana consumption.[115] In 1972, the report of the National Commission on Marijuana and Drug Abuse recommended decriminalization of consumption-related offenses.[116] In 1973, Oregon became the first state to decriminalize possession of small amounts of marijuana, and ten other states have followed suit. These ten states decriminalized marijuana using different methods.[117] For instance, Oregon, Maine, Alaska, and Nebraska provide only civil fines for the possession of small amounts of the drug for personal use. California, Colorado, Minnesota, Ohio, Mississippi, New York, and North Carolina have limited the permissible criminal sanction for the conduct to fines.[118] The Alaska Supreme Court ruled that possession by adults in the home for personal use is not an offense at all.

Marijuana has by far the lowest ratio of measured harm to total use of all illicit drugs, and it has state-recognized medicinal value.[119] A substantial fraction of all regular marijuana users become at least daily users for a time, but only few develop a chronic condition.[120] A few million Americans spend their waking hours under the influence of marijuana.[121] But even the existence of this rather obvious "problem" population must be inferred from data about the drug market rather than being directly observed in the form of deaths, injuries, crimes, and such.[122]

It is unlikely that decriminalization would lead to large increases in marijuana consumption.[123] Both survey evidence and the experience of decriminalized states suggest that fear of arrest plays an insignificant role in decreasing the use of marijuana.[124] Furthermore, if marijuana use were legal, the most dangerous health hazard its use poses, lung damage, might be reduced by encouraging the use of water-filtered smoking devices to replace the filterless rolled joint.[125]

Narcotics-Cocaine

Narcotics use is often linked to the moral deterioration of the addict's character.[126] The average narcotics addict in the United States in 1957 came from the lowest-income household, the lowest educational level, and the lowest social status.[127] Cocaine had been depicted with vicious sexual crimes, even though opiates physiologically depress the sexual appetite.[128] Today, cocaine is used by all socioeconomic groups, including students and professionals.

Cocaine achieved popularity in the United States as a general tonic for sinusitis and hay fever.[129] It was even used as a cure for opium, morphine, and alcohol habits. Cocaine's exhilarating properties made it a favorite ingredient of medicine, soda, wines, and more.[130]

The existence of the coca leaf has been known for centuries, but not until 1859 did Austrian physician Alfred Niemann succeeded in isolating cocaine.[131] Cocaine was soon widely recognized as an anesthetic.[132] In response to the high number of morphine-addicted Civil War veterans, an American physician successfully treated morphine addiction by using cocaine in 1878.[133] Sigmund Freud recommended the use of cocaine to treat opium addiction and melancholia.[134] Cocaine's uses became so diffuse that one county law allowed the equivalent of 29.03 grams of cocaine per person per year to meet an individual's legitimate medical needs.[135] Cocaine was an ingredient in many nonprescription medications sold to the public in both Europe and America.[136]

Cocaine was also used by intellectuals to increase mental awareness.[137] Freud himself used cocaine and wrote glowingly of the exhilaration and lasting euphoria it produced.[138] The famous *Vin Coca Mariani* was a mixture of wine and the Peruvian coca leaf.[139] The drink was popular and consumed by such notables as composer Charles Gounod and Pope Leo XIII.[140] Coca leaves were ingredients in popular soft drinks in the United States until 1906.[141] Cocaine use is still popular among intellectuals, artists, students, and members of the professional class who experiment with drugs.[142]

Because cocaine was not limited to physicians' prescriptions, the "lower classes," found they could obtain a jolt from it, rather than from hard liquor.[143] Bars began putting cocaine in hard liquor shots.[144] Cocaine was even sold door to door.[145]

This increased use of cocaine in the white population was accompanied by its increased use among blacks.[146] Pressure increased to control cocaine use out of fear that blacks would "overstep their bounds" under the influence of the drug and move into white society.[147] This fear of "cocainized" blacks coincided with the peak of lynchings, legal segregation, and voting laws, all designed to remove political and social power from them.[148]

Proponents of increased control over the drug's use introduced and perpetuated the myth that cocaine would make blacks resistant to .32-caliber bullets and foster violence, including sexual violence against white women.[149] This myth is said to have caused southern police departments to switch to .38-caliber revolvers.[150] Another myth was that cocaine improved pistol marksmanship.[151] These myths characterized not cocaine's effects but white fear of black people and served as justifications for repressing blacks.[152]

The Indians of South America chew coca leaves as a stimulant, an antidote for hunger and the fatigue resulting from working in high altitudes.[153] The practice of chewing the coca leaves is ancient.[154] An American botanist discovered coca leaves buried in prehistoric graves that date back 3,000 years.[155] The Spanish in Peru recognized that chewing of coca leaves increased the work capacity of their Indian slaves, and Indian miners were given a daily ration of the leaves.[156] The Indian chews the leaves mixed with lime and some cornstarch.[157] The lime flavors the mixture and helps release the cocaine in the leaves by forming an alkaline solution that activates the drug substance.[158] Commentators agree that the use of cocaine by these Indians reflects both social and environmental influences.[159] For instance, for Indians living in higher altitudes, the coca chewing acts both as a stimulant and as a hunger depressant.[160] When the Spanish arrived in Peru and observed this coca chewing, they outlawed it, believing it to be a "pagan practice."[161] However, once they realized that coca chewing increased the work capacity of their Indian slaves, the Spanish provided the Indian miners with a daily ration of the leaves.[162] It has been estimated that more than 90 percent of the Andes Indians chew coca.[163] The estimated production of Peru and Bolivia is more than 12,000 tons of coca a year, with most consumption domestic.[164]

Similarly, law-abiding middle-class and upper- middle-class employers also found practical uses for cocaine.[165] Both groups reportedly distributed cocaine to construction and mine workers to keep them going at a high pace and with little food.[166] Thus, cocaine was economically valuable before it was a key player in the black market.

When the Peruvian army banned coca use, Indians had no trouble adjusting when fed an adequate diet.[167] This does not mean that the use of coca may not lead to a psychological dependence.[168] However, the average coca-chewing Indian consumes only one-tenth as much cocaine as the drug user in the United States.[169]

Similar to marijuana, cocaine is becoming an "acceptable" drug for professionals.[170] These individuals can afford the drug and prefer it for various reasons.[171] Cocaine does not need to be injected with a hypodermic needle.[172] Additionally, cocaine has recreational value because it produces a temporary feeling of euphoria, reduces fatigue, and causes increased mental acuity.[173] Furthermore, the cocaine user is often more confident and open than without the drug.[174]

In 1922, Congress enacted legislation prohibiting the importation of cocaine and coca leaves.[175] This law was significant because it defined cocaine as a narcotic drug by law, even though pharmacologically it remained a nonnarcotic drug.[176] Additionally, the act increased penalties to a fine up to $5,000 and imprisonment for up to ten years.[177] Despite the seriousness of the drug problem, few efforts have been made to subject popular notions about drugs to rigorous scientific analysis.

III. LEGAL AUTHORITY PERMITTING DRUG PROHIBITION

Gradually, the United States Supreme Court broadened the federal government's constitutionally granted commerce and tax powers.[178] These decisions included upholding a federal tax on colored oleomargarine, federal prohibition against transportation of prostitutes across state lines, interstate transportation of lottery tickets, and importing liquor into a state where liquor importation was prohibited.[179]

Federal regulation of drug manufacture and distribution began in 1906 with enactment of the Pure Food and Drug Act.[180] The act deemed any article of food or drug as misbranded if it contained but did not disclose on the label alcohol, morphine, cocaine, heroin, or any derivatives or preparations of these substances.[181] The Pure Food and Drug Act curtailed the marketing of drugs and sodas that contained cocaine and/or opium in two ways.[182] First, by prohibiting interstate shipment of food and sodas containing cocaine and/or opium;[183] secondly, by requiring that any amounts of these drugs be noted on medicine labels.[184] This act placed all drugs in two classes, prescription only and those nonprescription drugs that could be sold over the counter. [185] This act was the legal basis for suppressing all sales of sedative drugs, particularly the barbiturates, except upon medical prescription.[186]

A joint committee set up by the State and Treasury Departments attempted to write a bill acceptable to the pharmaceutical trades, the medical profession, and the Internal Revenue Bureau, which would have enforcement responsibility.

The Harrison Narcotics Act of 1914 was enacted as U.S. support of the Hague Agreement and as a moral symbol of the government's views on drugs.[187] This act served more than fifty years as the basis for the entire federal scheme of drug control legislation.[188] At that time, the government was prohibited from imposing penal laws, so the Harrison Act punished manufacturers and sellers of opium and cocaine by requiring them to register, pay fees, and keep records of all such drugs in their possession.[189] The act required every person who produced, imported, manufactured, compounded, dealt in, dispensed, sold, distributed, or gave away opium or coca leaves or their derivatives (cocaine) to register with the Internal Revenue Service and to pay a special tax.[190] No grounds for refusal of registration were set out in the act.[191]

Registered parties must file returns identifying held quantities of all opium, coca leaves, and their derivatives, and these drugs could only be transferred with a special order form supplied by the transferee.[192] Only registered parties could obtain these special order forms from the Internal Revenue Service.[193] Consequently, all transfers of cocaine and opium must be between registered parties.[194] The regulations prohibited a consumer from registering under the act; consequently, consumers could only obtain a supply of such drugs through a duly registered physician, dentist, or veterinarian."Overnight, opiate addiction had become an illegal activity except in the narrowest of medical exceptions. Yet, thousands of bona fide opiate addicts existed in every region of the country requiring at least a short-term solution to their dilemma."[195]

The new interpretation left registered professionals as the only legal source of supply. In turn, registrants were heavily monitored through record-keeping provisions and sanctions for violations.[196] The Narcotics Division decided to close maintenance clinics and oppose treatment as an alternative in every case except among the aged and terminally ill.[197] The decision to close the clinics was grounded in the following considerations: (1) No medically proven specific treatment for narcotic addiction existed, but the public health service assured that any withdrawal method would get an addict off the drugs; (2) The danger of death in withdrawal cases was exaggerated, and authentic cases were hard to find; (3) After any method of withdrawal, addicts would usually return to drugs when available; (4) The chief source of drugs was still thought to be a small percentage of physicians who would write out a prescription for anyone; (5) The clinics were merely another supply source for those who wished drugs for comfort or pleasure.[198] The new laws left addicts stranded with a disease and no remedy, hence the emergence of the black market.

The Harrison Act became effective March 1, 1915.[199] Soon after, the federal government began prosecuting physicians for prescribing drugs to addicts. In *Webb et al. v. U.S.*, a retail druggist and practicing physician, Webb, had been indicted for conspiracy to violate the Harrison Act by providing maintenance supplies of morphine to an addict.[200] A divided court concluded that to call "such an order for the use of morphine a physician's order would be so plain a perversion of meaning that no discussion of the subject is required."[201] Three years after *Webb*, in 1922, the United States Supreme Court eliminated the intent of the physician as a defense if he should prescribe large amounts of narcotics for an addict.[202]

Public and congressional distinction between narcotic control and liquor prohibition was clearly shown during December 1914.[203] Part of a rush of legislation, the Harrison Act was approved in a few minutes, a fact not even noted in that week's *New York Times* summary of the session's work.[204] In contrast, the House set aside an entire day that month of December for debate on a resolution introduced to submit to the states a constitutional amendment mandating prohibition of alcohol.[205]

It is instructive to compare prohibition of alcohol with today's drug problem. Similar to modern drug prohibition, proponents lobby for intensified enforcement and punishment, while others call for outright repeal. Consequently, prisons become overcrowded, enforcement costs exceed the budget, dealers become rich, but the drug problem still thrives.

All in all, the Harrison Bill of 1913 had incorporated numerous compromises among the pharmaceutical trades, the medical profession, and the Internal Revenue Bureau.[206] The bill was passed and signed by the president in December 1914. Finally, the American government acknowledged its international promises to control opiates and cocaine traffic by federal law.[207]

The federal government created the Bureau of Narcotics from the old Narcotic Unit within the Treasury's Department's Bureau of Prohibition, to enforce the Harrison Act.[208] The federal government also has played an active role in states' enactment of drug prohibition laws.[209] For instance, the National Conference of Commissioners on Uniform State Laws promulgated the Uniform Narcotic Drug Act. This act criminalized the possession, use, and distribution of cocaine and opiates. The federal government was successful in creating uniformity of drug laws among the states, for example recommending the states use the act as a model in creating their own criminal drug laws.[210] The Bureau of Narcotics encouraged Congress to enact additional prohibition for it to enforce.[211] For instance, the Marijuana Tax Act, which criminalized cannabis was similar to laws prohibiting opiates and cocaine. The bureau reasoned that marijuana had "criminogenic" effects[212] The bureau's commissioner, Harry J. Anslinger, cited studies relating the ingestion of cannabis and the commission of violent and bizarre acts.[213] In lieu of criticisms of these studies promoting the idea of "reefer madness," Congress passed the act. Other historical reasons why the act was passed include anti-Mexican measures aimed at discouraging immigration into the southwest.[214] This is similar to the historical treatment of other substances, such as when cocaine raised the specter of the wild Negro, opium the devious Chinese, and morphine the tramps in the slums. These substances were associated with foreigners or other alien subgroups,[215] and fears emerged that use of these drugs was spreading into the "higher classes."[216]

No association between marijuana and crime or violence has ever been established.[217] The La Guardia report of 1944 exonerated marijuana as a dangerous drug.[218] The report's finding that "any tendency toward violence was expressed verbally" might be attributed to the fact that the studies were conducted under police guard.[219] The Task Force on Individual Acts of Violence, making a study for the National Commission on the Causes and Prevention of Violence, reviewed all current evidence and concluded that "the evidence will not support the theory that marijuana is a cause of crime and violence."[220]

In 1935, eleven years after the morphine clinics were closed, the government opened its first treatment facility for opium addicts in Lexington, Kentucky.[221] Three years later, in 1938, another facility opened in Fort Worth, Texas.[222] The primary reason for this federal aid to addiction was not to provide treatment, rather, these two facilities were built to house the many jailed addicts crowded into federal penitentiaries.[223] For example, three federal penitentiaries that had a total cell capacity of 3,738 before the Harrison Act, by 1928 maintained a population of 7,598.[224] Of the prisoners, about 2,300 were narcotics violators—1,600 addicted—and the prison system was not equipped to care for addicts.[225] Addicts caused problems by smuggling drugs into the prison and introducing drugs to nonaddicts.[226]

The Justice Department and the Federal Bureau of Narcotics supervised the operation of these farms by the Public Health Service.[227] Physicians were at odds with the Federal Bureau of Narcotics' "legal approach" toward addiction.[228] Not until the 1960s were the bars removed from the Lexington facility and the cells turned into rooms.[229] The cure rate at these hospitals was not impressive, but no well-established form of treatment was known.[230]

During the 1940s, the government was actively involved in a world war that resulted in only one additional drug prohibition. The purported link between crime and drugs fueled national movement toward a punitive approach to drug use, resulting in harsh penalties for nonmedicinal use. The Uniform Narcotic Drug Act was amended to include cannabis, and once again the states followed the lead of the federal government in criminalizing the cultivation, possession, use, and distribution of cannabis.[231]

Prior to 1951, the United States had two sets of penalties for drug offenses.[232] First, violations of the Harrison Act were punishable by fines of up to $2,000 and imprisonment for up to five years, or both.[233] Second, violations of the importation laws were punishable by a fine up to $5,000 and imprisonment up to ten years.[234]

With the 1951 amendments to the Narcotic Drugs Import and Export Act and the Harrison Act, Congress standardized penalties for all drug offenses.[235] Furthermore, in 1951, the Bureau of Narcotics' Commissioner Anslinger encouraged Congress to pass the Boggs Act.[236] The Boggs Act imposed mandatory minimum sentences on narcotics offenders.[237] Once again, states followed the paternalistic federal lead and enacted miniature Boggs Acts. In 1956, an unsatisfied Congress again increased federal narcotics laws.[238] As with the Narcotic Control Act of 1956, one could be sentenced to the death penalty for conviction of selling narcotics to anyone under eighteen years of age.[239] Adoption of these statutes has left the United States of America, land of the free, with one of the strictest narcotics policies in the world, imposing on the narcotics offender stiff mandatory minimum sentences normally considered for more serious violent crimes against persons or property.[240] Furthermore, to ensure that the drug trafficker would serve a full term in prison, Congress denied eligibility for a suspended sentence, probation, or parole even on first conviction.[241]

The 1960s were dominated by a more free-spirited, experimental view of drugs. In 1961, the American Bar Association and the American Medical Association published a combined report, *Drug Addiction: Crime or Disease?*[242] This report criticized the dominant law enforcement approach to addiction advocating a more balanced prevention policy.[243] Just one year after this report, President Kennedy convened the White House Conference on Narcotics and Drug Abuse, which promoted rehabilitation rather than punishment.[244] Legislation that authorized the involuntary civil commitment of narcotics addicts was enacted by the State of California (1961), the State of New York (1962), and Congress (1966). Although these laws and programs served a humanitarian and social control interest, poor treatment success and high operational costs led to their disappearance.[245] In response to the AMA/ABA report, Congress enacted the Narcotic Addict Rehabilitation Act in 1966.[246] The act permitted federal judges to condition criminal sentences of probationers and inmates on the participation in treatment programs available in Fort Worth and Lexington.[247] Unfortunately, as with civil commitment laws, this act has been deemphasized over the years.[248]

In the 1960s, depressant, stimulant, and hallucinogenic drugs were for the first time brought under federal control. This was done through the Drug Abuse Control Amendments of 1965,[249] which gave the Food and Drug Administration control over barbiturates, amphetamines, and other drugs from the manufacturer to the consumer.[250] This act limited the number of times a prescription could be refilled and made it criminal to possess the substances without a prescription.[251] The FDA then included peyote, mescaline, LSD, DMT, psilocybin, and certain tranquilizers.[252] Once again, the states followed the federal government's paternalistic lead and adopted uniform legislation regulating the possession, use, manufacture, and distribution of depressant, stimulant, and hallucinogenic drugs.[253]

Also in the 1960s, the international community agreed on a narcotics control compact.[254] The single convention replaced all earlier international agreements dealing with the control of narcotics.[255] It limited the production, manufacture, import, export, trade, distribution, use, and possession of opiates, cocaine, and cannabis drugs to medical purposes only.

In 1970, Congress passed the Comprehensive Drug Abuse Prevention and Control Act, more popularly labeled the Controlled Substances Act.[256] All existing federal drug laws were unified under this act, and all drugs subject to the act were labeled controlled substances. The Drug Abuse Act of 1970 rejected the Harrison Act's foundation on revenue powers and relied on the congressional interstate commerce power.[257] In the last half of the twentieth century, the interstate commerce clause's powers were substantially broadened so that its powers sustained strict regulation of drug use without the need to portray a police function as a revenue measure.[258]

The act subjects controlled substances to increasing levels of control based on abuse potential and lack of therapeutic usefulness. The act authorizes the attorney general and the secretary of health, education, and welfare to add or delete drugs based on abuse capacity. The rigid minimum penalties for drug offenders were reduced and education, research, and rehabilitation programs became the focus of government encouragement. That same year, the Uniform Controlled Substances Act was drafted and adopted by more than forty states.

The Uniform Controlled Substances Act replaces the Uniform Narcotic Drug Act. It was believed that because drug abuse had widened beyond traditional types of abused drugs such as heroin and marijuana, federal legislation should address a wide range of drugs. These drugs were grouped into five basic schedules, or classifications. This federal legislation required many states to amend existing legislation by adopting classifications similar to the federal approach.

Section 201 of the act, as adopted by all states that have enacted a Uniform Controlled Substances Act, provides the criteria to be used in controlling and classifying drugs into five distinct schedules.

In 1971, the international community agreed on a new international drug control pact.[259] The Vienna Convention on Psychotropic Substances regulates the production, manufacture, import, export, trade, distribution, use, and possession of depressant, stimulant, and hallucinogenic drugs.[260]

Throughout this time, the U.S. government created many offices and agencies to enforce drug-related legislation. Offices such as the Special

Action Office for Drug Abuse Prevention or agencies such as the Bureau of Narcotics and Dangerous Drugs (BNDD) formed from the consolidation of the Bureau of Narcotics and the Bureau of Drug Abuse Control.[261] However, all these offices and agencies failed to achieve the intended goal of coordinating federal drug law enforcement resources.[262] By executive order, the drug law enforcement resources of the Bureau of Narcotics and Dangerous Drugs, Office of Drug Abuse Law Enforcement, Bureau of Customs, and Office of National Narcotics Intelligence consolidated into a single federal enforcement agency, the Drug Enforcement Administration (DEA). All the functions performed by the predecessor agencies were integrated into this new agency.[263]

IV. DRUG PROHIBITION AND THE MORAL MAJORITY

From a plethora of periodical articles that oppose drug legalization, we draw only one conclusion: drug prohibition remains a moral crusade. The common thread in all these articles is the same prohibitionist arguments buttressed by the same premise, in namely that drug use leads to disorderly conduct. However, an objective evaluation demonstrates that drug laws, not drug use per se, causes social deviance.

Prohibitionists make blanket statements such as "Drugs themselves, not drug laws, cause the most damage to society," but no authority supports the "profound" statement aside from citing another prohibitionist article. No statistical, scientific, or sociological evidence is provided, only a subjective opinion masked in a statement that appeals to emotions. These emotions stem from an American childhood overflowing with media spin regarding every controversial issue in life.

Drug laws exist because people were more racist than interested in their right to use drugs, which is ironic considering prohibitionists proclaim society will deteriorate if the big paternalistic government fails to protect us from ourselves. For example, when marijuana was prohibited, as with many of the illicit drugs, no medical testimony was presented to Congress.[264] Drug prohibition is not the product of careful research and analysis, but a product of public prejudices and myths that remain unvalidated and unchallenged.

Another irony emerges, as well: drug laws create crime in an area that is a health issue. Even the *Washington Post* made "Early Skirmishes in the War on Drugs" the cover story for the newspaper's *health section*.[265] The journalist who wrote that story explains that the legislature's insistence on continuing to pass laws and pour money and manpower into making America "drug free" is a *mistake* because history tells a different story: "In 1830, alcohol consumption per person was estimated at two to three times what it is today, according to Dr. David F. Musto, professor of psychiatry and the history of medicine at the Yale School of Medicine's Child Studies Center." The journalist also alerts the reader of the campaign against opium between 1840 and 1914 followed with an increase from twelve grains annually per person in 1840 to fifty-two grains per person. One grain was considered a normal daily dose per person.[266]

The ABA and the AMA together stated that prohibition is not the answer, yet prohibitionists refuse to heed even their expert opinion. Why do prohibitionists insist on remaining ignorant if their goal truly is to help society? Wouldn't medical doctors know the best method for dealing with a health issue? Wouldn't lawyers know the legal method to solve a fundamental rights issue? Yet, the prohibitionists insist on stricter enforcement in lieu of the statistics from the other side. Every individual in America pays the cost of the " unwinnable" drug war with life, liberty, and property.

For the layman, a few terms must be defined at the outset of this debate. Decriminalization would make possession legal, or mildly punishable, while importing, processing, and distribution would remain illicit.[267] It is important to note that decriminalization would not eliminate the black market. Legalization covers making any psychoactive substance available to any buyer; however, most advocates of legalization would limit legal availability to adults and apply the new policy to only some of the currently illicit substances.[268] The term legalization also is used to describe the idea that addicts with established drug habits should have legal access to psychoactive drugs through clinics.[269] Advocates of decriminalization would keep distribution illegal, but end the arrests of consumers.[270]

Drug use only causes deviant behavior in deviants. A medical analysis of how particular drugs affect the human body supports this conclusion. Prohibitionists proclaim that "if recreational drugs were freely available, drug prohibitionists argue that the black market would be replaced by a 'black plague' of crime and drug overdose deaths." But, again they provide no statistical data, scientific or sociological, to support this broad assumption. A search through the *New York Times Index* 1895–1904, the years of peak drug use and minimum legal controls, for articles about the negative effects of cocaine use produced none.[271] Not one article was written on that topic in ten years, ironically, the ten years immediately preceding the moral crusade of prohibition. However, between 1979 and 1988, the peak years of the War on Drugs, 1,657 articles were written about the cocaine problem.[272]

Many factors contribute to the physiological and psychological effect a particular drug may have on a particular individual. The drug itself will have varying effects on the same person at different dosages.[273] However, a single drug dose may have effects different from those produced by its chronic repetitive administration.[274] Furthermore, society is composed of subcultures with differences in ethical, religious, and social characteristics.[275] These subcultures or reference groups influence the behavior of any individual to the degree he or she accepts their values and attitudes that then begin to govern the individual's conduct.[276]

Crime and violence do not emanate from some physiological effect of the drug, but the drug laws themselves. In May 1998, the United States Department of Justice in an article entitled "Addressing Community Gang Problems: A Practical Guide" stated "[t]he research community has found little evidence of a relationship between drug use in general and violent behavior."[277] Furthermore, the department's Bureau of Justice Assistance stated that systemic violence, the type of violence most commonly associated with gangs is a function of the illegal sale and distribution of drugs.[278] Examples include territorial issues relating to a gang's share of the illegal drug market or disputes arising from transactions between a buyer and seller.[279]

Today, the notion that marijuana causes crime "is no longer taken seriously by even the most ardent anti-marijuana propagandists."[280] Even heroin use has a neutral effect on the potential criminal tendencies of an individual.[281] Personality and setting are determinative of the individual's potential criminal tendencies, not drugs.[282] Although some evidence exists that wealthy persons or physicians become violent after using cocaine, thousands of them have used the drug. Further, the law of averages will explain that some people are violent and the use of a drug presents an excuse to indulge in those negative tendencies.

Antisocial conduct is too often placed on the drug rather than the person. Unfortunately, this is type of blame shifting has become typical of today's society. Lawyers employ any and every excuse in the book, from unpleasant childhood events to drug use, to justify their client's misconduct. For instance, rather than portray Klebold and Harris, the two student gunmen in the 1999 Columbine High School attack, as mentally unhealthy individuals who committed a heinous criminal act of violence, the media blames society. Instead, Klebold and Harris are portrayed as victims of peer pressure from the "jocks" and others. Witness accounts explain that "jocks" often wore white hats, and one student shot in the library was wearing a white baseball cap. Every adolescent and adult will experience some form of societal pressure, few of us retaliate with murder.

Statistics demonstrate that millions of people in this world with unsatisfactory childhoods use drugs but commit no antisocial acts. People with antisocial tendencies will have them regardless of drug use and those who do become involved in antisocial behavior would have done so anyway. Scapegoats are widely used and acceptable in today's society. Drugs represent just one of them.

Even the U.S. Department of Justice in a national report on drugs, crime, and the justice system has failed to objectively evaluate its own reports. For example, the first section of the book, in setting out to answer the question "[h]ow are drugs and crime related," states, "[d]rug use and crime are common aspects of a deviant lifestyle. [283] The likelihood and frequency of involvement in illegal activity is increased because drug users and offenders are exposed to situations that encourage crime." [284] Yes, the situation is the prohibition of drugs. That same report boasts that in 5.6 percent of all rapes, 4.7 percent assaults, and 9.1 percent of all robberies that occurred in 1990, the victim "perceived" that the offender was under the influence of drugs.[285] Therefore, 94.4 percent of all rapes, 95.3 percent of all assaults, and 90.9 percent of all robberies occur without even suspicion that the perpetrator was under the influence of drugs. These numbers indicate that drug use plays a minor role, not a major one in these violent crimes.

In contrast, offenders in crimes that involve money, such as prostitution, theft, stolen vehicle, and other stolen-property crimes, portray a different picture. Urinalysis results indicated that 79 percent of male and 81 percent of female offenders arrested for drug sale or possession, 68 percent of male and 58 percent of female offenders arrested for theft, 59 percent of both male and female offenders arrested for stolen property, and finally 60 percent of male and 65 percent of female offenders arrested for stolen vehicles tested positive for drug use.[286] All of these crimes benefit the offender by providing money necessary to buy illicit drugs. Such money is necessary in part because of inflated prohibition prices of illicit black market drugs.

The conclusion that drug use does not result in disorderly conduct is revealed by the difficulty in capturing drug users. Law enforcement officials have employed numerous techniques that walk a fine line of constitutionality to catch drug law violators. For instance, telephones must be wiretapped, undercover agents utilized, sting operations set up, and peering into private premises among many other methods of capture. All of these methods push the envelope of violating individual privacy. Law enforcement officers argue in court that they have no other way to capture these individuals, but if drugs really cause deviance, does it not seem counterintuitive that law enforcement officers must go to such great lengths to capture these individuals?

Another way drug laws cause deviant behavior is by forcing usually law-abiding citizens with health issues into the world of crime. These people are forced to deal with criminals in order to satisfy their habits; they commit crimes to pay high prices for illicit contraband. For example, black market cocaine cost between 50 and 100 times as much as legal "free market" cocaine in 1990.[287]

Drug laws encourage deviance by (1) criminalizing users of illegal drugs, creating disrespect for the law; (2) forcing users into daily contact with professional criminals, which often leads to arrest and prison records that make legitimate employment difficult to obtain; (3) discouraging legitimate employment because of the need to hustle for drug money;

(4) encouraging young people to become criminals by creating an extremely lucrative black market in drugs; (5) destroying, through drug crime, the economic viability of low-income neighborhoods, leaving young people fewer alternatives to working in the black market; and (6) removing drug-related dispute settlements from the legal process, creating a context of violence for buying and selling drugs.[288] How tempting of a lifestyle would this be if your mother was twenty-five years old, expecting her sixth child, and of course on welfare?

Drug laws encourage drug use. Regarding the effects of pre-prohibition drug use in the United States, Edward Brecher has stated the following: "[T]here was very little popular support for a law banning these substances. Powerful organizations for the suppression...of alcoholic stimulants exist through the land,...but there were no similar opiate organizations. The reason for this lack of demand for opiate prohibition was quite simple: the drugs were not viewed as a menace to society and...they were not in fact a menace."[289]

Drug laws cause drug-related violence. Violence that results from prohibition includes all the random shootings and murders associated with black market drug transactions: rip-offs, eliminating the competition, killing informers and suspected informers.[290] Drug laws result in the deaths of many law enforcement officers, users, and even innocent bystanders.[291] Almost if not all "drug-related murders" are the result of prohibition.[292] Similarly, alcohol prohibition in 1920 was accompanied by an increased murder rate.[293] It remained high throughout prohibition and then declined for eleven years afterwards.[294] Because the black market has no quality control, prohibition also kills by making drug use more dangerous.[295] Illegal drugs often contain poisons, often are of uncertain potency, and often are injected with dirty needles.[296]

Many deaths are caused by infections, accidental overdoses, and poisoning.[297] At least 3,500 people will die from AIDS each year as a result of the use of contaminated needles, a greater number than the combined death toll from cocaine and heroin (also inflated by prohibition).[298] But these deaths are only the beginning. In 1990, 250,000 drug users were infected with the AIDS virus.[299] As many as 2,400 to 3,000 deaths attributed to heroin and cocaine use each year are caused by black market factors.[300] In a prior study, the author concluded that drug prohibition is responsible for at least 8,250 deaths and $80 billion in economic loss each year, as well as pervasive corruption, systematic destruction of civil liberties, clogged courts and prisons, and a general breakdown of social order and community, particularly in the cities.[301]

Prohibition reduces the availability of certain types of drugs, but does nothing to curtail what causes people first to seek drugs. Consequently, people who are deprived of certain types of drugs seek out legal drugs as a substitute, often referred to as drug-switching.[302] These people will engage in other forms of addictive behavior such as drinking or smoking. Drinking alcohol and smoking tobacco are both addicting and health hazards. Furthermore, these legal drugs are responsible for more deaths each year than any of the illicit drugs combined. So, in choosing, the public pays a high price for this preference.

All of these negative effects will be abolished only with legalization. Decriminalization won't abolish the black market, because users will still need to obtain the drug through illegal channels. It is human nature to fight to control the use of one's own body, and if people want to take drugs they will and they do, doctors and lawyers alike, and of course all those politicians who "didn't inhale!" It must be insisted that the prevention of mere drug use without evidence of actual harm does not qualify as harm prevented by prohibition.

Legalization would enable the government to put more money into education and treatment. This is logical, it is generally accepted that only medical treatment will cure an addict's addiction and education is the key to all society's ills. In 1986, the U.S. annual cost of drug abuse rose 40 percent from $60 billion to $100 billion.[303] No comprehensive cost-benefit analysis supports prohibition.[304]

In 1992, about 750,000 of the 28 million illegal drug users are arrested every year.[305] Between one-quarter and one-third of all felony charges involve drug offenses.[306] The Supreme Court has held a term of life imprisonment without parole for the offense of possessing 677 grams of cocaine is not cruel and unusual punishment, leaving the severity of the sentence with almost no limits.[307] As a result, the courts have become clogged, prisons overcrowded, and violent criminals set free to make room for drug-related crime offenders.

The U.S. Sentencing Commission estimated that within fifteen years the Anti-Drug Abuse Act passed by Congress in 1986 would cause the proportion of inmates incarcerated for drug violations to increase from one-third to one-half of all defendant's sentenced to federal prison.[308] At the end of 1986, an estimated 43 percent of the 445,780 adults serving time were classified as serious drug abusers.[309] The costs of punishment threaten to drain the treasury, as each prisoner requires expenditures of between $10,000 and $40,000 per year.[310] It costs taxpayers approximately $109,000 for a new inmate to serve a six-year prison term.[311] The Supreme Court has upheld the practice of including the entire weight of the substance or mixture when calculating the quantity of the drug for purposes of sentencing.[312]

INTERNATIONAL DRUG POLICY

Prior to the twentieth century, little effort was made to address drug production or trafficking through international law.[313] Now, nearly all nation members in the United Nations are party to one or more U.N. drug treaties.[314] This congruence does not exist, however, because these countries all hold the same beliefs about drug use.

The massive international trade of drugs was initiated by the Dutch and British.[315] Imperial Britain became a major producer state through acquisition of India, home to much of the world's opium production capacity.[316] The primary importer was China, though Britain on occasion maintained market access to Chinese users against the Chinese government's wishes, with the opium wars being one result.[317]

Opium was the first drug to receive sustained abolitionist attention. Opposition to the opium trade developed first in the West among religious groups, such as the Quakers.[318] A strong anti-opium movement began in the late nineteenth century, ultimately culminating in the Shanghai Conference of 1909, the first international conference on drug trafficking, and the 1912 Hague Opium Convention, the first international treaty on the subject.[319] Drugs were increasingly considered evil and corrosive to human life and progress.[320] A leading treatise on international drug control states, "The anti-opium movement was a struggle against a deepseated evil which was founded on a colossal economic motive. This movement was motivated purely by philanthropic ideals."[321]

A primary mover behind the early twentieth-century effort to address drugs through international law was the United States.[322] Opium, marijuana, and cocaine use were linked with ethnic and racial minorities in the United States, in particular with those of Asian, Latin American, or African descent, and hence drug prohibition efforts were fed by xenophobia, racism, and anti-immigrant sentiments.[323]

Global consumption of narcotics and psychoactive substances is at an all-time high. This is particularly true in the United States: the world's largest consumer.[324] The Clinton Administration, like its recent predecessors, made drug control a major priority.[325] The United States' antidrug budget increased from $53 million in 1970 to $8.2 billion in 1995, an increase of some 15,000 percent in nominal terms.[326] Even the editors of the *New York Times* suggested in 1998 that, at least as far as cocaine was concerned, traditional U.S. policy was failing.[327]

HISTORICAL FOUNDATIONS OF DRUG CONTROL

In 1914, U.S. Secretary of State William Jennings Bryan, "a man of deep prohibitionist and missionary convictions and sympathies," urged that the Harrison Narcotic Act be enacted to fulfill U.S. obligations under the new Hague Opium Convention.[328] Consequently, domestic and international drug law enforcement was born.

The Anti-Drug Campaign was first manifested through the League of Nations and then through the United Nations.[329] In the aftermath of the

Hague Convention, prior to World War II, international treaties were negotiated at drug control conventions in Geneva, Switzerland, in 1925, 1931, and 1936.

Hague Opium Convention (1912)

In 1909, U.S. authorities, in an attempt to enact international legislation to complement domestic drug prohibition laws, opened an international opium conference in Shanghai with the participation of thirteen powers.[330] Among the nations that gathered at the conference, the United States, Great Britain, and China dominated.[331] Documentation presenting the opium problem in the world was only approximate and followed the U.S. format.[332] Neither presentation of the various reports nor the discussion to which they gave rise demonstrated the conflict of interests between the participating countries.[333] The debate revolved around the type of control to be advocated, prohibition or regulation, the latter being pressed by the British, eager to protect their Indian-Chinese trade.[334] The conference ended in nine resolutions governing the prohibition of opium smoking and control of trade.[335]

The Shanghai resolutions required follow-up, and another meeting was convened three years later in the Hague.[336] The origin of drug control policies in the United States, England, and the Netherlands can be traced to the Hague Opium Convention of 1912, which sought to solve the opium problems of China and the Far East.[337] Until then, antidrug legislation was virtually nonexistent throughout the nations of the globe.[338] Again, the United States, through its diplomatic channels, made all the preparations.[339] Conflicting interests were already apparent at this preparatory stage, such as the meeting being postponed when the British attempted to delay the convention until the conclusion of an agreement consolidating the ten-year reduction of the Indian-Chinese trade.[340] Britain had a large economic interest in the opium trade.[341] The signing parties of the Hague Convention, in a limited number, agreed to regulate production and distribution of raw opium and medical products derived therefrom, and to prohibit trade in treated opium used for nonmedical purposes.[342]

The text of the Hague convention called for domestic, rather than international regulations controlling production and distribution.[343] Because of the peculiar ratification procedure maneuvered by the German delegation, the Hague Convention took effect after World War I began.[344] However, numerous countries became parties to the Hague convention through their ratification of the Versailles Treaty.[345] The British government took the lead in securing the ratification of the convention by this method.[346]

Geneva Convention (1931 and 1935)

The representatives of fifty-seven nations decided to control artificially produced drugs and to limit their use only to medical purposes.[347]

International cooperation in the prosecution of drug dealers was promoted, as well as the specialization of narcotics divisions within enforcement agencies.[348] The 1925 Geneva Convention governed regulation of drug distribution, and the 1931 Limitation Convention limited the manufacture of opiates to the amounts necessary to meet medical and scientific needs.[349]

Single Convention on Narcotic Drugs, New York (1961)

Adopted by 70 nations and ratified by 133, the Single Convention on Narcotic Drugs has become a model for antidrug policies.[350] Its purpose is to replace all previous agreements and to impose a general and absolute prohibition on all known drugs, including cannabis cultivations.[351] Furthermore, for those countries that traditionally cultivated cannabis and coca, deadlines were set.[352] The convention mandated "adequate punishment" for serious crimes dealing with every activity linked to drugs.[353] In addition to earlier treaties, the Single Convention included oversight provisions broadening the focus from solely opium to the raw material of natural narcotic drugs.[354] Finally, this convention states that every country, even those that did not sign it, has an obligation to fight against production of illicit drugs within their own territories.[355]

The Single Convention achieved more than the unification of treaties, it established a new policy toward cannabis prohibition.[356] Implementation of the Single Convention was assigned to the International Narcotics Control Board, itself a unification of prior agencies.[357] The Single Convention was amended in 1972 to strengthen provisions relating to producing and trafficking of illicit narcotics.[358] The amendment also addressed treatment and rehabilitation of drug abusers.[359]

Convention on Psychotropic Substances, Vienna (1971)

The Single Convention failed to include certain substances causing "disquiet" in several countries.[360] The 1971 Psychotropic Substances Convention extended international control to synthetic hallucinogens, stimulants, and sedatives.[361] This convention evolved from the Single Convention and sought to differentiate among those substances completely prohibited except for limited scientific and medical purposes and those whose manufacture, distribution, and use were merely curtailed.[362] This convention includes a list of generally forbidden substances, such as hallucinogens, amphetamines, THC, and barbiturates.[363] Although the two conventions contain some limited provisions relating to punishment of traffickers, they are mainly regulatory and provide no basis for comprehensive national action aimed at punishing distribution and use.[364]

Convention Against the Illicit Traffic of Narcotic Drugs, Vienna (1988)

This is latest agreement was ratified by fifty nations in 1991.[365] In promoting drug policy cooperation among nations, it calls for the following: (1) that the parties deem not only the production and trade of drugs, but also their possession and purchase as penal violations if the latter are done with intent to deliver the drugs to other people; (2) that the organization and financing of such activities, along with the use or conversion of profits derived therefrom, be deemed penal violations; (3) that the possession of drugs for personal use be of itself a crime, but that together with punishment therefore, social rehabilitative treatment measures must be adopted; and (4) that similar measures can replace penal sanction when "minor violations" occur.[366] The United Nations enacted the Convention Against Illicit Traffic in Narcotic Drugs and Psychotropic Substances in 1988 (Narcotics Convention) in recognition that the two aforementioned conventions lacked the ability to regulate trafficking.[367]

The Narcotics Convention calls upon party states to take specific law enforcement measures to improve their ability to identify, arrest, prosecute, and convict those who traffic in drugs across national boundaries.[368] These measures include establishing drug-related criminal offenses under domestic law, making these offenses the basis for international extradition between states party to the Narcotics Convention, providing for mutual legal assistance in the investigation and prosecution of covered offenses, and facilitating the seizure and confiscation of proceeds from illegal trafficking.[369]

EUROPEAN LEGISLATION

With few exceptions, European drug policies since World War II have been relatively liberal toward drug users, and during the first half of the 1990s became more so.[370]

Sweden

Sweden is the only European county that still has a strict prohibition drug policy similar to that of the United States. It also shares some of the secondary harms resulting from the prohibition.

The Narcotic Drugs Act of 1968 still forms the basis of Swedish drug policy. The 1970s Swedish narcotics debate reflected two differing ideologies. First, the Swedish Association for Help and Assistance to Drug Abusers emphasized that drug abuse should be seen as a result of adverse social experiences and that solutions should be sought by improving societal conditions and through voluntary therapy.[371] The other group, the

National Association for a Drug-Free Society, demanded the continued use of the criminal justice system, rejecting the idea of therapy. In their view, problematic consumers are ordinary people who have been improperly brought up, and therefore treatment was a matter of teaching.[372]

In the early 1970s, the main thrust of police activity addressed the kingpins of drug trade, rather than consumers and dealers.[373] In the early 1980s, law enforcement strategy changed, and to this day emphasis is on street-level intervention.[374] Arresting problematic consumers makes imposing statistics, gives the impression of determination, energy, and drive, and is thought to scare off experimenters.[375] Since the early 1980s, narcotics debate has diminished and either/or thinking seems to be the rule in Sweden.[376] In other words, either you support prohibitions or you are a liberal.[377] Sound familiar?

Use of Sweden's criminal justice system in drug policy has repeatedly expanded. The Narcotic Drug Act of 1968 has been modified repeatedly, partially because of the international conventions and partially by Swedish initiative.[378] Currently, supply, production, acquisition, procurement, transport, storage, possession, and consumption of illegal drugs are punishable offenses.[379] Furthermore, penalties have increased from a one-year maximum imprisonment in 1966, to up to sixteen years today.[380] In the early 1980s, Swedish courts had sentenced drug-related prisoners to a total of 1,000 years imprisonment.[381] By the mid-1990s, this figure doubled and parole was no longer granted after half the sentence was served.[382]

Sweden currently has three methadone maintenance programs.[383] In spite of an official narcotics report condemning needle exchange as social approval of drug use, a needle exchange program started in Sweden in the 1980s and currently operates in two Swedish cities.[384]

Italy

As with other European countries, the spread of illegal drugs in Italy occurred gradually from the late 1960s onward and did not initially cause any particular concern.[385] The Italian drug law of 1975 provided for impunity—exemption from punishment—for a person who committed crimes connected with drugs but was found in possession of a "moderate" amount of illegal drugs for personal use.[386] This law included French-based rules that mandated addicts be sent to the National Health Service by court order. Interestingly, the Catholic Church encouraged this ideology as viewing drug addicts as afflicted people in need of treatment.[387] However, in 1990, the law was changed to forbid the personal use of drugs, too.[388]

In 1990, Law 162 was enacted, which provided for a range of penalties for users.[389] The law had at its very heart the belief that traffickers could not be defeated as long as users were not pulled into the enforcement net and prosecuted.[390] Furthermore, it was argued that drug users were a danger to themselves and others. Thus, they must be identified by society through the police task force.[391]

Because in the spring of 1993 more than 50,000 prisoners, many of whom were drug addicts, populated the 35,000 available places in the Italian prison system, the Italian people voted in favor of canceling the portion of the law that dealt with punishment of drug consumers.[392] Now, simple possession of a moderate but undefined dose of an illicit drug is punishable by only minor sanctions such as suspension of driver's license or passport.[393] Concrete evidence of intent to distribute must exist before the judge can impose more serious penalties.[394] However, when the amount of the illegal drug possessed is greater than the average daily dose, its intended sale is presumed and traditional criminal penalties are applied.[395]

The drug question has declined as a major policy issue in Italy. Many ascribe the receding fears to recent successes against the Mafia.[396] Italian drug trafficking was long considered, and to a certain degree is still considered, a major activity of the Mafiosi organized crime networks.[397] However, studies on specific local markets demonstrated that Mafia organizations are not at all involved in some heroin markets.[398] In fact, studies indicate that drug markets are not monopolies because of the many dealers and the many competing importers and wholesalers.[399]

France

The French law of December 31, 1970, as amended in 1987, provides for penalties of up to one year in jail for possession of illegal drugs and prison sentences ranging from two to ten years for trade in illegal drugs.[400] However, the drug addict arrested for possession can avoid liability through forced rehabilitation.[401] Furthermore, in efforts to prevent AIDS, the sale of syringes was liberalized in 1988.[402]

United Kingdom

Opiate dependence was first seen as a problem in the United Kingdom at the turn of the century.[403] Although opiates were readily available in medications for pain relief and sleep aids, prior to this time little evidence spoke of morphine or heroin dependence.[404] However, just across the Atlantic Ocean, America was implementing a prohibitionist approach to a perceived drug problem, and Britain was influenced into signing the first Opium Convention in The Hague in 1912.[405] Participation in the Hague Convention obliged the British government to prepare legislation to control drugs.[406] The result was the first Dangerous Drugs Act of 1920.

The British Dangerous Drugs Act of 1920 followed the "medical model" of drug control, in contrast to the "criminal model" adopted by the United

States (the 1914 Harrison Act).[407] Private physicians were allowed discretion in prescribing heroin and other controlled substances for their patients. The system worked fairly well for the next forty years.[408] That is, the number of users remained low, they received quality-controlled drugs under medical supervision, and no substantial black market developed.[409]

In England, heroin and cocaine have been dispensed legally through a medical framework ever since their discovery and acceptance as medicines.[410] Treating drug addicts through traditional medical practice as part of Britain's National Health Service (NHS) is philosophically rooted in Great Britain's 1924 Rolleston Committee report.[411] The Rolleston Committee of 1926 examined the issue of replacement prescribing by physicians.[412] This report recognized two facts: (1) that drug addiction is a "chronic, relapsing disease," and (2) that "the indefinitely prolonged administration of morphine or heroin may be necessary" for a segment of the addict population.[413] Though the Rolleston report was without statutory power, it removed from doctors the risk of prosecution should they continue to prescribe replacement opiates.[414] It also defined opiate addiction as a medical problem.[415] This situation allowed the relatively small numbers of opiate addicts in the United Kingdom to be managed by physicians until the 1960s.[416]

In 1968, the treatment of addicts was removed from the NHS to a "clinic system" managed by psychiatrists.[417] Thereafter, an addict must enroll in a drug dependence clinic to obtain maintenance.[418] This change in policy was a response to the recommendations of the so-called Second Brain Committee.

In the early 1960s, concern over use of illicit drugs led to two interdepartmental committees, the first in 1961 and another in 1965.[419] Because these committees were chaired by Sir Russell Brain, they became known respectively as the First and Second Brain Committees.[420] Although the First Brain Committee reported in 1961 that the extent of the British drug problem was of little concern at that time, the Second Brain Committee recognized that a new group of younger recreational users had emerged, and its addicts were being managed by physicians.[421] Consequently, the committee recommended (1) compulsory notification of heroin and cocaine addicts to a central register; (2) specialist treatment centers staffed by doctors with specialized interest in addiction; and (3) the prescribing of heroin and cocaine restricted to licensed specialist doctors.[422] Gradually, the psychiatrists developed a philosophy of "less is better" and began to reduce the amounts prescribed to addicts.[423] Additionally, rather than prescribing injectable opiates, they followed the lead of the U.S. treatment community by prescribing oral methadone, or physeptone.[424]

The Dangerous Drugs Act of 1967, the Misuse of Drugs Act of 1971, and the Misuse of Drugs Regulations promulgated in 1973 all constituted a battery of legislation enacted in response to the Second Brain Committee report.[425] The Dangerous Drugs Act of 1967 set up Drug Dependence Units between 1968 and 1970, in which physicians treated the majority of addicts with opiates but could not prescribe heroin or cocaine.[426] The Misuse of Drugs Act of 1971, Misuse of Drugs Regulation of 1973, and the Misuse of Drugs Order of 1977, classifies drugs into three categories: (1) cocaine and opiates; (2) cannabis and hallucinogens, barbiturates, amphetamines; and (3) pharmaceuticals.[427] As amended, the act has offenses relating to production, cultivation, supply, and possession. For each of these, *mens rea* is an element in the commission of the offense. Although penalties against trafficking are severe, as in Ireland, personal use is permitted except for opium.[428] Finally, the Misuse of Drugs Regulations required any physician attending a person and having reasonable grounds to consider that the patient is addicted to one of fourteen drugs enumerated in the Misuse of Drugs Act must notify the chief medical officer.[429] Despite these initiatives, the number of drug addicts in the United Kingdom continued to rise, and by the late 1970s had doubled from of the figure before the 1971 Misuse of Drugs Act.[430] In spite of this staggering statistic, the British government exerted further restrictions over controlled substances. The Misuse of Drugs Regulations of 1985 divided controlled substances into five schedules, each of which has specific requirements governing import and export, production, supply, possession, prescribing and the record keeping associated with these activities.[431]

Although the nation as a whole has seen sanctions increase for illicit drug use and trafficking, an alternative to this conservative British trend has developed in Liverpool, England, partly in response to the AIDS crisis.[432] By the mid-1980s, HIV and AIDS were becoming a public health concern.[433] In Scotland, the 1986 McLelland Committee Report emphasized the need to improve the availability of clean injecting equipment, such as needle exchange services, and reduce the spread of HIV via contaminated needles.[434] The Advisory Council on the Misuse of Drugs, established as part of the Misuse of Drugs Act in 1971, acknowledged 1988 that the spread of HIV was a greater potential danger than drug misuse itself.[435]

The harm reduction concept does not support or condone drug use, rather, it recognizes although the ultimate goal for drug users may be to become drug free, for many this is an unrealistic short-term goal.[436] Instead, patients make smaller changes while moving toward a drug-free state, improving their situation with each change.[437] The *harm reduction model* is composed of five essential components: (1) committed drug addicts are prescribed and maintained on drugs; (2) through counseling, addicts are encouraged to "kick" their habits and lead drug-free lives; (3) intravenous drug users are provided with clean syringes and hypodermic needles so as to prevent the spread of HIV; (4) drug users are educated about how HIV is contracted and spread; and (5) drug users are empowered to act and think for themselves.[438] As of 1990, no cases of HIV had been reported among intravenous drug users in England's Merseyside region for the past five years.[439] The Liverpool experience demonstrated that drug maintenance for drug addicts can be synonymous with drug treatment.

In accordance with the harm-reduction model, the United Kingdom minimizes the negative effects of drug use through education. The NHS Health Advisory Service recognized that drug education and drug prevention are two complementary but distinct concepts.[440] Education was defined as "having the overall aim of preventing people from harming themselves by the use of substances," and prevention was defined as "prevention of dependent forms of substance use and misuse and prevention of physical and psychiatric disorders that may be related to substance use and misuse."[441] These definitions reflect the view that the goal of minimal incidence of drug-related harm is more practical than one of no drug use whatsoever, and education is critical to minimizing drug-related harm.

Germany

The drug control law of 1971, updated in 1981, punishes illegal distribution of drugs with imprisonment from three to ten years.[442] However, penalties may be omitted if the guilty party possessed a minimum amount for personal use.[443] Every available indicator showed that, after years of stagnation, illicit drug use increased after 1987, reaching a saturation point by 1992.[444] Germany followed the Amsterdam experience and in 1992, the Federal Drug Enforcement Act was reformed.[445] Under the revised law, the prosecutor's office can drop a case where further trial is obviously counterproductive.[446] Rehabilitative treatment may be imposed.[447] Even a sentence of less than two years for crimes connected with drug addiction, such as theft, can be exchanged for therapy.[448]

In April 1994, the German Constitutional Court ruled that the police and prosecution authorities do not have absolute duty to bring charges against cannabis users, thus bringing this European country even closer to the policy of others such as Britain.[449]

Spain

In accordance with the rest of Europe, Spain's law of March 24, 1988, states that the use and detention for personal use of illegal drugs is not punishable.[450] Spain also distinguishes between "light" and "heavy" drugs, imprisoning offenders for two to eight years for the latter and only four months to four years for the former.[451]

Holland

In the 1960s, two committees were appointed to clarify any existing narcotics problems in the Netherlands and make policy recommendations.[452] The Hulsman Committee, formed in 1969 and consisting of a working group within the state-sponsored Institution of Mental Health, was appointed under the chairmanship of law professor Loek Hulsman.[453] The Hulsman Committee warned against placing more than minimal reliance on the penal law in controlling the drug problem.[454] It predicted that the threat of law enforcement would not only fail to deter people from engaging in drug use in their private life, but for various reasons would also fail to control the supply side of the drug market.[455] The second commission, the "Working Group on Narcotics Substances" or Baan Committee, appointed by the government and with official status, in 1972 proposed a revised form of the strictly prohibitionist "Opium Act" of 1928.[456] This proposal came before parliament in 1976, but drug control had already relaxed in practice during this four-year time lapse.[457]

The Dutch *Opiumwet* (Opium Act) of 1928, as amended, remains the main official control of drugs, though it has been amended many times, most notably in 1976.[458] The revised Opium Act of 1976 reflected the recommendations and warnings of the Hulsman and Baan Committees.[459] The Netherlands adopted a policy based on two principles: (1) Drug use is considered primarily a public health issue rather than a judicial problem; and (2) A distinction is made between "hard" drugs, which involve an unacceptable degree of risk, and cannabis products, which are known as "soft" drugs.[460] It passed, after a long debate in parliament, by a vote of almost three to one.[461] It also fulfilled all the demands of the international conventions, setting out punishments for possession, trade, cultivation, importation, and exportation.[462]

The drug control laws of 1976 and 1985, grants the state attorney the ability not to prosecute offenders possessing an amount for personal use.[463] The United Nations treaties only demand the law be on the books, not that they be enforced.[464] The Single Convention acknowledges explicitly that enforcement of statutes may be limited based on principles fundamentally part of a nation's sovereignty.[465] The Schengen Agreement works in a similar fashion, mandating enforcement but acknowledging national sovereignty.[466]

The Dutch maintain severe punishment for trafficking: imprisonment of up to twelve years for 'heavy" drugs and four years for "light."[467] Since 1976, the punishment for breach of the *Opiumwet* has depended on whether a drug is classified as list 1 or 2.[468] The most lenient penalties address list 2 drugs, basically cannabis products and psychotropic substances.[469] List 1 covers drugs such as heroin and cocaine.[470] The low punishments for possession and trafficking in small amounts of cannabis reflect the compromise between the government, which fears international condemnation if cannabis is not controlled, and those in favor of legalization of the drug.[471] Marijuana and hashish laws are not enforced by Dutch authorities.[472] This nonenforcement was authorized by the expediency principle and it empowered the public prosecutor's office to refrain from initiating criminal proceedings if in the public interest.[473] However, public guidelines were established to assist prosecutors with these discretionary decisions.[474] As a result, cannabis was already listed on menus and available at numerous coffeehouses throughout the Netherlands for purchase.[475] It is also available at youth centers, but under no circumstances is the sale of cannabis to children under age sixteen permitted.[476]

In efforts to prevent youth from venturing into the back market, Dutch authorities sought to create an above-ground market where cannabis could be used without fear.[477] Because the central aim of Dutch policy is still "the prevention and reduction of harm caused by drugs by reducing dangers of their use both to the community and to the individual," a 1995 memorandum published by the Dutch government sets out guidelines concerning the coffeehouses, the above-ground market, and personal consumption.[478] For instance, no coffee shops are permitted near schools, the maximum purchase for personal consumption was limited to five grams, and bona fide coffee shops with a stock of only a few hundred grams would not be investigated.[479] Interestingly, coffeehouses were prohibited from selling alcohol.[480] Currently, Amsterdam, Arnhem, Maastricht, and various other municipalities are drafting legislation to provide for a licensing system for coffeehouse.[481] A license merely entitles the holder to a coffee shop, not to sell soft drugs.[482] However, a license may not be issued to anyone with a police record, and license holders must observe the coffee shop rules.[483]

The Dutch published data that compared the U.S. National High School Survey conducted by NIDA (the National Institute on Drug Abuse of the U.S. Department of Health and Human Services) with a similar survey of Dutch youth.[484] The data revealed that both cannabis and cocaine use by U.S. secondary school students is considerably higher than that of their Dutch counterparts.[485] Furthermore, regarding past-month drug use prevalence, U.S. youths use cannabis and cocaine at significantly greater rates than do Dutch youths. For example, the ratio of U.S. to Dutch past-month use rates range from 2.9 times as great (for thirteen- to fifteen-year-olds who have used cannabis) to fourteen times as great (for seventeen- to eighteen-year-olds who have used cocaine).[486] Comparison of lifetime prevalence yields similar results.[487] Hence, Dutch authorities appear successful in preventing youths from entering the black market by creating an above-ground safe market where only cannabis is accessible.

Dutch doctors are permitted to prescribe any drug for those who are ill or injured.[488] Addicts can only be given methadone; prescribing heroin is not allowed but is generally tolerated.[489] The goal even for problematic consumers of opiates is to keep them as integrated in society as possible.[490] A major instrument for realizing this aim is methadone offered on a reduction basis (gradual decrease in dosage) and on a maintenance basis (a constant dose).[491] These programs do not try to prevent all heroin use, rather they aim at substituting acceptable drugs (methadone) and activities (contact with social/medical professional) for unacceptable drugs (heroin) and unacceptable activities (contact with criminal dealers).[492]

The Dutch also have a national needle exchange program in place for intravenous drug users.[493] Needle exchange was based on the principle assumptions of Dutch drug policy that drug use cannot be completely eliminated and that the ranks of potential problematic consumers are small, thus needle exchange could limit one of the risks.[494] Needle exchange programs appear to lead to safer injection practices. The feared negative side effects, such as increased use of needles because of increased availability, have not occurred.[495]

Although the principle goal of the war on drugs is to prevent all consumption of psychoactive drugs, the major objective of Dutch drug policy is to minimize problems with use. The emphasis is placed on individuals making well-informed choices,[496] whereas before current drug policies were initiated, drug education was an extension of rather old-fashioned information about alcohol, threatening and rigid, and aimed at total abstinence. The Netherlands has changed their strategies in recognition that young people today are knowledgeable.[497] Consistent with this effort, Dutch education efforts are devoid of moralizing messages and value judgments, and focus instead on the need to rationally calculate the costs versus the benefits of using drugs.[498] Even addicts convicted of crimes can choose between a prison term and voluntary treatment in an open or closed institution.[499]

This policy is considered a success in the Netherlands. In practice, the policy has helped stabilize the number of cannabis users and has led to the proliferation of coffee shops.[500] Furthermore, it seems to have prevented cannabis users from making the transition to hard drugs.[501] This recognition emerges from the fact that relatively few cannabis are users of soft drugs, and from the fact that relatively few cannabis users are addicted to hard drugs.[502]

Other Countries

Although minor differences exist, legislation of other European states provides for various forms of punishment for drug traffickers, but in accordance with the rest of Europe, therapy for addicts is universally offered.[503] Greece, Malta, Cyprus, and Portugal use long penalties of up to fourteen or twenty years' imprisonment for trafficking.[504] In contrast, Austria, Luxembourg, and Switzerland have much shorter drug trafficking penalties of three to five years.[505] Penalties in Norway range from fourteen days to twenty years in the case of heavy trafficking and money laundering.[506]

The United States has a bilateral extradition treaty with the following countries, identified as major illicit-drug countries: Bahamas, Belize, Bolivia, Brazil, Bermuda, Colombia, Dominican Republic, Ecuador, Guatemala, Haiti, Jamaica, Mexico, Nigeria, Pakistan, Panama, Paraguay, Peru, Thailand, and Venezuela.[507] The remaining countries of Afghanistan, Aruba, Cambodia, China, Hong Kong, India, Taiwan, and Vietnam have no extradition treaty with the United States and, therefore, no opportunity for formal extradition.[508] The United States has encountered great difficulties in obtaining custody of foreign drug traffickers through use of extradition treaties.[509] Europe has many multilateral and bilateral initiatives that have a direct impact on drug policy. Most important in this respect are the Schengen Agreement of 1985 and Convention of 1990, the Maastricht Treaty on the European Union, and the activities of the Council of Europe.

In the area of drugs, the Schengen Agreement/Convention is directed at harmonization of legislation and policy.[510] Negotiations included strong pressure placed on the Netherlands to alter its policies, which were considered out of line with the strict drug enforcement in all other states.[511] Each state was permitted to decide policy within its own borders but allow for collective responsibility for the effects of that policy for other Schengen countries.[512] The Schengen Convention of 1990 stresses a permissive approach in another Schengen state, and requires each state to combat illegal import and export of drugs to the territory of other parties.[513]

The vast majority of European nations have decriminalized possession of drugs in an amount that is presumed for personal consumption, which includes enough to share with a friend.[514] As with many other activities, the European do not share the U.S. either/or belief system.

If we expand our vision beyond North America, we find that all of the psychoactives now legal and widely enjoyed were at one time illegal and feared. Coffee and chocolate were viewed with suspicion when they first became available in Europe and the Near East.[515] In terms similar to those used with reference to "hippie drugs" in the 1960s, they were associated with laziness and promiscuity.[516] In the seventeenth century, visiting a coffeehouse was a capital offense in what are now Egypt, Saudi Arabia, and Turkey, places where coffeehouses are important components of society and business.[517] More than 200 years ago, Frederick II of Prussia tried to ban coffee, which he believed threatened the balance of trade, commercial breweries, and fitness of soldiers.[518] He created a coffee monopoly and a special police force whose mission was to sniff out illegal coffee-roasting establishments.[519] These measures were unpopular, and corruption flourished within the special police force.[520] Yet, people continued drinking coffee. Sound familiar?

Many cultures, such as Mexican Indian tribes and the Native American Church, hold peyote as a sacrament.[521] Beer is an important offering for many African and South American tribes.[522] Music and psychoactive substances were combined in the Shamanic rituals of Latin America and tribal initiations and celebrations in Africa. Drug use and youth culture have been intertwined for decades in Western culture. The present links between dance and drugs can be traced to the 1970s all-nighters in Southport, England, at the height of Northern Soul, a movement resulting from the white working-class youth of 1970s Northern England and African-American soul recordings of the previous decade.[523] Amphetamines helped people to feel they could make the most of the night. Some felt the need for a boost of energy after having traveled for several hours or worked all day before reaching an event.[524]

Marijuana has long been used as an energizer by sugarcane harvesters in Jamaica and by laborers in Costa Rica.[525] In contrast, early United States prohibitionist propaganda portrayed cannabis as leading to uncontrollable lust and lack of motivation.[526] Meanwhile, poets whose works form part of many schoolchildren's education have supped laudanum from pewter goblets, and their psychoactive experiences have become part of innumerable English literature examinations.[527] A few decades later, contributors to the fields of art, psychology, literature, and science openly reporting their drug use as an influence upon their work.[528]

Recreational drug use reflects the attitudes, values, and beliefs of the society. Today's fast-paced, competitive, technological society has given birth to raves, laser light shows, and techno music, consisting of fast repetitive beats. The 1980s saw economic change, conservatism, individual attainment, and competitive drive.[529] Drug use moved away from hallucinations toward stimulation.[530] In the late 1980s the youth Acid House movement reflected in its style and speed a fast-moving and constantly changing, constantly competing society.[531] Clubs and parties integrated sweating heat, lights flashing at frightening speed to keep up with the beat, glowsticks, waving hands, and whistles, the raves of the 1990s and the millennium. The music fosters a sense of belonging, a shared experience among these clubbers.

Europe has responded and accepted this newly emerged culture. The London Drug Policy Forum's *Dance 'til Dawn Safely* document of 1996 is a set of guidelines for running safer dance events and providing better venues.[532] These guidelines were modeled against a set of guidelines produced by the Scottish Drug Forum for the same purpose.[533] The Scottish guidelines include advice concerning security, health and safety, environmental issues, information provision, and support.[534] These guidelines call for so-called chill-out facilities for people to cool down and relax to avoid confusion or uncomfortable feelings resulting from the crowded environment.[535] This can be just as important to nondrug user clubbers.

The American government has permitted drug use to become too politicized. The American War on Drugs is nothing more than a political platform that helped Presidents Reagan and Bush win election. Politics have stifled the enactment of effective drug policy. For instance, in Germany, the political parties, the police, and the medical profession used the drug issue to further their own institutional objectives by a process of problem amplification.[536] A contrary process of deescalating the significance of the drug problem occurred in the Netherlands.[537] The Social Democrats were allowed to realize their liberal interests in moral issues because their Christian Democratic partners in the coalition cabinet did not choose to use the drugs issue "as a self-serving socio-political symbol."[538]

The American War on Drugs is failing miserably and needs to be objectively reevaluated. A comparison of the results of the Swedish strict prohibition policy and the Netherlands decriminalization policy demonstrates the point. Sweden and the Netherlands have similarities in political and social welfare systems, but vast differences in narcotics policy.[539] Statistics published by the European Monitoring Centre for Drugs and Drug Addiction in 1997 show that Sweden's rate was estimated between 1.6 and 2.3 per 1,000, while the Dutch figure was 1.6–1.8, similar in order of magnitude of problematic consumers.[540]

It is time for the U.S. Congress to "get with the times" and accept two critical facts. First, the War on Drugs has failed. Second, recreational drug use is not only possible, it exists both in America and in other nations. It exists among a population of students and professionals alike. This is common knowledge. As Confucius said, education is the cure to all of society's ills. Similarly, the cure to the drug problem is to never let it become one. This cannot be done by cutting off supply, because it has been proven that the supply cannot be cut off. Rather, educate the public about the effects of drugs, both good and bad. The public can then make personal, informed decisions about what, when, and how to use drugs.

The Netherlands has proven that a normalization approach is practical. The Dutch implementation of a harm-reduction policy toward drug use is being followed by many other European nations. It is time America buried the hatchet and joined our European counterparts.

NOTES

1. Stephen R. Kandall and Wendy Chavkin, Illicit Drugs in America: History, Impact on Women and Infants, and Treatment Strategies for Women, 43 *Hastings L.J.* 615, 1992.

2. *Id.*

3. Group for the Advancement of Psychiatry, *Drug Misuse: A Psychiatric*

View of a Dilemma, Gap Report 80 (New York: Charles Scribner's Sons, 1971), p. 17.
See also, http://www.groupadpsych.org/publications.htm.

   4. *Id.*

   5. David F. Musto, M.D., *The American Disease: Origins of Narcotic Control* (Yale University Press, 1973), p. 1.

   6. *Id.*

   7. *Id.,* p. 2.

   8. William Butler Eldridge, *Narcotics and the Law: A Critique of the American Experiment in Narcotic Drug Control* (2d ed., 1967), p. 3.

   9. *Id.*

   10. GAP, *Drug Misuse: A Psychiatric View of a Dilemma* (New York: Scribner, 1971), p. 17.

   11. *Id.*

   12. Eldridge, *supra* note 8, p. 4.

   13. GAP, *supra* note 10, p. 18.

   14. *Id.*

   15. *Id.*

   16. Musto, *supra* note 5, p. 2.

   17. William O. Walker III, *Drug Control in the Americas* (Albuquerque: University of New Mexico Press, Revised edition, 1989), p. 1.

   18. GAP, *supra* note 10, p. 18.

   19. Musto, *supra* note 5, p. 2.

   20. *Id.*

   21. *Criminal Justice and Drugs: The Unresolved Connection* (James C. Weissman and Robert L. DuPont, eds., Port Washington, N.Y.: Kennikat Press, 1982), p. 31.

   22. *Id.*

   23. Musto, *supra* note 5, p. 2.

   24. *Id.*

   25. Weissman and DuPont, *supra* note 21, p. 32.

   26. *Id.*

   27. *Id.*

   28. *Id.*

   29. *Id.*

   30. *Id.*

   31. *Id.,* p. 33.

   32. *Id.*

   33. *Id.,* p. 34.

   34. *Id.,* p. 35.

   35. *Id.*

   36. *Id.*

   37. Musto, *supra* note 5, p. 7.

   38. Weissman and DuPont, *supra* note 21, p. 35.

   39. *Id.,* p. 36.

   40. *Id.,* p. 37.

   41. *Id.*

   42. *Id.*

   43. *Id.*

   44. *Id.,* p. 38.

45. *Id.*
46. *Id.*
47. Musto, *supra* note 5, p. 3.
48. *Id.*
49. *Id.*
50. *Id.*
51. *Id.*
52. *Id.*
53. *Id.*
54. Weissman and DuPont, *supra* note 21, p. 38.
55. *Id.*
56. Richard J. Bonnie, *Marijuana Use and Criminal Sanctions: Essays on the Theory and Practice of Decriminalization* (Charlottesville, Va.: The Michie Company, 1980) p. 1.
57. 56 *Va. L. Rev.* 971, 1010.
58. *Id.*
59. *Id.,* p. 1011.
60. *Id.*
61. *Id.*
62. *Id.*
63. *Id.,* p. 1010.
64. *Id.*
65. Musto, *supra* note 5, p. 216.
66. *Id.*
67. *Id.,* p. 218.
68. 56 *Va. L. Rev.* 971, 1011.
69. *Id.*
70. *Id.*
71. *Id.*
72. *Id.,* p. 1012.
73. *Id.*
74. Musto, *supra* note 5, p. 219.
75. *Id.*
76. *Id.*
77. 56 *Va. L. Rev.* 971, 1012.
78. *Id.*
79. *Id.,* p. 1014.
80. *Id.*
81. Musto, *supra* note 5, p. 219.
82. 56 *Va. L. Rev.* 971, 1012.
83. *Id.,* p. 1014.
84. *Id.*
85. *Id.,* p. 1014.
86. *Id.*
87. *Id.*
88. *Id.*
89. *Id.*
90. Musto, *supra* note 5, p. 220.

91. *Id.*
92. GAP, *supra* note 10, p. 30.
93. 56 *Va. L. Rev.* 971, 1016.
94. *New York Times,* Jan. 3, 1937.
95. *Id.*
96. Bonnie, *supra* note 56, p. 1.
97. Musto, *supra* note 5, p. 221.
98. *Id.*
99. 56 *Va. L. Rev.* 1010.
100. Bonnie, *supra* note 56, p. 1.
101. *Id.,* p. 3.
102. 56 *Va. L. Rev.* 971, p. 1018.
103. *Id.*
104. *Id.,* p. 1019.
105. *Id.*
106. *Id.,* p. 1022.
107. *Id.*
108. *State* v. *Bonoa,* 172 La. 955 (1931).
109. 56 *Va. L. Rev.* 971, p. 1023.
110. *Id.*
111. 56 *Va. L. Rev.* 971, p. 1024.
112. *Id.*
113. *Id.*
114. Bonnie, *supra* note 56, p. 1.
115. *Id.,* p. 2.
116. *Id.*
117. James C. Weissman, *Drug Abuse, the Law, and Treatment Alternatives* (Cincinnati: Criminal Justice Studies, Anderson Publishing, 1978), p. 124.
118. *Id.*
119. Mark A. R. Kleinman and Aaron J. Saiger, Drug Legalization: The Importance of Asking the Right Question, 18 *Hofstra L. Rev.* 527, 1990.
120. *Id.*
121. *Id.*
122. *Id.*
123. *Id.,* p. 557.
124. *Id.*
125. *Id.*
126. Eldridge, *supra* note 8, p. 8.
127. *Id.*
128. *Id.,* p. 20.
129. Musto, *supra* note 5, p. 7.
130. *Id.*
131. Gerald. T. McLaughlin, Cocaine: The History and Regulation of a Dangerous Drug, 58 *Cornell L. Rev.* 544, 1973.
132. *Id.,* p. 545.
133. *Id.*
134. *Id.*
135. *Id.*

136. *Id.*
137. *Id.*
138. *Id.*
139. *Id.*, p. 546.
140. *Id.*
141. *Id.*
142. *Id.*, p. 555.
143. Musto, *supra* note 5, p. 8.
144. *Id.*
145. *Id.*
146. Kandall and Chavkin, *supra* note 1, p. 619.
147. *Id.*
148. Musto, *supra* note 5, p. 7.
149. Kandall and Chavkin, *supra* note 1, p. 619.
150. Musto, *supra* note 5, p. 7.
151. *Id.*
152. *Id.*
153. McLaughlin, *supra* note 131, p. 539.
154. *Id.*
155. *Id.* p. 540.
156. *Id.*
157. *Id.*, p. 541.
158. *Id.*
159. *Id.*, p. 542.
160. *Id.*
161. *Id.*, p. 540.
162. *Id.*
163. *Id.*, p. 541.
164. *Id.*
165. Musto, *supra* note 5, p. 8.
166. *Id.*
167. McLaughlin, *supra* note 131, p. 542.
168. *Id.*, p. 543.
169. *Id.*
170. *Id.*, p. 556.
171. *Id.*
172. *Id.*
173. *Id.*
174. *Id.*
175. *Id.*, p. 563.
176. *Id.*
177. *Id.*
178. Musto, *supra* note 5, p. 9.
179. *Id.*
180. Weissman, *supra* note 117, p. 116.
181. McLaughlin, *supra* note 131, p. 559.
182. *Id.*
183. *Id.*

184. *Id.*

185. Harvey R. Levine, *Legal Dimensions of Drug Abuse* (Springfield, Ill.: Thomas 1974) Chapter 3, p. 21.

186. *Id.*

187. Weissman, *supra* note 117, p. 117.

188. McLaughlin, *supra* note 131, p. 561.

189. *Id.*

190. *Id.*

191. *Id.*

192. *Id.*

193. *Id.,* p. 562.

194. *Id.*

195. Weissman, *supra* note 117, p. 117.

196. Musto, *supra* note 5, p. 122.

197. *Id.,* p. 148.

198. *Id.*

199. Musto, *supra* note 5, p. 121.

200. *Webb* v. *U.S.,* 249 U.S. 96 (1922).

201. *Id.*

202. *U.S.* v. *Behrman,* 258 U.S. 280 (1922).

203. Musto, *supra* note 5, p. 66.

204. *Id.*

205. *Id.*

206. Musto, *supra* note 5, p. 59.

207. *Id.,* p. 61.

208. Weissman, *supra* note 117, p. 118.

209. *Id.*

210. *Id.,* p. 119.

211. *Id.*

212. *Id.*

213. *Id.*

214. *Id.*

215. Musto, *supra* note 5, p. 65.

216. *Id.*

217. GAP, *supra* note 10, p. 30.

218. *Id.*

219. *Id.*

220. *Id.*

221. Weissman, *supra* note 117, p. 119.

222. *Id.*

223. Musto, *supra* note 5, p. 204.

224. *Id.*

225. *Id.*

226. *Id.*

227. *Id.,* p. 206.

228. *Id.*

229. *Id.*

230. *Id.*

231. Weissman, *supra* note 117, p. 120.

232. McLaughlin, *supra* note 131, p. 564.

233. *Id.*

234. *Id.*

235. *Id.*

236. Weissman, *supra* note 117, p. 120.

237. *Id.*

238. McLaughlin, *supra* note 131, p. 565.

239. Weissman, *supra* note 117, p. 120.

240. *Id.*, p. 121.

241. Act of July 18, 1956 (repealed 1970), 22 U.S.C. 24, I, § 1750–1753(a); See also U.S. Code collection at http://www4.law.cornell.edu/uscode/22/1750to1753a.htm.

242. Weissman, *supra* note 117, p. 121.

243. *Id.*

244. *Id.*

245. *Id.*

246. *Id.*, p. 122.

247. *Id.*

248. *Id.*

249. *Id.*

250. Levine, *supra* note 185, p. 21.

251. *Id.*

252. *Id.*

253. Weissman, *supra* note 117, p. 123.

254. *Id.*, p. 121.

255. *Id.*, p. 122.

256. *Id.*, p. 124.

257. Musto, *supra* note 5, p. 10.

258. *Id.*

259. Weissman, *supra* note 117, p. 124.

260. *Id.*

261. *Id.*, p. 123.

262. *Id.*, p. 124.

263. *Id.*, p. 123.

264. James Ostrowski, A Symposium on Drug Decriminalization: The Moral and Practical for Drug Legalization, 18 *Hofstra L. Rev.* 607, 1990.

265. Wendy Melillo, Early Skirmishes in the War on Drugs, *Washington Post*, November 4, 1986, p. Z14.

266. *Id.*

267. Kleinman and Saiger, *supra* note 119, p. 556.

268. *Id.*, p. 529.

269. *Id.*, p. 530.

270. *Id.*

271. Ostrowski, *supra* note 264, p. 613.

272. *Id.*

273. Douglas Matheson, and Meredith Davison, *The Behavioral Effects of Drugs* (Holt, Rinehart and Winston, 1972), p. 3.

274. *Id.*

275. *Id.*

276. *Id.*

277. U.S. Dept. of Justice, Office of Justice Programs, Bureau of Justice Assistance, *Addressing Community Gang Problems: A Practical Guide* (May 1998), p. 22. See also, http://www.ncjrs.org/pdffiles/164273.pdf.

278. *Id.*, p. 23.

279. *Id.*

280. Ostrowski, *supra* note 264, p. 124.

281. *Id.*

282. *Id.*, p. 652.

283. U.S. Dept. of Justice, *supra* note 277, p. 2.

284. *Id.*, p. 5.

285. *Id.*

286. *Id.*, p. 7.

287. Ostrowski, *supra* note 264, p. 648.

288. *Id.*, p. 649.

289. *Id.*, p. 612.

290. *Id.*, p. 649.

291. *Id.*, p. 641.

292. *Id.*

293. *Id.*

294. *Id.*

295. *Id.*, p. 652.

296. *Id.*

297. *Id.*

298. *Id.*, p. 653.

299. *Id.*, p. 655.

300. *Id.*, p. 654.

301. *Id.*, p. 611.

302. *Id.*, p. 620.

303. *Altered States of Mind: Critical Observations of the Drug War* (Peter Kraska, ed., New York: Garland Publishing, 1993), p. 14.

304. Ostrowski, *supra* note 264, p. 612.

305. Douglas N. Husak, *Drugs and Rights* (Cambridge University Press, 1992), p. 11.

306. *Id.*

307. *Harmelin* v. *Michigan,* 111 S. Ct. 2680 (1991).

308. Husak, *supra* note 305, p. 11.

309. Kraska, *supra* note 303, p. 50.

310. Husak, *supra* note 305, p. 11.

311. *Id.*, p. 12.

312. *Chapman et al.* v. *U.S.,* 111 S. Ct. 2680 (1991).

313. Kal Raustiala, Law, Liberalization & International Narcotics Trafficking, 32 *NYU J. Int'l. L. & Pol.,* 89, 1999.

314. *Id.*, p. 94.

315. *Id.*, p. 94.

316. *Id.*, p. 94.

317. *Id.*, p. 94.

318. *Id.*, p. 95.

319. Joseph P. Shereda, The Internalization of the War on Drugs and Its Potential for Successfully Addressing Drug Trafficking and Related Crimes in South Africa, 31 *Geo. Wash. J. Int'l. & Econ.* 297, 306, 1998.

320. Raustiala, *supra* note 325, p. 95.

321. Syamal Kumar Chatterjee, *Legal Aspects of International Drug Control* (Hingham, Mass.: Kluwer Boston, 1981), p. 22.

322. Raustiala, *supra* note 325, p. 96.

323. *Id.*

324. *Id.*, p. 98.

325. *Id.*

326. Raustiala, *supra* note 325, p. 98.

327. Editorial, Illusions of a War Against Cocaine, *N.Y. Times,* Jan. 24, 1998, p. A14.

328. Kraska, *supra* note 303, p. 209.

329. *Id.*

330. Kettil Bruun, Lynn Pan, and Ingemar Rexed, *The Gentlemen's Club: International Control of Drugs and Alcohol* (Chicago: University of Chicago Press, 1975), p. 10.

331. *Id.*

332. *Id.*

333. *Id.*

334. *Id.*, pp. 10–11.

335. *Id.*, p. 11.

336. *Id.*

337. Kraska, *supra* note 303, p. 207.

338. *Id.*

339. Bruun, Pan and Rexed, *supra* note 342, p. 11.

340. *Id.*, pp. 11–12.

341. *Criminal Justice in Europe: A Comparative Study* (Phil Fennell et al., eds., Oxford: Clarendon Press; New York: Oxford University Press, 1995), p. 149.

342. Mario Garavelli, Drug Abuse in Italy and Europe in a Comparative Context, 4 *Ind. Int'l. & Comp. L. Rev.* 277, 1994.

343. Bruun, Pan and Rexed, *supra* note 342, p. 12.

344. *Id.*

345. *Id.*

346. *Id.*

347. Garavelli, *supra* note 354, p. 280.

348. *Id.*

349. Bruun, Pan, and Rexed, *supra* note 342, p. 14.

350. Garavelli, *supra* note 354, p. 280.

351. *Id.*

352. *Id.*

353. *Id.*

354. *Id.*

355. Garavelli, *supra* note 354, p. 280.

356. Bruun, Pan, and Rexed, *supra* note 342, p. 17.

357. *Id.*

358. Shereda, *supra* note 331, p. 306.

359. *Id.*

360. Bruun, Pan, and Rexed, *supra* note 342, p. 17.

361. Shereda, *supra* note 331, p. 306.

362. *Id.*

363. Garavelli, *supra* note 354, p. 280.

364. Shereda, *supra* note 331, p. 306.

365. Garavelli, *supra* note 354, p. 281.

366. Id., p. 281.

367. Shereda, *supra* note 331, p. 307.

368. *Id.*, p. 306.

369. *Id.*

370. *European Drug Policies and Enforcement* (Nicholas Dorn, Jørgen Jepsen, and Ernesto Savona, eds., Houndsmill, Basingstoke, Hampshire: Macmillan; New York: St. Martin's Press, 1996), p. 2.

371. Ted Golberg, *Demystifying Drugs: A Psychosocial Perspective* (New York: St. Martin's Press, 1999), p. 178.

372. *Id.*

373. *Id.*

374. *Id.*, p. 179.

375. *Id.*

376. *Id.*

377. *Id.*

378. *Id.*, p. 196.

379. *Id.*

380. *Id.*

381. *Id.*

382. *Id.*

383. *Id.*, p. 177.

384. *Id.*, p. 203.

385. Dorn, Jepsen, and Savona, *supra* note 382, p. 119.

386. Garavelli, *supra* note 354, p. 283.

387. *Id.*

388. *Id.*

389. Dorn, Jepsen, and Savona, *supra* note 382, p. 121.

390. *Id.*

391. *Id.*

392. Garavelli, *supra* note 354, p. 284.

393. *Id.*

394. *Id.*, pp. 284–285.

395. *Id.*

396. Dorn, Jepsen and Savona, *supra* note 382, p. 122.

397. *Id.*

398. *Id.*, p. 124.

399. *Id.*, p. 125.
400. Garavelli, *supra* note 354, p. 285.
401. *Id.*
402. *Id.*
403. *Illegal Drug Use in the United Kingdom: Prevention, Treatment and Enforcement* (Cameron Stark, Brian A. Kidd, and Roger A. D. Sykes, eds., Aldershot, England; Brookfield, Vt.: Ashgate 1999), p. 17.
404. *Id.*
405. *Id.*
406. *Id.*
407. Kraska, *supra* note 303, p. 207.
408. *The Crisis in Drug Prohibition* (David Boaz, ed., Washington, D.C.: Cato Institute, 1990), p. 72.
409. *Id.*
410. Kraska, *supra* note 303, p. 208.
411. *Id.*, p. 213.
412. Stark, Kidd, and Sykes, *supra* note 415, p. 17.
413. Kraska, *supra* note 303, p. 213.
414. Stark, Kidd, and Sykes, *supra* note 415, p. 18.
415. *Id.*
416. *Id.*
417. Kraska, *supra* note 303, p. 213.
418. *Id.*
419. Stark, Kidd, and Sykes, *supra* note 415, pp. 18–19.
420. *Id.*, p. 18.
421. *Id.*, p. 19.
422. *Id.*
423. Id., pp. 19–20.
424. *Id.*
425. *Id.*, pp. 19–20.
426. *Id.*, p. 19.
427. Garavelli, *supra* note 354, p. 285.
428. *Id.*
429. Stark, Kidd, and Sykes, *supra* note 415, p. 20.
430. *Id.*, p. 21.
431. *Id.*
432. Kraska, *supra* note 303, p. 215.
433. Stark, Kidd, and Sykes, *supra* note 415, p. 22.
434. *Id.*
435. *Id.*
436. *Id.*, p. 58.
437. *Id.*
438. Kraska, *supra* note 303, p. 215.
439. *Id.*
440. Stark, Kidd, and Sykes, *supra* note 415, p. 28.
441. *Id.*
442. Garavelli, *supra* note 354, p. 286.

443. *Id.*

444. Dorn, Jepsen, and Savona, *supra* note 382, p. 56.

445. *Id.*

446. *Id.*

447. Garavelli, *supra* note 354, p. 286.

448. *Id.*

449. Dorn, Jepsen, and Savona, *supra* note 382, p. 2.

450. Garavelli, *supra* note 354, p. 286.

451. *Id.*

452. Golberg, *supra* note 383, p. 216.

453. *Id.*

454. *Id.*

455. *Id.*

456. *Id.*, pp. 216–217.

457. *Id.*

458. Christopher Harding, et al., *Criminal Justice in Europe: A Comparative Study* (Oxford: Clarendon Press; New York: Oxford University Press, 1995) p. 151.

459. Golberg, *supra* note 383, p. 218.

460. Dorn, Jepsen, and Savona, *supra* note 382, p. 97.

461. Golberg, *supra* note 383, p. 218.

462. Harding, *supra* note 470, p. 151.

463. Garavelli, *supra* note 354, pp. 286–287.

464. Golberg, *supra* note 383, p. 227.

465. *Id.*

466. *Id.*

467. Garavelli, *supra* note 354, pp. 277–287.

468. Harding, *supra* note 470, p. 151.

469. *Id.*

470. *Id.*

471. *Id.*

472. Kraska, *supra* note 303, p. 218.

473. Golberg, *supra* note 383, p. 224.

474. Dorn, Jepsen, and Savona, *supra* note 382, p. 97.

475. *Id.*

476. *Id.*

477. Kraska, *supra* note 303, p. 219.

478. Golberg, *supra* note 383, p. 220.

479. *Id.*

480. *Id.*

481. Dorn, Jepsen, and Savona, *supra* note 382, p. 99.

482. *Id.*

483. *Id.*

484. Kraska, *supra* note 303, p. 219.

485. *Id.*, p. 220.

486. *Id.*

487. *Id.*

488. Harding, *supra* note 470, p. 152.

489. *Id.*

490. Goldberg, *supra* note 383, p. 229.

491. *Id.*

492. *Id.*

493. Kraska, *supra* note 303, p. 221.

494. Golberg, *supra* note 383, p. 231.

495. *Id.*

496. *Id.*

497. *Id.*, p. 233.

498. *Id.*

499. *Id.*, p. 220.

500. Dorn, Jepsen, and Savona, *supra* note 382, p. 100.

501. *Id.*

502. *Id.*

503. Garavelli, *supra* note 354, pp. 277–284.

504. *Id.*

505. *Id.*

506. *Id.*

507. Eric Pinkard, The Death Penalty for Drug Kingpins: Constitutional and International Implications, 24 *Vt. L. Rev.* 1, 14, 1999.

508. *Id.*

509. *Id.*

510. Harding, *supra* note 470, p. 164.

511. *Id.*, p. 165.

512. *Id.*

513. *Id.*

514. *Drugs: Should We Legalize, Decriminalize, or Deregulate?* (Jeffrey A. Schaler, ed., Amherst, N.Y.: Prometheus Books, 1998), p. 142.

515. *Id.*

516. *Id.*

517. *Id.*

518. Golberg, *supra* note 383, p. 193.

519. *Id.*

520. *Id.*

521. Schaler, *supra* note 526, p. 142.

522. *Id.*

523. Stark, Kidd, and Sykes, *supra* note 415, p. 154.

524. *Id.*

525. Schaler, *supra* note 526, p. 142.

526. *Id.*

527. Stark, Kidd, and Sykes, *supra* note 415, p. 154.

528. *Id.*

529. *Id.*, p. 155.

530. *Id.*

531. *Id.*

532. *Id.*, p. 157.

533. *Id.*

534. *Id.*
535. *Id.*
536. Golberg, *supra* note 383, p. 219).
537. *Id.*
538. *Id.*
539. *Id.*, p. 245.
540. Golberg, *supra* note 383, p. 245. Chapter 4.

Chapter 4

Prostitution: The History of Criminalization

The origin of prostitution is debatable. How prostitution is defined determines how old the practice is. Some theorists contend that prostitution can be found in the animal kingdom. Female primates and younger males have been observed offering sexual services to males for food or to avoid attack. If "presentation," behavior—females and younger males offering sexual contact to dominant members to avoid attack or for food—is a form of prostitution, then prostitution is older than humans.[1]

Another controversy involves the beginnings of society. In the wake of research by Charles Darwin and others in the nineteenth century, many scholars began to challenge the Judeo-Christian story of creation, particularly the fact that it ignored millions of years.[2] From this came theories of the beginnings of mankind and, of interest for this discussion, whether those beginnings were patriarchal or matriarchal. Theorists who advocate matriarchal systems as the origins of society claim that the roots of prostitution go back to the time of goddess worship.

Within these societies, religion, culture, and sex were closely intertwined and sexual rituals were prominent components to spiritual worship.[3] The great goddess Inanna (later known as Ishtar), goddess of fertility, was heavily associated with promiscuity and prostitution.[4] The women who lived and worked in the temples performed sexual rites as part of their worship.[5] Some theorists claim that these women, followers of Ishtar, were the first prostitutes. These sacred prostitutes were originally regarded as priestesses and women of the highest rank.[6] According to advocates of the goddess theory, female promiscuity and the idea of prostitution did not become stigmatized until men took over and society evolved into the patriarchal system.[7]

What constitutes prostitution is a matter of definition, and throughout history, prostitution has been defined in many different ways. In a society where female promiscuity is tolerated, fewer sexual activities are classified as prostitution.[8] For prostitution to thrive as it has in the United States, it generally requires a moral code that condemns promiscuity in women and tolerates it in men, and at the same time rewards promiscuous women with money or other means.[9]

The Near East

The people who lived in the ancient Near East are considered the founders of Western civilization. The earliest people lived in Babylonia, an area sometimes referred to as Mesopotamia.[10]

Here, what has been called sacred prostitution was part of worship activity in the temples. These priestesses reenacted the annual growth and harvest cycle by having sexual intercourse with priests or rulers.[11] These temple prostitutes earned their keep by receiving food, wine, oil and other precious goods from worshippers who laid these items at their feet before participating in sexual rituals. The *harimtu*, who worked outside of the temples, are considered the world's first streetwalkers. Religion had been woven deeply into the profession of a prostitute, and these women were thought of as holy women working under the goddess Ishtar.[12]

The first written reference to prostitution appears in the Hammurabic Code, the earliest law code to survive. Although it did not set rules regarding the prostitute, it did recognize her.[13] The code, from the town of Eshunna in 1700 B.C., gave insight into relationships between men and women and the purpose of marriage (procreation, not companionship). Women were considered property of men, be it their fathers, their brothers, or their husbands.[14] A wife was punished more for her husband's adultery than he was. If a husband was caught fornicating with an unmarried woman, the husband's wife was given to the father of the unmarried woman as restitution for the damage of his property.[15]

Because women were property, prostitution was looked upon as a necessary part of life in Babylonia. Female virginity and chastity were valuable commodities to be bought and sold.[16] Seventh-century B.C. documents indicate that wealthier men made profits from selling the sexual services of their slaves. Not-so-wealthy men sold their daughters into prostitution.[17]

As prostitution became more of a commercial enterprise, a class system evolved among prostitutes. The highest class, of course, being the temple prostitutes, followed by concubines and courtesans. The next step down were women who worked in the taverns, and the lowest class were slave prostitutes.[18]

Although extant writings are less clear, Egyptian temple life may also have included sacred prostitution.[19] For the most part, the average Egyptian was monogamous, although lifelong celibacy was not necessarily encouraged.[20]

Egyptian women had more freedom than the women of Babylonia. Records indicate that a few held positions such as house superintendent or dining hall director. Several Egyptian women became famous prostitutes. Among them was a woman called Rhodopis.[21] Rhodopis came to Egypt as a Greek slave. She attained her freedom and continued to work as a courtesan. She made such a fortune that she was able to build a pyramid for herself.[22] Another such was Cheops' daughter. Herodotus, the fifth-century Greek historian, told the story of Cheops, a twenty-sixth-century B.C. king of Egypt who ran short on money when building his pyramid and sent his daughter to the brothels to make up the difference. She decided that she, too, deserved a monument and ordered all her customers to give her a stone in addition to her fee. Legend has it that she built a pyramid more than 150 feet tall.[23]

Whether or not religious or temple prostitution carried over into the Jewish culture is debatable, but prostitution is frequently mentioned in the Bible.[24] Generally, just as others of the Near East, the Jewish people seemed to accept prostitution as a fact of life.[25] Prostitutes were easily spotted in the streets of ancient Palestine. They wore bright, colorful clothing, and many of them sang or played the harp in the city streets. Prostitution houses were a common sight in the city and were marked with red emblems. Overall, prostitution was tolerated, but female promiscuity was not. Parents whose daughters became prostitutes were looked down upon, and women who were not virgins on their marriages were punished.[26]

The double standard was prevalent in Palestine as elsewhere in the Near East. The rape of a virgin woman was a crime, not against the woman herself but against the man who possessed her—it was a property crime. The rapist could be forced to pay for his crimes or forced to marry the woman.[27] The biblical book of Proverbs warns men to be wary of "strange women" or any woman other than one's own wife.[28] Harlotry, according to the Bible, is the lesser of two evils. Prostitution was considered a protective institution because it allowed young males to explore their sexuality without exploiting the good, pure women of society.[29]

Ancient Greece

Ancient Greece was so fully a male-oriented society, it is no wonder that the Greeks were fascinated with prostitutes. Sex was considered important for good health and vitality. It was a socially acceptable way for men to "take care of their excess sexual energy."[30]

Prostitution was seen as a natural part of life. Most of the Greek states regulated prostitution and taxed the brothels. Solon, who ruled Athens at the turn of the sixth century, introduced laws in Greek society to regulate women; dividing the "good" from the "bad."[31] This division, intended to protect "good" women, ultimately made them prisoners of their home. It was inappropriate at that time for women, other than prostitutes, to lead a public life.[32]

Athenian wives and wives-to-be were allowed out of the house only for the occasional funeral or religious activity. These women were not even allowed to go to the marketplace—men or slaves did all the shopping. Solon's view of women was clear: they were wives or whores, period. Women living independently of men—slaves, poor women, and foreign women—were all considered whores.[33]

Solon sought to reap the benefits of prostitution by setting up state-run brothels. It is said that the brothels financially supported the military.[34] The women who worked in the state-run brothels were typically slaves, and many were Asian war captives.[35] The women lived in cramped cells, and their fees were paid directly to the *pronobosceion*, the male state official who managed the brothel.

In spite of Solon's attempts to control the entire sex-for-sale industry, women and boys walked the streets of Athens, competing for a portion of the market Solon's regulation sought to dominate.[36] Perhaps the most independent women of Athens were the famous *hetairae*, the elite whores of ancient Greece. These were the only women in Greece allowed to manage their own affairs and to stroll through the city streets. They were known for their beauty and intellect as well as their lovemaking.[37] Phryne, considered the most beautiful hetaire in Athens, went to trial for disrobing in public during an impersonation of Aphrodite. During her trial, Hyperides, her defender, saw little hope that her case would prevail, so he tore off her clothes to expose her breasts to the court. Apparently, the judges were so taken with the beauty of them that they could not find her guilty.[38]

If the *hetairae* were the top prostitutes in Greece, then the *porne* were the bottom rung on the prostitution ladder. They did, however, have an interesting way of advertising their services: on the soles of their sandals they engraved the words "Follow Me" so that they left a seductive trail in their wake.[39]

Greece, as described in its early writings, clearly embraced the double standards that allow prostitution to flourish. Wives and mothers were kept pure by banishment from the society that created another set of women—the prostitutes and courtesans—who served as companions and lovers. Although they were segregated from the "good" women, prostitutes received considerable freedoms that good women were not allowed.[40] Men often went to symposiums, lavish drinking parties, in which wild orgies often occurred. Of course, their wives were not allowed; the women who attended were the *hetairae*.[41]

In Greek philosophy we see the beginnings of the idea that sex is an evil to be avoided.[42] Pythagoras, philosopher, magician, and scientist who lived during the sixteenth century B.C., taught that the world could be divided into opposing principles: good and bad, right and wrong, limited and unlimited, light and dark, men and women. Limited, light, and men were good; unlimited, dark, and women were bad. Plato believed that true love was distinct from physical love, and that true happiness could only be found through controlling one's physical urges.[43]

Romans

Prostitution was accepted as a necessary business in Roman culture, but the prostitutes in Rome were not admired and looked upon as goddesses, as they had been in Greek society. Romans definitely considered prostitutes on the low rung of the class ladder.[44] Many of the prostitutes in Rome were actually slaves, and their owners simply rented them out.[45]

Under Gaius Caligula in the first century, prostitutes were taxed one client's worth of fees to the state.[46] Romans were the first Europeans to require prostitutes to register with the state.[47] Although supposed to register with state officials, called *aediles*, few did. The *aediles* looked after the brothels, making sure they opened and closed at the proper times and checking to see that the women donned proper clothing.[48]

Outside of the brothels, the women would sit or stand where potential clients could see them. The word *prostitute* comes from this time, meaning "to set forth in public ... or to be exposed for sale." There were two kinds of brothels: one in which independent prostitutes paid a fee to the *leno* or *lena* (proprietor of the house), and the other, where the prostitutes were actually slaves to the brothels and were paid a small amount from the *lenos*. Most of the prostitutes in Rome were slaves brought in from Syria and Egypt and who were bought and sold at the auctions.[49]

Romans viewed the lower-class prostitutes as insatiable, sex-craving, mad women. Higher-class courtesans were by no means sought after by the Romans as the *hetairae* were by the Greeks. The Romans were more of a family-focused society, and Roman women had more freedom than Greek women did. They accompanied their husbands on social outings and were allowed educations. Men did not look to prostitutes for intellectual stimulation, but merely for their sexual services.[50]

So as not to be confused with proper Roman women, prostitutes were required to wear short toga-like gowns, similar to those that men wore. The prostitutes also were forbidden from approaching the temple of Juno for fear that the temple would be polluted.[51]

Cato the Censor, the self-appointed guardian of Roman morals, thought of prostitution similarly to the Jewish interpretation: he believed that prostitution protected the idea of marriage. Brothels provided an outlet for young, unmarried men to explore their sexuality without bothering "other men's wives."[52]

Although she may have had more rights than her Greek counterpart, a Roman woman was still considered the property of her husband.[53] Marriages were arranged, and the desire for sex outside of marriage may have reflected marriages entered into out of obligation, not love.[54] Prostitutes in Rome were looked down upon, in part because the proper women of Rome wanted to be distinguished from them, thus creating an even deeper demarcation between good women and bad women. The Romans tolerated prostitution but enforced the Greek idea that sexuality (particularly that of females) is dangerous and evil.[55]

Christianity

Christianity, built on both Jewish and pagan traditions, survived the fall of the Roman Empire. According to writer Elizabeth Fisher, "Christianity took the Jewish mistrust of women and added its own repressions, in a much stricter interpretation of Hebrew mores. Significant was the fact that the idealization of chastity was transformed into a loathing for the body and a severe condemnation of sexual acts."[56]

Christianity adopted as doctrine philosopher Musonious Rufus's notion that sex within marriage is permissible for the purpose of procreation, but that sex for pleasure should be forbidden. Saint Paul, who helped shape the Christian Church, taught that celibacy was the ideal state for mankind.[57] Saint Paul also saw women as naturally inferior—man was not of the woman, woman was of the man. Clement of Alexandria took the idea further and stated that "every woman ought to be filled with shame at the thought that she is a woman." Saint John Chrysostom said, "Among all the savage beasts, none is found so harmful as woman."[58]

Strangely, the Church accepted many prostitutes who repented of their sinful lives. Mary Magdalene became the New Testament example of the converted sinner.[59] Mary Magdalene was a prostitute, but she was also the first person to notice that Jesus' grave was empty and the first to witness his reappearance. Possibly because of her influence, the Christian Church began to pity the prostitute rather than merely condemn her.

Several prostitutes were actually sainted.[60] Saint Mary the Egyptian worked in a brothel from the age of twelve. At thirty-nine, one of her clients brought her the message of Jesus Christ. She journeyed to Jerusalem and retired as a hermit in the desert. Legend has it that her sainthood allowed her to live for seventeen years off just three loaves of bread.[61]

In an attempt to bridge the gap of beliefs among early Christians, a group of men came together to interpret the Scriptures. These men became known as the church fathers or patristics.[62] They defined prostitution as promiscuous behavior, not necessarily accepting payment for sex. Saint Jerome said that a whore was a woman who was available to many men.[63] The church father most outspoken on the subject of prostitution was Saint Augustine (A.D. 354–439). Before converting to Christianity, Augustine was a part of the Manichaean sect. During this time, he kept a mistress who gave birth to his son. At one time, he stated, "Grant me chastity, oh, Lord, but not now!"[64] His mother pressured him into leaving his mistress and son and becoming a Christian. Upon doing so, Augustine swore to be celibate for the rest of his life, claiming that the only purpose for intercourse was procreation. A married couple having intercourse for pleasure was just as sinful as a man having intercourse with a prostitute. Surprisingly, Saint Augustine found a reason for prostitution. Although he believed nothing was as shameful as prostitution, he believed that without it, lust would overtake society. Saint Augustine was of the opinion that removing prostitution from society would give rise to other patterns of sexual relationships.[65]

Despite any possible function prostitution might serve in society, the church fathers adopted the idea that prostitutes must be banned from the Church. The converted prostitute, of course, they would welcome.

Medieval Europe

The *Corpus Juris Civilis* codified Roman law and gave prostitution legal basis in Christian Europe (Christianity was the official state religion).[66] The code of laws emerged under Emperor Justinian in the A.D. sixth century and recognized prostitution as legal but sought to punish third parties by banning procuresses and brothel keepers.[67] The Justinian legislation also sought to put into law a distinction between concubines and prostitutes, the former protected as an informal type of marriage.[68]

Unlike Greek theater, women were allowed to portray themselves in the Byzantine theaters. The church fathers became so disgusted with chorus girls dancing with little or no clothing on stage that they claimed all actresses were prostitutes. However, not all prostitutes were actresses. Many worked on the streets or in the *xenones*, hostels in which travelers stayed. Other houses existed solely for the purpose of prostitution.[69]

In the Byzantine Empire, prostitution was condemned, but the prostitute was not. Hope remained that she would reform herself, so the law allowed former prostitutes to marry and many houses of refuge were created in order to assist the prostitute out of her sinful life.[70]

Farther west, the Germans affected many ideas and concepts of Roman law. Germans had adopted the idea of women as property and even declared that a man who caught his wife with another had the right to execute her and her lover. Prostitution was initially considered a family issue, but eventually became a crime against the public mores of society.[71]

Alaric II, king of the Visigoths, created the Alaric Code, which threatened prostitutes and their customers with whippings if caught in the act. In fact, the code stated that prostitutes were subject to up to 300 whip blows, the highest number of whip blows allowed.[72]

As the German tribes began adopting Christianity, questions of sexual morality were left up to the Church. One method of dealing with sin was confession. In early Christianity, confession was public, in front of the congregation. Some sins required that the confessor be banned from the fellowship for a specified amount of time. Initially, many members believed that fornicators and adulterers should be banned from the Church forever.[73]

Questions concerning the definition of prostitution proved complex. The Church was not sure how to define a concubine in comparison to a prostitute or the difference between fornication and prostitution. Medieval lawyers attempted to interpret Roman law in terms of Christian morality. The medieval canon lawyers regarded intercourse as part of natural law. They believed that sexual desire led to sin, and that marriage only provided an outlet. Followers of Saint Augustine and the canon lawyers also believed that sexual pleasure, even within marriage, was a sin.[74]

Many of these lawyers were also clerics who believed that sexuality was different for men than for women. Women were considered more susceptible to sexual desires and requiring to be looked after by men. The canon lawyers did not fault the prostitute for her sins, but instead wanted to punish those who profited from her falls from grace—the pimps, the brothel keepers, and the regular customers.[75]

During this period, prostitutes were not expected to obey the law, being considered below the law. A prostitute could not accuse someone of committing a crime, could not own property, and could not answer for herself under the law. She was, however, legally permitted to keep money she received for her services.[76]

Many European rulers attempted to regulate prostitution. In 1158, Holy Roman Emperor Frederick Barbarossa punished prostitutes traveling with the army. When caught in the act, the prostitute was ordered to have her nose cut off in an attempt to make her less attractive. A soldier caught in the act sometimes had a finger cut off or an eye removed.[77]

Alfonso IX of Castile (1188–1230) set a legal example that many European rulers followed. Those involved in selling prostitutes were exiled from the kingdom; landlords who rented to prostitutes were fined and their houses were seized; brothel keepers had to free their women and find them husbands or else face the possibility of execution; husbands prostituting their wives were executed; and pimps were flogged or sent to galleys. The women who supported the pimps were publicly whipped and their clothes destroyed.[78]

In 1254, in Paris, King Louis IX passed an edict threatening to exile prostitutes and brothel keepers. As a result, many brothels shut down. When the men complained that sexual violence had erupted and that wives and daughters were no longer safe, Louis IX repealed the edict.[79] He then attempted to regulate prostitution by instilling a dress code and prohibiting prostitutes from living in certain parts of the city. Under Louis' son, Philip, prostitution for a short time became a misdemeanor, but the program was abandoned and France went back to state regulation of prostitution.[80]

In 1347, Queen Joanna established a regulation in Naples and Provence that required state brothels to keep prostitutes off the street. Any time a prostitute left the brothel, she was to wear a red knot on her left shoulder. Prostitutes who failed to live in a brothel or wear the red knot were paraded through town with red knots on their shoulder and drums playing to their public whipping. A second offense merited banishment from the city.[81]

Renaissance

It has been documented that in thirteenth-century Paris student-clerics shared the same lodging houses with prostitutes. A writer in 1230, Jacques de Vitty describes "buildings that house a college upstairs and a brothel downstairs; on the ground floor professors are lecturing while below them the prostitutes exercise their shameful trade."[82]

Church gatherings often included an entourage of prostitutes. It was reported that more than 1,500 prostitutes traveled across Europe at the Council of Constance in 1414 and could make more than 800 gold ducats each night.[83]

Prostitution thrived in Rome and in the Vatican itself. Many prostitutes lived in church-owned homes. The clergy had realized, as had kings, that if prostitution were outlawed they would lose a great source of profit (and pleasure).[84]

Northern Italy became the birthplace of a new era of classicism and reason in the fourteenth and fifteenth centuries. These men made remarkable breakthroughs in science and technology, ending the Middle Ages.[85] Similarities to ancient Greece can be seen in the portrayal of women in Renaissance Italy. Like the Athenian wives, these women were confined to their homes, except on holidays when they were allowed to attend church with their husbands. Inevitably, we again see the rise of high-class courtesans, this time called the *cortegiane* of Venice. These women were rich and independent and, like their ancient Greek counterparts, the *hetairae*, they socialized with the men whose wives were forbidden to leave home.[86] Among Venetian courtesans, the trade was passed down from mother to daughter. These women had to have beauty and intellect in order to qualify to live as a cortegiane.[87]

Thomas Coryat, an English traveler of the late sixteenth century, estimated 20,000 prostitutes in Venice.[88] Because the demand for prostitutes was so large, the Venetian authorities imported foreign women and housed them in buildings under the supervision of a madam. These women received pay only after the government and the madam took their share.[89]

Reformation

The Reformation in sixteenth-century Europe was a period of religious change. Martin Luther (1483–1546) was known as the leader of the early Protestant movement. Although he viewed marriage with more favor than the early church fathers, he thought sexual intercourse unclean.[90]

Luther saw a woman's role as the bearer of children and the means to man's sexual relief.[91] John Calvin (1509–64), Luther's French counterpart, viewed women more as lifetime "associates" of men rather than simply childbearers or remedies of sexual desires.[92] Although the Protestants were much more likely to praise marriage than the early church fathers, they were much less tolerant of promiscuity and prostitution.[93]

Luther was a harsh critic of prostitution. He said that if he were a judge, he would order severe punishment for prostitutes. "Let the government, if it wishes to be Christian, punish whoredom, rape, and adultery, at least when they occur openly: if they still occur in secret, the government is not to be blamed."[94]

Luther was reluctant for the Church to become involved in the state enforcement of morals while Calvin was more aggressive in his attempts to eliminate prostitution. In Geneva in 1566, under the rule of Calvin, adultery, blasphemy, witchcraft, and heresy were punishable by death. Prostitutes were driven from the city. Dancing and theatergoing were banned and clothing colors were regulated by law.[95]

Lutheranism spread throughout Germany as Calvin's teachings conquered Switzerland. John Knox took Calvin's teachings to Scotland, and English Henry VIII broke away from Rome and created the Anglican Church.[96]

This new sense of morality developed in Catholic countries as well under the veil of the Counter Reformation.[97] Pope Pius V ordered everyone engaged in prostitution to leave the city of Rome in 1566. (This demand was later rescinded due to the potentially massive defection.)[98]

Also during the sixteenth century, syphilis hit.[99] Although many theories account for its origins, its appearance coupled with the Reformation resulted in action against prostitution.[100] The Imperial Diet of the Holy Roman Empire issued an edict that prohibited all extramarital sexual relations, including prostitution and concubinage. London's public houses were closed in 1546, and those in Paris were closed in 1560. Punishment for prostitution was severe during this time. Common was a punishment called *accabussade*, in which a woman found guilty of prostitution was forced to wear a bonnet with feathers and a sign on her back stating that she was a prostitute. With her hands tied behind her back, she was forced to march through town to the banks of a river. There, the prostitute was forced to undress and placed in a cage in which she was dunked until she nearly drowned. After three dunkings, the woman was left lying naked for the townspeople to scorn.[101]

In 1561, Charles IX abolished the remaining brothels throughout France. Henry VIII and Emperor Charles V of Germany also began enforcing criminal laws against prostitution.[102] Henry VIII even went so far as to require any woman caught trading sex with a soldier to be branded on her face with hot irons.[103]

Brothels disappeared at the beginning of the sixteenth century, but as the fear of venereal disease waned and the Reformation lost its luster, legally recognized and regulated prostitution returned.[104] At this time, the first mention of child brothels in England is made. These brothels supplied rich clients with girls between the ages of seven and fourteen, either stolen from their families or sold by poor parents.[105]

At the turn of the seventeenth century, prostitution was widespread. Puritanism emerged in opposition to the supposedly morally lacking English establishment. Protestantism took behavior to the utmost extreme—all pleasure was considered sinful. William Stubbes, Puritan author, pointed out sins in every aspect of life, including holidays and dancing:

Dancing, as it is used (or rather abused) in these days, is an introduction to whoredom, a preparative to wantonness, a provocative to uncleanness, and an introite to all kinds of lewdness....For what clipping, what culling, what kissing and bussing, what smouching and slobbering one another, what filthy groping and unclean handling is not practiced everywhere in these dancings...and shewed forth in their bawdy gestures of one to another.[106]

Stubbes lobbied for prostitutes "to be cauterized and seared with a hot iron on the cheek, forehead or some other part of their body that might be seen, to the end [that] the honest chaste Christians might be discerned from the adulterous children of Satan."[107]

The appropriate female behavior was spelled out in W. Whatley's *The Blushing Bride* (1617): "If ever thou purpose to be a good wife, to live comfortably, set down this with thyself: mine husband is my superior, my better; he hath authority and rule over me; nature hath given it to him....God hath given it to him."[108] The Puritans left behind large volumes of court records in which they prosecuted their neighbors for immoral behavior.[109] Snooping and spying were common among the Puritans and seen as acts necessary to guard society's morality. Families in which women were absent were observed closely in case the women might be working as prostitutes.[110]

Eighteenth-Century Europe

During the seventeenth and eighteenth centuries, it is well documented that European kings and princes indulged quite heavily in sex outside of marriage.[111] Henry IV (1589–1610) is said to have set the tone for his successors. During his lifetime (a mere twenty-one years), Henry had approximately fifty-six mistresses, three of whom were nuns.[112]

Prostitution was technically illegal in France, but the laws were modified in 1684 to distinguish between the professional prostitute and the poor or underage girls who had no other means for making a living. The police could go after any professional but could not go after the other girls without official complaint. Professional prostitutes could be exiled, imprisoned, whipped, or have their heads shaved.[113] Records of prostitution in eighteenth-century Paris are derived from reports madams were required to submit each week to the police.[114]

Certain aristocrats of the eighteenth century were fond of sexual experimentation. The most famous Parisian brothel was the house of Madame Gourdan on the Rue des Deux Portes, which catered to wealthy, powerful clients. Madame Gourdan's whores advertised their services to potential clients by posing in provocative positions.[115] Respectable clients visited the house unnoticed through a secret passage that led to the brothel from a home on a different street. The brothel housed sexual statues and pictures, a peep room for voyeurs, and a chamber of horrors for those who enjoyed a little beating with their intercourse.[116]

Many prostitutes not living in brothels congregated at the Palais Royal, where an estimated 1,500 girls gathered each day.[117] In 1778, French officials passed a law that prohibited women from soliciting in the streets and boardinghouses from allowing unmarried men and women to sleep together.[118] State-licensed brothels were still permitted, which makes it likely that these laws were created to eliminate competition rather than limit prostitution.

In England, prostitutes solicited anywhere a crowd gathered: at public shows, church gatherings, plays, and parks.[119] The general attitude toward the prostitute during this period was one of pity over condemnation. A general acceptance allowed that gentlemen could have their way with poor, lower-class women, even those unwilling. In an attempt to stop involuntary prostitution, Queen Elizabeth ordered that no waitress or laundress under the age of forty could go into a gentleman's chamber at a public inn, and that men caught in uncompromising positions were punished instead of the women. These laws were rarely enforced.[120]

Miss Fawkland, a famous English madam, ensured her prostitutes were thoroughly trained before they worked in one of her houses. She maintained three houses of three specialties: the first, the "Temple of Aurora," featured girls between the ages of eleven and sixteen. Elderly clients were allowed to fondle the girls but no more. Second was the "Temple of Flora," in which girls over the age of sixteen were housed in a luxurious brothel. The third house, the "Temple of Mysteries," catered to extraordinary tastes and fetishes, including sadomasochism.[121]

Widespread prostitution in the eighteenth century existed alongside and correlated somewhat with widespread illegitimacy. Illegitimate births were on the rise around 1750 and continued to increase until about 1850.[122]

Many thinkers in the eighteenth century struggled for the solution to prevalent promiscuity, prostitution, and illegitimacy.[123] Men from the middle classes distinguished themselves from the loose aristocrats by defining themselves as the "moral" class and idealizing the family and female chastity. The progressive thinkers of the Enlightenment, which originated in France, looked back to ancient Greece for inspiration. Once again, women were separated from men and kept at home. Jean-Jacques Rousseau, a leader of the Enlightenment, wrote, "Women are made for the delight of men, and the bearing of children is their proper business...motherhood is a total career and commitment in itself." It is "indecent," Rousseau wrote, for a woman to seek the company of a man, whether she is married to him or not.[124]

This familiar view of women as meek and subservient once again created a need for prostitutes and mistresses to fulfill man's desires in ways that the virtuous wife and mother was forbidden. Bernard Manville, physician, wrote a pamphlet entitled *A Modest Defence of Public Stews*, in which he said that the greatest problem of prostitution is the risk of passing disease to innocent wives and children. Manville proposed state-regulated brothels. The "abuse and ill management" of private, unregulated prostitution, he claimed, resulted in illegitimate births, the alienated affections of wives and husbands, the temptation to live beyond one's means, warped virtues, and the ruin of young virgins.[125]

Mandeville believed all of the above could be eliminated by legalizing prostitution. His plan proposed approximately 100 brothels in London, each housing about twenty women. Each house would be overseen by a matron and associated with two physicians and four surgeons for regular exams of the women. Mandeville argued that his plan would prevent boys from masturbating, protect against venereal disease, and "halt the debauching of modest women."[126]

Sir John Fielding, a London magistrate, proposed a "severe Industry" for poor girls and reformed prostitutes to make a living. The "severe Industry" was a public laundry in which the women would earn a living doing laundry while learning how to cook, knit, and clean in hopes that they would one day become submissive and dutiful wives.[127]

Fielding encouraged the passing of the *Disorderly Houses Act of 1752*, which stated that any house, room, or garden in London or Westminster that allowed music, dancing, or other entertainment without a license would be regarded as a disorderly house (brothel) and punished accordingly.[128]

Age of Reform: Nineteenth-Century Europe

In 1796, Paris instituted a new Register of Prostitutes. Agents were employed whose task was merely to find and register prostitutes in the city. In 1798, two physicians were hired to examine the prostitutes, and in 1802, a dispensary was created at which all prostitutes were supposed to submit to weekly examinations.[129] These regulations were not recognizable in law. The Napoleonic Code of 1810 never mentioned prostitution.[130]

Control of prostitution was left to a Morals Bureau.[131] The bureau attempted to confine prostitution to the brothels, to register and license every prostitute, and to submit each prostitute to compulsory medical inspection. Diseased prostitutes were sent to a hospital for treatment and when cured went back to work. Each prostitute carried a card signed by the medical inspector and stamped with a date as proof of a clean health record. Prostitutes were required to show these cards to anyone who requested to see them.[132] Unfortunately, the medical inspections themselves likely transmitted sexual disease; rubber gloves and aseptic techniques were unheard of until late in the nineteenth century.[133]

A new concern over venereal disease had emerged, particularly from military authorities. The British navy customarily invited prostitutes aboard ships in port.[134] The British Parliament enacted the Contagious Diseases Preventions Acts in 1864, 1866, and 1869. The 1866 act required all prostitutes to register and submit to regular medical inspections. A special unit of police was to enforce the act, and any woman must submit to an examination or be sent to jail. The act was generally limited to military towns, and London was not included. It was repealed in 1886.[135] Critics of regulation claim that it never dealt well with venereal disease, it failed to reduce illegitimacy, and it was not cost effective.[136] Supporters held fast to the idea that prostitution was a necessary evil.

Berlin established a system of regulation similar to that of Paris. The Berlin regulations of 1792 stated that a procuress must have permission from the police to open a brothel, and a landlord must have police permission to rent a room to a prostitute. Prostitutes faced up to three months in jail for transmitting a venereal disease to a client and also had to pay the client's medical treatment.[137]

Most European cities adopted similar regulations with varying specific details. For example, in Paris and Berlin, a woman could be forced by her husband to register as a prostitute. A woman in Budapest could register only with her husband's consent, and in Munich and Vienna a married woman could not register at all.

The high-class prostitutes of the nineteenth century rarely had run-ins with the authorities. Numerous wealthy clients assisted a fair number of nineteenth-century courtesans to personal wealth. The highest rank of prostitute, of course, was the royal mistress. England's George IV was the leader of a group known as the Bucks, or Corinthians, who spent a good deal of time chasing the "Fashionable Impures," or Cyprians, the elite courtesans.[138]

United States of America

Early American attitudes toward sexuality and promiscuity resembled those in Europe. Prostitution was a problem for colonial authorities almost from the beginning of settlement.[139]

The puritanical colonial environment perpetuated a male-dominated society in which women relied on men for physical protection, financial support, and spiritual guidance.[140] Prostitution in early America was considered neither a profession nor a vice, but a temporary sin from which a woman could reform.

As early as 1699, New Amsterdam, Boston, and Philadelphia passed laws that made nightwalking an offense. The first American ban on brothels went into effect in 1672.

As the eighteenth century progressed, Americans became less concerned with punishing prostitutes. It was not uncommon for men to have mistresses or to visit prostitutes. Some European prostitutes were sent to America for punishment. In 1721, twenty-five prostitutes were sent from a corrections facility in Paris to become the wives of French residents in the Louisiana territory. Those who failed to convert to the role of good wife were whipped.

Prostitution in America began to organize in the late eighteenth century when industrialization began to change society. Americans left the smaller villages and towns to find work in the large cities. The fact that many early American societies were predominantly male encouraged the rapid growth of prostitution. Most early settlers in the American West were males seeking their fortune. Many of the men saved a percentage of their wages to send back to their homes in order to bring families and girl-friends to the new land. Meanwhile, these men were alone, and many spent a portion of their paychecks on alcohol and prostitutes.[141] Often, the first women to arrive in early American colonies were prostitutes, or perhaps prostitution was the only way immigrant women could succeed without the financial support of a man.[142] Women had few employment opportunities. Some of them turned to prostitution rather than take a garment trade job for two dollars per week. Patricia Cline Cohen, author of *The Murder of Helen Jewett*, said that few such women probably went to the city to become prostitutes, but once there saw how hard it was to survive, and that the richest of women were often the prostitutes. Some prostitutes made nearly $1,000 per night.[143]

Whorehouses became popular in the cities. More than 200 brothels operated in lower Manhattan alone.[144] In New York, landlords discovered the lucrative business of renting to a madam: such arrangements could earn four times as much rent for a row house.[145]

Parlor houses were top-of-the-line brothels and attracted the wealthiest of clients. The ladies here charged at least five dollars per night, which was more than the average working man made in one week. Bawdy houses, on the other hand, were the bottom-of-the-barrel. Madams here herded the men through like cattle. These ladies would see as many as thirty men in one night.[146]

Prostitution was considered vagrancy, and therefore illegal. It was common for the police and city officials to look the other way if they received a share of the profits.[147] Although the majority accepted prostitution as a necessary evil, two antiprostitution movements appeared in the 1830s. The first was led by divinity student John McDowall in 1832. This reform movement created the Magdalene Society in New York. The society distributed sensational papers and recruited volunteers to save prostitutes from their sins. The second movement, in 1834, began when the New York Moral Reform bought out McDowall's paper. By 1839, the female-run organization had national status and contended that prostitution was the product of oversexed males. By the 1840s, the Moral Reformers changed their tune. They began to portray prostitution as a result of economic inequity between the sexes. They advocated increased salaries for women and the opening of traditionally male occupations to females. The reformers created houses for prostitutes looking for respectable work where women could inculcate both morals and new job skills.[148]

In 1858, prostitution in New York brought in an estimated $6.3 million per year—more than the shipbuilding and brewing industries combined.[149] In addition, an estimated 75 percent of New York males had some type of social disease.[150]

The Victorian era, beginning in the 1870s, marked the second wave of prostitution reform in the American colonies. Reformers sought not to eliminate but to regulate prostitution as necessary to protect "respectable" women. The result was red-light districts. Medical authorities and researchers argued that prostitutes should be registered, licensed, and forced to comply with regular medical examinations.[151] Prominent in this movement was the physician W. W. Sanger, who believed that regulation was necessary to prevent venereal disease.[152] The only city in the United State to officially adopt the European idea of regulation was St. Louis. On July 5, 1870, the city council passed the Social Evil Ordinance, in which physicians were appointed to examine registered prostitutes and send those diseased to a Social Evil Hospital until cured. The ordinance was nullified in 1874 following a petition signed by 100,000 people.[153]

It seemed as if regulation was going to sweep the nation; for a time New York, Chicago, Cincinnati, San Francisco, and Philadelphia all contemplated such legislation. The public, however, failed to support what meant accepting prostitution itself, and the idea of regulation slowly gave way to ideas of abolition.[154] Concerned citizens in New York mistrusted corrupt police and decided to take matters into their own hands. Led by Anthony Comstock, the Society for the Suppression of Vice was born.[155]

The last two decades of the nineteenth century are sometimes called the movement toward "social purity." Male reformers blamed prostitution on feminine sexuality, while the feminists blamed it on male domination.[156]

With the failure of regulation, many cities turned to segregation. Although red-light districts were against the law in most American communities, authorities tolerated them because not only did they supposedly protect the general community from immorality, but also authorities could better keep an eye on prostitution contained in a district.[157] The police periodically raided brothels and arrested prostitutes, but in most cases, a brothel that closed down eventually reopened after the attention died down.[158] The 1916 Vice Report of Bridgeport, Connecticut, states that "A segregated district...is really a protection of the morality of the womanhood of the city, for without it rape would be a common and clandestine immorality would increase."[159]

By 1900, great political and social changes were occurring in America, including the rationalization of the prostitute. Whereas she was once viewed as a fallen woman, many began to see her as a victim. Americans had a hard time believing that anyone would willingly go into prostitution, thus came the notion of white slavery. James R. Petersen, author of *The Century of Sex*, said that the media helped perpetuate the idea that the public had to fight to keep white women safe from sex.[160]

In 1910, Congress passed both the Mann Act and the Mary Act. The Mann Act prevented the transportation of women into other states for immoral purposes. Fifteen hundred men, including actor Charlie Chaplin, were arrested under this statute.[161] The Mary Act prohibited prostitution in military establishments.[162]

Congress empowered a then little-known agency called the Bureau of Investigations (now known as the Federal Bureau of Investigation), to interview inmates of American brothels to determine whether or not these women had come into prostitution willingly or were in fact slaves. Of

1,106 prostitutes interviewed, only 6 said they were prostitutes involuntarily. Others cited low wages and family problems as reasons for prostituting.[163]

Prostitution went through major changes with the invention of the telephone. By 1913, a brothel was just a telephone call away. Some girls left their brothels and madams to go into business for themselves; all they needed was a business card and a telephone. Here, we start seeing the term "call girl."[164]

New Orleans has a reputation for being an exotic, seductive town. Officials there forced all sex business into one district of town eventually known as Storyville. In 1907, business was booming and an estimated $10 million was made each year in the notorious red-light district. At least 1,500 girls worked in Storyville at that time, charging anything from twenty-five cents to ten dollars per sex act. At the train station, blue books made available to visitors described where to go in New Orleans for what kind of sexual pleasures.[165]

Districted or segregated prostitution gradually disappeared from most cities in the early part of the twentieth century. In 1911, the Chicago Vice Commission urged the city to adopt a policy of repression and rid of its "evil conditions." Similar actions took place in New York and around the country.[166]

In 1916, 40,000 prostitutes died of syphilis. During this same year, New Orleans officials attempt to segregate Storyville into black and white districts. Willie Piazza, a rich and well-known madam, led the fight against segregation of the red-light district and won. However, the mayor of New Orleans shut down the entire district in 1917 following a military order that forbade any brothels within five miles of a military camp.[167]

The prohibition era forced prostitution underground. Following World War II, marriages rose and commercial sex evaporated from the public eye.

The criminalization of prostitution transformed the prostitute's status from moral deviant to criminal. Prostitutes, rejected in society, became trapped in a cycle of poverty and crime that established the basis for modern prostitution.[168] Prostitution remains illegal in the United States everywhere except for a few counties in Nevada. In 1999, the best-known brothel in America, the Mustang Ranch in Reno, Nevada, closed its doors.

PROSTITUTION LAWS

A discussion of prostitution laws requires at the outset definition of the various degrees of prostitution criminalization: legalization, decriminalization, regulation, and abolition. First, *legalization* refers to a system of criminal regulation and government control over prostitution.[169] This system typically legalizes one type of prostitution while continuing to criminalize others that fall outside the legal definition. Legalized prostitution exists in Switzerland and Taiwan.[170]

Activists and prostitutes'-rights advocates typically refer to *decriminalization* as the elimination of laws that make prostitution illegal by rescinding laws against consensual sexual activity among adults.[171] *Regulation* typically refers to control of prostitution through criminal codes and sanctions, although the term also sometimes refers to civil regulation and self-regulation.[172]

Abolitionism is the idea of eradicating both the whole institution of prostitution and the selling of sexual services.[173] Typically, abolitionists see prostitution as a violent and exploitative practice that employs people who had abusive childhoods.[174]

United States of America

In 1910, Congress passed both the Mann Act and the Mary Act. The Mann Act, officially known as the White Slave Traffic Act, forbade the transportation of women across state lines for "immoral purposes."[175] In 1986, the act was amended and its title changed to Transportation for Illegal Sexual Activity and Related Crimes. The act now forbids transporting any individual, not just women, in interstate or foreign commerce "with intent that such individual engage in prostitution, or in any sexual activity for which any person can be charged with a criminal offense." [176]

Except for certain counties in Nevada, prostitution is illegal in the United States,[177] as well as various activities linked to prostitution. Most states have stricter codes against pimping and pandering than against prostitution.[178] Many states treat patronizing a prostitute to the same degree of punishment as prostitution.[179] Almost all states have criminalized patronizing in the past forty years.[180]

Prostitution is usually a misdemeanor, although many states make certain aspects of pimping and pandering felonies.[181] A current trend in prostitution statutes is a felony charge against prostitutes and patrons who knowingly engage in commercial sex while infected with HIV.

The constitutionality of prostitution statutes has been questioned in American courts. Cases such as *Griswold* v. *Connecticut*[182] alleged that the state's statutes against prostitution violated the constitutional right to privacy.[183] The court disagreed. A few prostitution statutes have been deemed "unconstitutionally vague," however, where the statute cites "immoral acts" but fails to define an "immoral act."[184] In other cases, defendants have claimed freedom to offer sexual activity under the First Amendment's free speech clause. Again, these challenges are typically unsuccessful.[185]

During the 1990s, many communities began to impose different sanctions against patrons, or buyers, of prostitution.[186] These sanctions included impounding a patron's car, revoking a patron's driver's license, and publicizing a patron's picture.[187] These penalties have created new concerns of due process, because many communities impose the sanctions upon arrest rather than conviction.[188] When prosecuted, most patrons faced with the threat of public humiliation will typically plead out on a lesser charge.[189]

Nevada is the only state that currently regulates prostitution in some of its counties. In 1971, a state law that regulates gambling and dance halls in Nevada was amended to prohibit counties with populations greater than 250,000 to license houses of "ill fame or repute."[190] The Nevada Supreme Court determined that this language allows counties with less than 250,000 residents to license brothels.[191] Of the seventeen counties with less than 250, 000 residents: four counties prohibit prostitution; six counties ban it in unincorporated areas; and seven counties permit prostitution throughout the county.[192] Approximately 1,000 women worked in Nevada's thirty-three licensed brothels during 1999.[193]

Since 1986, no prostitutes in Nevada's licensed brothels have tested HIV positive.[194] State law requires these women to register with the police and to submit to weekly health exams as well as to monthly HIV tests.[195]

Although the United States as a whole criminalizes prostitution, historically, the country has tolerated commercial sexual services for military men in time of war.[196] During World War II, the regulation of prostitution resembled regulation in parts of Nevada today.[197] In 1942, 250,000 men stood in line at brothels on Hotel Street, in Hawaii, and paid $3 for three minutes of intimacy.[198] In 1944, when civilian authorities reclaimed control, brothels closed down.[199]

Other Countries

Around the world, attitudes toward prostitution vary. In Great Britain, selling sex has never been a criminal act.[200] The 1954 Wolffenden Report recommended keeping prostitution legal but recommended harsher criminal sanctions against "public nuisance" acts associated with prostitution.[201] Parliament has increased penalties on public solicitation; many prostitutes in Great Britain now rely on advertising and agents to sell their services.[202]

The Canadian attitude is similar to that of Great Britain. In 1972, prohibitions on commercial sex were eliminated and a ban on solicitation enacted.[203] The Royal Commission on the Status of Women recommended repeal of "futile and stigmatizing" Canadian solicitation statutes.[204]

Prior to the 1960s, prostitution in France was regulated with licensing and health exams.[205] During the 1960s, the brothels in France were closed and the government enacted harsh penalties against procuring, pandering, and pimping.[206] These laws are rarely enforced, however, and commercial sex in France is not uncommon.[207]

Sweden has no criminal laws against consensual sex among adults as long as the actions are not abusive or exploitative.[208] Despite an absence of criminal prohibitions on selling sex, Sweden has hardly any commercial sex.[209]

Since the 1970s, most Australian states have repealed laws that made commercial sex a crime.[210] In 1985, a committee consulted with prostitute collectives and conducted surveys and interviews to create the *Report of the Inquiry of the Victorian Government*.[211] The inquiry produced five recommendations: First, to repeal most sanctions against prostitute-related activities including the use of one's home to engage in commercial sex, the use of brothels, and living off the earnings of prostitution.[212] The inquiry commission wanted these specific sanctions repealed because it found that women who work in brothels are often less vulnerable to violence. The sanction against living off prostitution punished the children and spouses of prostitutes.[213]

Second, the inquiry advocated laws against public solicitation and loitering but called for zoning of particular areas designated for street solicitation.[214] Third, the inquiry recommended that brothels be subject to the same zoning laws as any other group home.[215] Fourth, the inquiry recommended that prostitutes need not be licensed. The inquiry argued that when prostitutes are licensed, they become subject to stigmatization that in turn makes it more difficult for them to leave the business.[216] Finally, the inquiry recommended new offenses against prostitution of minors and intimidation or assault against any prostitute.[217]

Historically, Japan is tolerant of commercial sex.[218] In 1956, Japan adopted a Prostitution Prevention Law that primarily targets third parties who thrive off prostitution, but the law is not enforced by the authorities.[219] Although the law itself has not officially changed, in practice commercial sex in Japan has been decriminalized.[220]

During the 1980s, prostitution telephone clubs emerged in Japan.[221] Since 1996, Japanese law requires registration of telephone clubs and prohibits anyone under age eighteen from using the service to arrange for a date.[222]

NOTES

1. Vern and Bonnie Bullough, *Women and Prostitution: A Social History* (Prometheus Books, 1987), p. 1.

2. Id.

3. Nickie Roberts, *Whores in History: Prostitution in Western Society* (London: HarperCollins Publishers, 1992), p. 3.

4. Bullough, *supra* note 60, p. 14.

5. Roberts, *supra* note 62, p. 4.

6. *Id.*

7. Bullough, *supra* note 60, pp. 4–6.

8. Bullough, *supra* note 60, p. 14.

9. *Id.*

10. Bullough, *supra* note 60, p. 15.

11. Bullough *supra* note 60, p. 19 (citing Friedrich Engels, *The Origins of the Family, Private Property and the State In the Light of the Researches of Lewis H. Morgan* (reprinted, New York: International Publishers, 4th ed., 1942), p. 50).

12. Roberts, *supra* note 62, p. 7; and Bullough, *supra* note 60, p. 20.

13. Bullough, *supra* note 60, p. 16.

14. Bullough *supra* note 60, p. 17 [citing J. J. Bachofen, *"Mother Right" in Myth, Religion, and Mother Right, Selected Writings of Bachofen* (Ralph Manheim, translator, Princeton, N.J.: Princeton University Press, 1967) series nos. 84, 86].

15. *Id.*

16. Bullough, *supra* note 60, p. 21.

17. Bullough, *supra* note 60, p. 20 [citing Robert Briffault, *The Mothers: A Study of the Origins of Sentiments and Institutions* (3 vols., vol. III, New York: Macmillan, 1927)], pp. 21–13.

18. Bullough, *supra* note 60, pp. 22–23.

19. Bullough, *supra* note 60, p. 25 [citing Robert Briffault, *The Mothers: A Study of the Origins of Sentiments and Institutions* (3 vols., vol. III, New York: Macmillan, 1927)], pp. 76–78.

20. Bullough, *supra* note 60, pp. 22–23.

21. Bullough, *supra* note 60, p. 26.

22. Bullough, *supra* note 60, p. 27.

23. Bullough, *supra* note 60, p. 26.

24. Bullough, *supra* note 60, p. 27.

25. Vern L. and Bonnie Bullough, *Sin, Sickness & Sanity: A History of Sexual Attitudes* (New York: New American Library, 1977), p. 137.

26. Bullough, *supra* note 60, pp. 30–31.

27. Bullough, *supra* note 60, p. 31.

28. Bullough, *supra* note 60, p. 32.

29. Bullough, *supra* note 60, p. 33.

30. Interview of Dan Garrison, classics professor at Northwestern University, in *History's Mysteries: The History of Prostitution* (History Channel, television broadcast, Nov. 13, 2000).

31. Roberts, *supra* note 62, p. 14.

32. Bullough, *supra* note 60, p. 14.

33. Roberts, *supra* note 62, p. 15.

34. *Id.*

35. Roberts, *supra* note 62, p. 16.

36. Roberts, *supra* note 62, pp. 17–18.

37. Roberts, *supra* note 62, p. 20.

38. Bullough, *supra* note 60, p. 42.

39. *History's Mysteries: The History of Prostitution, supra* note 89.

40. Bullough, *supra* note 60, pp. 44–45.

41. *History's Mysteries: The History of Prostitution, supra* note 89.

42. Bullough, *supra* note 60, p. 45.

43. Bullough, *supra* note 60, p. 46 [citing Plato, Symposium (211B), edited and translated by W. R. M. Lamb] (London: William Heinemann, 1953).

44. Bullough, *supra* note 60, p. 48.

45. Interview of Professor Ruth Mazo Karras, author of *Common Women,* on *History's Mysteries: The History of Prostitution* (History Channel, television broadcast, Nov. 13, 2000).

46. Bullough, *supra* note 60, p. 49 (citing Suetonius, "Gaius Caligula," *Lives of the Caesars,* XL, edited and translated by J. C. Rolfe, 2 vols. (London: William Heinemann, 1950–51); and Pauly-Wissowa, *Real Encyclopaedie, der classichen Altertumwissenschaft* (Stuttgart: J. B. Metzler, 1914–1961) vol. XL, p. 1022).

47. Roberts, *supra* note 62, p. 41.

48. Roberts, *supra* note 62, p. 43.

49. Bullough, *supra* note 60, p. 50 (citing Pauly-Wissowa, *supra* note 105, op. cit., vol. XV, p. 1025).

50. Bullough, *supra* note 60, pp. 51–54.

51. Bullough, *supra* note 60, p. 54 (citing Aulus Gellius, *Attic Nights,* IV, iii, edited and translated by John C. Rolfe, 3 vols.) (reprinted, London: William Heinemann, 1952–1960).

52. Bullough, *supra* note 60, p. 55.

53. See generally, Bullough, *supra* note 60, pp. 52–59.

54. Bullough, *supra* note 60, p. 59.

55. *Id.*

56. Roberts, *supra* note 62, p. 57 (citing Elizabeth Fisher, *Woman's Creation: Sexual Evolution and the Shaping of Society)* (Garden City, N.Y.: Anchor Press, 1979, p. 379).

57. Roberts, *supra* note 62, p. 58 (citing I Timothy 2, 11–12).

58. Roberts, *supra* note 62, pp. 59–60.

59. Bullough, *supra* note 60, p. 63.

60. Roberts, *supra* note 62, p. 62.

61. *Id.*

62. Bullough, *supra* note 60, p. 65.

63. Bullough, *supra* note 60, p. 69.

64. *History's Mysteries: The History of Prostitution. supra* note 104.

65. Bullough, *supra* note 60, p. 70 (citing St. Augustine, *De Ordine,* II, iv, 12, in Migne, *Patrologa Latina,* XXXII).

66. Bullough, *supra* note 60, p. 110.

67. Bullough, *supra* note 84, p. 140.

68. Bullough, *supra* note 84, p. 110.

69. Bullough, *supra* note 84, p. 113.

70. Bullough, *supra* note 84, p. 114.

71. Bullough, *supra* note 84, p. 115.

72. Magdalene Meretrix, *A Brief History of Medieval Whores,* 1 (1999), http://www.realm-of-shade.com.

73. Bullough, *supra* note 84, p. 118.

74. Bullough, *supra* note 84, pp. 118–19.

75. Bullough, *supra* note 84, p. 119.

76. Bullough, *supra* note 84, p. 120.

77. Bullough, *supra* note 84. p. 123 (citing Iwan Bloch, *Die Prostitution,* 2 vols.) (Berlin: Louis Marcus, 1912, vol. I, pp. 676, 722).

78. Bullough, *supra* note 84, pp. 123–24.

79. Meretrix , *supra* note 131, p. 2.

80. Bullough, *supra* note 84, pp. 122–23.

81. Bullough, *supra* note 84, p. 127.

82. Roberts, *supra* note 62, p. 84 (citing Bullough, *supra* note 84, pp. 114–15).

83. Roberts, *supra* note 62, p. 85.

84. Roberts, *supra* note 62, p. 87.

85. Roberts, *supra* note 62, pp. 100–101.

86. Roberts, *supra* note 62, p. 101.

87. Roberts, *supra* note 62, p. 106.

88. Roberts, *supra* note 62, p. 103.

89. Roberts, *supra* note 62, p. 105.

90. Bullough, *supra* note 84, pp. 139–40.

91. Bullough, *supra* note 84, p. 141.

92. *Id.*

93. *Id.*

94. Bullough, *supra* note 84, p. 142 [quoting Martin Luther, *Letters of Spiritual Counsel* Theodore G. Tappert. ed. and, trans. (Philadelphia: Westminster Press, 1955, p. 293)].

95. Bullough, *supra* note 84, pp. 142–43.

96. Roberts, *supra* note 62, p. 111.

97. *Id.*

98. Bullough, *supra* note 84, p. 146 (citing Preserved Smith, *The Age of Reformation* (New York: Henry Holt, 1920), pp. 506–07).

99. Bullough, *supra* note 84, p. 147.

100. Bullough, *supra* note 84, pp. 148–52.

101. Bullough, *supra* note 84, pp. 152–53.

102. Roberts, *supra* note 62, p. 116.

103. Roberts, *supra* note 62, p. 118 (citing Nicolas Ome, The Reformation and the Red Light, *History Today,* March 1997, p. 40).

104. See generally, Bullough, *supra* note 84, pp. 153–55.

105. Roberts, *supra* note 62, p. 123.

106. Roberts, *supra* note 62, p. 129 (quoting G. R. Quaife, *Wanton Wenches and Wayward Wives* (London 1979 pp. 84–6).

107. Roberts, *supra* note 62, p. 130 (quoting Gamini Sallgado, *The Elizabethan Underworld)* (London 1984, pp. 56–7).

108. Roberts, *supra* note 62, p. 131 (quoting Lawrence Stone, *The Family, Sex and Marriage in England 1500–1800)* (London, 1977, p. 109).

109. Roberts, *supra* note 62, p. 131.

110. Roberts, *supra* note 62, pp. 132–33.

111. See generally Bullough, *supra* note 84, pp. 157–66.

112. *Id.*

113. Bullough, *supra* note 84, p. 167.

114. Bullough, *supra* note 84, p. 170.

115. Roberts, *supra* note 62, p. 156.

116. Bullough, *supra* note 84, p. 169.

117. Bullough, *supra* note 84, p. 170.

118. Bullough, *supra* note 84, p. 172 (citing A. J. B. Parent-Duchatelet, *De la prostitution dans la ville de Paris,* 2 vols. (Paris: J.B. Bailliere, 1837) vol. II, pp. 466–71).

119. Bullough, *supra* note 84, p. 173.

120. Bullough, *supra* note 84, p. 174.

121. Roberts, *supra* note 62, p. 158.

122. Bullough, *supra* note 84, p. 180.

123. Bullough, *supra* note 84, p. 182.

124. Roberts, *supra* note 62, pp. 164–65.

125. Bullough, *supra* note 84, p. 182.

126. Bullough, *supra* note 84, p. 183.

127. Roberts, *supra* note 62, p. 185.

128. Roberts, *supra* note 62, p. 186.

129. Bullough, *supra* note 84, p. 188.

130. Bullough, *supra* note 84, p. 123.

131. Bullough, *supra* note 84, p. 189.

132. Bullough, *supra* note 84, p. 190.

133. Bullough, *supra* note 84, p. 194.

134. *Id.*

135. Bullough, *supra* note 84, p. 195.

136. Bullough, *supra* note 84, p. 197.

137. Bullough, *supra* note 84, p. 191.

138. Bullough, *supra* note 84, pp. 200–01.

139. Bullough, *supra* note 84, p. 212.

140. *Prostitution: The American Occupation of Womanhood,* http://www.pimpz.org/prostitution.

141. Bullough, *supra* note 84, p. 216.

142. Bullough, *supra* note 84, p. 217.

143. Interview of Patricia Cline Cohen on *History's Mysteries: The History of Prostitution* (History Channel, television broadcast, Nov. 13, 2000).

144. *Id.*

145. Interview of Timothy J. Gilfoyle, author of *City of Eros* on *History's Mysteries: The History of Prostitution* (History Channel, television broadcast, Nov. 13, 2000).

146. *Id.*

147. *Id.*

148. *Prostitution: The American Occupation of Womanhood, supra* note 199, p. 2.

149. *History's Mysteries: The History of Prostitution, supra* note 204.

150. *Id.*

151. *Prostitution: The American Occupation of Womanhood, supra* note 199, p. 2.

152. Bullough, *supra* note 84, p. 222.

153. Bullough, *supra* note 84, p. 223.

154. *Prostitution: The American Occupation of Womanhood, supra* note 199, p. 3.

155. *History's Mysteries: The History of Prostitution, supra* note 204.

156. *Prostitution: The American Occupation of Womanhood, supra* note 199, p. 3.

157. Bullough, *supra* note 84, p. 224.

158. Bullough, *supra* note 84, p. 225.

159. *Prostitution: The American Occupation of Womanhood, supra* note 199, p. 3.

160. Interview of James R. Petersen, author of *The Century of Sex* on *History's Mysteries: The History of Prostitution* (History Channel, television broadcast, Nov. 13, 2000).

161. *Id.*

162. *Prostitution: The American Occupation of Womanhood, supra* note 199, p. 4.

163. *History's Mysteries: The History of Prostitution, supra* note 219.

164. *Id.*

165. *Id.*

166. Bullough, *supra* note 84, p. 227.

167. *History's Mysteries: The History of Prostitution, supra* note 219.

168. *Prostitution: The American Occupation of Womanhood, supra* note 199, p. 4.

169. Carol Leigh, A First Hand Look at the San Francisco Task Force Report on Prostitution, 10 *Hastings Women's L.J.* 59 , 59–60 Winter 1999.

170. *Id.*

171. *Id.*

172. *Id.*

173. *Id.*

174. *Id.*

175. Richard A. Posner, *Sex and Reason* (Cambridge, Mass.: Harvard University Press, 1998, 1992) p. 79.

176. Posner, *supra* note 236.

177. Posner and Silbaugh, *supra* note 47, p. 155.

178. *Id.*

179. Posner and Silbaugh, *supra* note 47, p. 156.

180. Posner and Silbaugh, *supra* note 47, pp. 156–87.

181. *Id.*

182. *Griswold* v. *Connecticut*, 381 U.S. 479, 85 S.Ct 1678 (U.S. Conn, 1965).

183. Posner and Silbaugh, *supra* note 47, p. 156.

184. *Id.*

185. *Id.*

186. Sylvia A. Law, Commercial Sex: Beyond Decriminalization, 73 *S. Cal. L. Rev.* 523, 567, March 2000.

187. Law, *supra* note 248, p. 568.

188. *Id.*

189. *Id.*

190. Law, *supra* note 248, pp. 559–60.

191. *Id.*

192. *Id.*

193. *Id.*

194. *Id.*

195. *Id.*

196. Law, *supra* note 248, p. 564.

197. Law, *supra* note 248, p. 562.

198. Law, *supra* note 248, p. 564.

199. *Id.*

200. Law, *supra* note 248, p. 554.

201. *Id.*
202. Law, *supra* note 248, p. 555.
203. *Id.*
204. *Id.*
205. *Id.*
206. *Id.*
207. Law, *supra* note 248, p. 556.
208. *Id.*
209. *Id.*
210. Law, *supra* note 248, p. 557.
211. *Id.*
212. *Id.*
213. Law, *supra* note 248, p. 558.
214. *Id.*
215. Law, *supra* note 248, p. 559.
216. *Id.*
217. *Id.*
218. Law, *supra* note 248, p. 556.
219. *Id.*
220. *Id.*
221. *Id.*
222. *Id.* Chapter 5.

Chapter 5

Gambling: The History of Criminalization

The history of gambling could fill volumes upon volumes of books. The desire to gamble has been suggested by some authorities as based on psychological stimuli inherent in human nature.[1] Certainly, the psychological stimuli are strong enough for gambling to have prevailed throughout thousands of years of human culture.

Our English words *gaming* and *gambling* derive from the Middle English word *game,* to amuse oneself. Gambling consists of three elements: consideration, chance, and reward. The lottery is probably the best example of pure gambling. *Consideration* is the cost of the ticket. The random selection or drawing of the ticket renders a result based on *chance.* The *reward* is the lucky winner's prize.[2]

Since before the time of Christ, gambling activity existed and prevailed in many cultures. Ancient Egyptians, Chinese, Japanese, Hebrews, Greeks, Romans, and Early Germanic tribes enjoyed games of chance. An ancient drawing on the wall of a burial vault in Beni Hasan, Egypt, dating about 2500 B.C. depicts a ball under one of several cups. British excavations in London have recovered remnants of 2,000-year-old dice games.[3] Other estimations that dice games appeared between the eras of poets Homer and Aristophanes, about 2300 B.C., rest on the fact that Homer never wrote of dice or similar games, and Aristophanes, the latter of the two, did.[4] "Loaded" dice were found in a Pompeii excavation site along with a tavern decorated with an ancient painting of a quarrel breaking out between two men playing dice.[5] Some authorities even suggest that certain uncovered artifacts dating from the Stone Age were used for gambling.

Governments have been regulating gambling since its inception. Records from India indicate a governmental department to regulate gambling in 321 B.C. The governmental department included a superintendent of public games who supplied dice and collected a fee of 5 percent of the receipts. Richard I of England and Phillip of France issued joint regulations to control gambling in the Christian army in 1190 during the Crusades. In England, proclamations or legislative enactments designed to control gambling were set forth in 1388, 1477, 1494, 1503, 1511, 1535, 1541, 1664, and 1699. In 1388, King Richard II enacted legislation directing all laborers and serving men to abandon "hand and foot ball, coits, dice, throwing of stone Keyles, and other such importune games," and concentrate on archery (probably for the preparation for war). In 1477, Edward IV added new games to the prohibited list, but in 1494 Henry VII created an exception allowing the games to be played at Christmastime. In the proclamation of 1541, Henry VIII repealed the various earlier gambling statutes and consolidated gambling law under a new, comprehensive statute. Gambling continued and thrived despite the proclamations.

In 1603, the common law of gambling and the government's ability to regulate gambling were changed by the decision in the Case of Monopolies, which held that all games were legal unless expressly made illegal by legislature. A slight modification to a prohibited game would make the game legal until the legislature could respond. Legislation, unsuccessful in preventing gambling, was aimed at controlling fraud and limiting wager amounts.[6]

In 1661, the Statute of Charles II, enacted to regulate fraudulent or excessive gambling, permitted gambling for any amount of money. However, the act was designed to protect the "younger sort" from "sundry, idle, loose, and disorderly persons...to the loss of their precious time and utter ruin of their estates and fortunes." It allowed the victim of cheating or fraud in gaming to sue for recovery of three times the sum lost. If the victim's suit succeeded, he would walk home with one-half the amount recovered. The crown would keep the other half. Furthermore, any person could sue in the victim's place and recover the victim's share as a reward if the victim failed to sue the fraudulent party within six months of the loss. The statute also regulated gambling debts and contracts. Gambling debts on credit in excess of £100 were judicially unenforceable, while the contracts for payment of the debt were "utterly void of none effect."

In 1699, William III prohibited lotteries by statute, which prescribed punishment for operating or participating in a lottery. Lotteries had been around well before the sixteenth century; the earliest were conducted by merchants hoping to dispose of excess stock. Soon after, governments recognized their profitability. Likewise, governments found lotteries attractive because they were easily controlled and their profitability was enhanced by monopoly power and wide coverage. Besides, they were an excellent source of revenue, being largely recession proof and far more popular than taxes.

William's statute exemplified the belief that lotteries were a dangerous form of gambling that deserved special attention. The preamble to the legislation stated

> Whereas several evil-disposed persons, for divers years last past, have set up many mischievous and unlawful games, called lotteries...in most of the eminent towns and places in England...and have thereby most unjustly and fraudulently got themselves great sums of money from the children and servants of several gentlemen, traders and merchants, and from other unwary persons, to the utter ruin and impoverishment of many families, and to the reproach of the English laws and government, by color of several patents or grants under the great seal of England...which said grants or patents are against the common good, trade, welfare and peace of his Majesty's kingdoms; for remedy whereof be if enacted, adjudged and declared...That all such lotteries, and all other lotteries are common and public nuisances, and that all grants, patents and licenses for such lotteries, are void and against the law.

However, the act authorized several charitable lotteries for the duration of their charters.

No matter the regulations, gambling remained popular especially with the British gentry. However, the large transfers of property involved in the gambling between gentlemen disrupted England's land-based aristocracy. To remedy the problem, Queen Anne enacted the Statute of Anne, which prevented large transfers of wealth. The statute provided "All Notes, Bills, Bonds, Judgments, Mortgages, or other Securities or Conveyances whatsoever" given in payment of gambling debts of more than £100 were "void, frustrate, or none Effect for all Intents and Purposes." The restrictions failed to curtail gambling but did end large transfers of wealth. The Statute of Anne and other common law doctrines became part of the law of every state in the New World.

GAMBLING IN THE NEW WORLD

Colonial Period

Gambling in the United States has a long history. The Puritans in the New World drafted the earliest gambling regulations. Their regulations were designed to attack unproductive use of time—not gambling. Idleness they reckoned a waste of time. However, colonists would gamble when it could be of good use, such as lotteries to finance public works.

In 1612, James I gave his permission for a lottery in the Virginia colony. The king chartered the Virginia Company of London to raise revenue for the benefit and support of the Jamestown settlement. One authorized means of raising the money was by conducting lotteries throughout England. Lotteries were the "real and substantial food, by which Virginia hath been nourished," as one American colonist noted. However, the nourishment became a burden on the British economy because the British purchased the tickets but did not receive any benefits from the profits. Accordingly, the Virginia Company's charter was revoked in 1624, and colonists soon turned to domestic lotteries.

Between 1746 and the Civil War, lotteries funded many public works, including road building; construction of bridges, canals, hospitals, light-houses and jails; promotions of literature; improvements to river naviga-tion; and development of schools, colleges, and even churches. In 1748, Philadelphia held a lottery to purchase cannons for the city's defense. In 1750, additions to Yale were financed by a Connecticut state lottery. Uni-versities such as Harvard, Dartmouth, Brown, and Union also benefited from public lotteries during this era. Lotteries provided funds for 47 col-leges, 300 elementary schools, and 200 church groups. The construction of Washington, D.C., was also financed by lotteries.

By 1832, approximately 420 lotteries existed in eight states. Their popu-larity leads to various forms of abuse. Deviant lottery operators would sell large blocks of tickets with no intention of holding a raffle and would flee with the proceeds. Lottery fraud was abundant; taking the form of fixed games or prizes inferior to those advertised. Thus, the majority of early gambling prohibition legislation focused on lotteries.

In the mid-1800s, serious lottery opposition began to mount. The oppo-sition was spurred by a general social reform that moved for peace, women's rights, education, and abolition of slavery. The U.S. Department of Justice noted:

In 1842, Democrats swept to power because of their opposition to lotteries. The lot-teries in turn were portrayed merely as an adjunct to a corrupt monopolistic bank-ing system dominated by the wealthy Whig power elite. The great moral fervor of the 1830s produced may reform movement....[A] class element [also] entered the picture. Lotteries, like corporations, made men wealthy without physical work. The poor, who worked hard for their fatback and beans, resented the state's approval of activities that made men wealthy without sweat. Thus, anti-lottery leaders were often enemies of all forms of speculation.

In 1833, Pennsylvania and Massachusetts passed statutes prohibiting lottery tickets sales and lottery operations. In 1834, New York followed with its prohibition, and by 1840, lotteries were prohibited in most states. However, Louisiana continued to run its infamous lottery, known as "The Serpent." The lottery was charted for a period of twenty-five years. By 1877, tickets were sold in almost every state in the nation. The Louisiana lottery at that time was a nationwide monopoly making estimated annual profits of up to $13 million and paying out more than $3 million per year.

The amount of money the lottery brought to the state made Louisiana lawmakers unwilling or unable to close it down. Lottery officials made generous donations to state projects. It is also speculated that The Serpent was run by the New York gambling syndicate and the operators controlled newspapers, banks, and public officials. In 1879, lottery officials even obtained ratification of a constitutional amendment expressly authorizing the lottery to continue until 1895.

The prohibitions on lotteries throughout the nation failed to prevent people from playing the Louisiana lottery. Ninety-three percent of the lottery's gross revenue came from outside Louisiana. The lottery was so well known that "a winning ticket was accepted everywhere in the country as the equivalent of a certified check."

Because Louisiana relied heavily on the lottery and the legislature refused to shut it down, reformers lobbied for federal intervention. President Harrison urged Congress to act. In 1890, Congress prohibited all distribution of lottery tickets by mail and in 1895 took the last step that ended the Louisiana lottery and banned all lottery material from interstate commerce. The Supreme Court upheld both acts. It also reaffirmed the states' use of police powers to control gambling. Government-sponsored gambling finally had met its end in the United States until the mid-1960s.

Modern Era

After the interstate commerce ban on lottery tickets, punch boards, prize cards, and gaming devices, gaming persisted as a localized endeavor despite general public disfavor. The cradle of gaming at this time was New Orleans. However, New Orleans continued to license gaming houses as well as other vices commonly housed in such dwellings.

The next wave of gambling in the United States began in the 1930s when Nevada legalized casino gambling. A unique partnership between the State of Nevada and Bugsy Siegal and Myer Lansky resulted in the first gambling casino in Nevada, the Flamingo. During its construction, Bugsy Siegal reportedly said in reference to the barren desert, "What you see here today is nothing...in ten years time, this'll be the biggest gambling center in the world." Bugsy's prediction was correct in that Las Vegas quickly became a nationally prominent entertainment vacation for relatively modest fees.

By the end of the 1930s twenty states had legalized pari-mutuel betting at horse tracks. The next major expansion of gaming occurred when New Jersey enacted gaming subject to strict zoning, rationalized as urban redevelopment. This began an era of locality-restricted legalized gambling. New Hampshire's state lottery, in 1964, spurred a radical change in the social perception of gaming. Once again, state legislatures promoted gaming as a means of financing state government. For example, Mississippi riverboat gaming business expanded once the government gave its approval and promoted the gaming as a direct state revenue source.

During this era, gambling for the benefit of recognized charities grew, as well. Churches in particular promoted charity gambling through bingo nights and annual lotteries to benefit congregations.

Despite the existence of a few legalized avenues of gaming, illegal gaming continued. The federal government began dealing with illegal gambling on a national level in 1948. Congress passed a statute that prohibited gambling ships operating off the coasts of the United States. Much of the legislation aimed at preventing the rise and establishment of organized criminal operations. In 1950, the Special Senate Committee to Investigate Organized Crime in Interstate Commerce began hearings that produced statutes that targeted organized crime. This series of statutes, known as the Johnson Act, prohibited the interstate transportation of gambling devices. In particular, the Johnson Act prohibited use of mails, federal wire, and wireless communications frequencies, or interstate commerce to transport gaming equipment devices or carry on gaming activities. The legislative intent was to support the states in their regulation of gambling activity. The legislation allowed sovereign states to seek exemption from the act, thereby delegating the regulation of gaming to the states.

Nevada took advantage of exemption from the Johnson Act, which required states to make an affirmative statement legitimizing gaming. Nevada had no problem stating that gaming was vitally important to the state's economy and general welfare of its citizens. The federal legislation exempted Nevada from most applicable federal regulations regarding transportation, possession, and use of gaming devices in interstate commerce.

In the 1950s, the federal government created statutes to control the spread to gambling by authorizing the Internal Revenue Service to monitor and tax betting through excise and occupational stamp taxes. In the 1960s, the federal government began a crusade against organized crime, focusing on the belief that illegal gambling provided much of the revenue for organized crime syndicates. Congress passed into legislation three statutes that attacked interstate gambling facilities and prohibited use of interstate public communications facilities to transmit wagering information. In 1968, the Omnibus Crime Control and Safe Streets Act passed, allowing the Federal Bureau of Investigation to use wiretapping in order to catch bookmakers.

In 1970, federal control over interstate gambling expanded with the Organized Crime Control Act. The act defined a gambling business as one that involves five or more persons in conducting, financing, directing, managing, or ownership, and that does a gross volume of $2,000 per day or that operates continuously over a thirty-day period and that violates the law of the state where it occurs. The act prohibits those involved in these operations from conspiring to obstruct justice.

These statutes of the United States Code did not apply to states that had legislated legal lotteries and gambling into operation. New Hampshire reintroduced the state lottery in 1964. New York and New Jersey followed by introducing lotteries in 1967 and 1970, respectively. These lotteries were unsuccessful until New Jersey developed a computer-based weekly game in 1971. Cheaper tickets, convenient sales, more prizes, and a large jackpot helped the new style of lotto succeed. By 1974, eleven states had jumped on the bandwagon. Currently, lotteries are popular forms of gambling in at least thirty-three states. Gambling fever is high, with several states allowing pari-mutuel betting, casino gambling, riverboat gambling, or other forms of licensed or state-sponsored gambling.

Indian Gaming

Opening the Door for Indian Gaming: The Seminole and Carbazon Decisions

The struggle for tribal autonomy has been a reoccurring theme in Native American history. The legal relationship between tribes and federal and state governments has certainly been far from consistent. Throughout the nineteenth and twentieth centuries, Native Americans have been the victims of federal policy that has varied between policies of assimilation and paternalism and promoting self-sufficiency and autonomy. The *consent principle*, a policy of gaining tribal consent before acquiring lands or exercising political authority, was quickly eroded in the early nineteenth century as the federal government began a policy of removal and forced many Native Americans to move west.[7] The later decades of the nineteenth century marked the beginning of assimilation policies and distribution of private land allotments among tribes.[8] The federal government's paternalistic relationship with Native Americans changed significantly during the 1960s as the federal government began to promote tribal self-sufficiency and preservation of distinct tribal cultures.[9] Though the concept of tribal self-sufficiency was a promising way to promote autonomy, Native Americans still suffered from poor economic development. Their unique political status with the federal government, which has been characterized as "that of a ward to his guardian,"[10] permitted Native Americans to pursue gaming without state interference. Native American tribes viewed gaming as a viable reaction to federal encouragement of economic and political self-sufficiency. However, the states, which have throughout history claimed a right to regulate illegal activities taking place on their land, voiced strong opposition to Indian gaming. Thus, in the past twenty years, Indian gaming has served as the forum for the struggle between Native American autonomy and state attempts to regulate Native American activities.

This latest struggle began with the 1979 opening of a high-stakes bingo hall by the Seminole tribe of Florida, which led to the 1981 landmark decision of *Seminole Tribe* v. *Butterworth*.[11] The Seminole tribe sought an injunction against a Broward County, Florida, sheriff from enforcing a Florida statute that regulated bingo games and would have prevented the tribe from continuing its gaming operation. The crucial issue in *Butterworth* was whether the state could enforce its legislation of gaming on Indian lands. In 1953, Congress had passed Public Law 280, which transferred criminal and civil authority over Indian lands from the federal government to five states.[12] It was later held in *Bryan* v. *Itasca County*[13] that Public Law 280 gave states no jurisdiction over purely regulatory matters.[14] The *Bryan* court distinguished between criminal/prohibitory laws, which the state could enforce on Indian lands, and civil/regulatory laws, which it could not.[15] This distinction became important in *Butterworth* because the Supreme Court analyzed Florida's bingo statute in light of the criminal/prohibitory and civil/regulatory scheme of the *Bryan* court, reiterating the general proposition that states cannot *regulate* Indian activity.[16] The court held that, because Florida law allowed bingo activities in civic, charitable, religious, and other forms, bingo did not violate public policy and therefore was "regulatory" in nature.[17] The court concluded that the Florida statute could therefore not be enforced on Indian land.[18]

The Supreme Court affirmed the criminal/prohibitory and civil/regulatory scheme of the *Butterworth* decision six years later in *California* v. *Carbazon Band of Mission* Indians. The Carbazon and Marongo tribes sought a declaratory judgment that neither California nor Riverside County could enforce gambling laws on Indian reservations.[19] The Carbazon and Marongo tribes sought a declaratory judgment that neither California nor Riverside County could enforce gambling laws on Indian reservations.[20] The court stated that "[S]tate jurisdiction is pre-empted ... if it interferes or is incompatible with federal and tribal interests reflected in federal law, unless the state interests at stake are sufficient to justify the assertion of state authority."[21] The court held that the state interest in preventing bingo enterprises and organized crime was not a compelling enough reason to regulate tribal bingo when compared with the federal and tribal interests in supporting such enterprises.[22] The *Carbazon* court was not persuaded by arguments that high-stakes bingo was a misdemeanor under California law and therefore fell within the criminal/prohibitory classification.[23] Because California permitted certain gaming activities, and even promoted gambling activity with a state-run lottery, the court concluded that its laws were merely regulatory and thus unenforceable on Indian lands.[24] The *Carbazon* decision essentially gave tribes the green light for gaming activities as long as the state they were located in did not expressly prohibit the activity.[25]

Congressional Response: The Indian Gaming Regulatory Act (IGRA)

The year following the *Carbazon* decision Congress reacted to state concerns of unregulated Indian gaming by passing the Indian Gambling Regulatory Act (IGRA).[26] The act was to "provide a statutory basis for the operation of gaming by Indian tribes as a means of promoting tribal economic development, self-sufficiency, and strong tribal government,"[27] while at time shield gaming from "organized crime and other corrupting influences."[28] IGRA set up a three-tiered classification of gaming on Indian reservations. Class I gaming consist of "social games solely for prizes of minimal value or traditional forms of Indian gaming engaged in by individuals as part of, or in connection with, tribal ceremonies or celebrations."[29] The act gives exclusive jurisdiction over this type of gaming to the Indian tribes that operate the activities.[30] Class II gaming consists of games such as bingo, lotto, punch boards, tip jars, and other similar games.[31] Card games explicitly authorized or not explicitly prohibited by the state are included in Class II gaming[32] provided they are played in conformity with state regulations as to operation hours, wager limitations, and pot sizes.[33] Congress made clear that banking card games, such as blackjack or baccarat are not included in Class II gaming,[34] as well as "electronic or electromechanical facsimiles of any game of chance or slot machine of any kind."[35] Class II gaming is permissible only if the state in which a tribe is located allows such gaming for any purpose,[36] and if the tribe adopts an ordinance approved by the chairman of the National Indian Gaming Commission (NIGC).[37] An important provision of the act is that a Class II gaming ordinance will be approved only if the net revenues of gaming operations are used exclusively to fund tribal government operations, provide for the general welfare of the tribe, promote economic development, benefit charitable organizations, or help fund local governmental agencies.[38] Tribes must also submit to an annual audit and comply with various background checks.[39] Regulation of Class II gaming falls entirely within jurisdiction of the NIGC.

Any gaming that does not fit in Class I or Class II, including lucrative casino games such as blackjack and slot machines, is Class III gaming under IGRA.[40] Class III gaming, like Class II gaming, requires that a tribe adopt a resolution approved by the NIGC chairman [41] and that the state in which they reside permits that type of gaming "for any purpose."[42] Thus, if a state permits charity blackjack gambling, a tribe may seek to have that game included in its casino operations. Before a tribe may operate Class III gaming, however, it must form a compact with the state, subject to the

approval of the secretary of the interior.[43] This final requirement has generated the most criticism from both states and the Indian tribes. Once a
tribe approves a gaming ordinance, a state must negotiate in good faith
with the tribe in determining the governing of gaming activities.[44] The
compact reached between the tribe and the state must include provisions
regarding application of civil laws and regulation, taxation, remedies for
breach of contract, and standards for the operation of gaming facilities.[45]
After a 180-day period from when the tribe requests a state to enter into
negotiations, a tribe may initiate a cause of action if a state has not
responded to the request or failed to respond in good faith.[46] United States
district courts have jurisdiction over any cause of action arising from a
state's failure to negotiate in good faith.[47] In considering "good faith" on
the part of the state, the court may take into account "the public interest,
public safety, criminality, financial integrity, and adverse economic
impacts on existing gaming activities," as well as the state demand for
direct taxation.[48] If the court finds that the state has not negotiated in good
faith, the court must order a compact to be concluded within sixty days.[49]
Failing agreement after sixty days, both the state and the tribe must submit their last best offer to a court-appointed mediator.[50] If the state does
not consent within sixty days to the mediator's proposed compact, the
secretary of the interior must describe procedures consistent with the
mediator's proposed compact, the provisions of the act, and "the relevant
provisions of the laws of the state."[51]

IGRA: Continual Disputes Between States and Tribes

Indians oppose the compact provision because, they argue, it undermines their sovereignty by forcibly subjecting them to state regulation and
violating the federal trust doctrine toward Indians.[52] Many argue that
tribal economic sovereignty has a direct effect on legal and political sovereignty.[53] Thus, they believe that tribes should be left to determine how to
best develop their own economy without restrictive legislation such as
IGRA.[54] They consider tribal sovereignty the impetus for creating an economic niche for Indians and believe that continual congressional legislation and court decisions jeopardize prosperity and erode Indian rights.[55]

States object to IGRA's compacting provision in part on the grounds
that it violates the Tenth Amendment by making negotiation regarding
regulation of Indian activity compulsory. The thrust of this argument is
that Congress has the power, and indeed the responsibility, to regulate
Indian affairs via the Indian Commerce clause. The states argue that by
compelling negotiation, the federal government requires states to admin-
ister a regulation scheme that is federal in nature and that undermines
their sovereignty.[56] This argument, though, has had only marginal success
because the courts are hesitant to elevate a requirement to negotiate in

good faith to the status of requiring enactment or enforcement of federal law.[57]

States have made a stronger argument that IGRA violates the Eleventh Amendment by attempting to grant federal court jurisdiction over a state that has not consented to suit. In 1989, in *Pennsylvania v. Union Gas, Co.*,[58] the Supreme Court held that Congress may, via the Article I interstate commerce clause, abrogate a state's Eleventh Amendment immunity right.[59] The debate soon turned to whether legislation such as IGRA, exercised under the Indian commerce clause could be interpreted as an appropriate vehicle to abrogate Eleventh Amendment immunity. In essence, it was unclear whether the Union Gas holding could be read to include acts made exclusively under the Indian commerce clause.[60] This question was answered in 1996 in *Seminole Tribe of Florida v. Florida*.[61] When the State of Florida refused to enter negotiations for a tribal-state compact, the Seminole tribe sued the state alleging that it violated the good faith requirement of IGRA.[62] The Seminole tribe argued that Congress had abrogated the state's Eleventh Amendment immunity when it enacted IGRA and that the *Union Gas* holding includes acts made pursuant to the Indian commerce clause.[63] The Court of Appeals for the Eleventh Circuit had held that the *Union Gas* decision did not extend to the Indian commerce clause and therefore Congress could not abrogate the state's Eleventh Amendment immunity under IGRA.[64] The Supreme Court disagreed with the court of appeals that a distinction between the Indian commerce clause and the interstate commerce clause made *Union Gas* inapplicable.[65] However, the Court strongly criticized the plurality decision of the *Union Gas* decision and ultimately overruled it,[66] thereby eliminating tribes' ability to bring suit against states in federal court.

The impact of the *Seminole* decision on Indian gaming is not yet clear. The Supreme Court did not specifically address the applicability of the remaining IGRA procedures in ruling that the act did not abrogate a state's Eleventh Amendment immunity. Though tribes can no longer sue a state in federal Court, one interpretation of the IGRA is that the secretary of the interior may now directly prescribe a regulation scheme for gaming operations.[67] The State of Florida recently challenged this interpretation and filed suit against the secretary of the interior for issuing rules regarding Class III gaming without a compact with the state.[68] Governor Jeb Bush is an ardent critic of casino gambling in Florida and argues that only the state may regulate tribal gambling.[69] In light such strong state opposition and the uncertainties of legal recourse for tribes after the *Seminole* decision, Congress is expected to amend IGRA. Some scholars argue that in amending IGRA, Congress should entirely leave out the state's role in regulation, using its plenary power to regulate gaming without the states if the states continue to frustrate IGRA.[70] However, proposed amendments to IGRA seem to indicate that the states will have more, rather than less, regulation power over Indian gaming.[71] Until such time, many states will likely attempt to prevent unregulated Class III gaming, especially in the states where casino operations exist without compacts.[72]

In California, Indian gaming has become a hot political topic. When the state threatened to shut down casinos operating without a compact, the tribes sought approval from California voters to operate video and banking card games. Proposition 5 became one of the most highly financed campaigns in the state's history. Indian tribes spent $63.2 million for the campaign, while the opponents to the measure, which included many Las Vegas casinos, spent $25.4 million.[73] The proposition passed with overwhelming voter support, but was ultimately struck down by the California Supreme Court. The court held that a constitutional amendment, rather than a revision of the state statute, would be required to change California's gaming law. A vote on the amendment was set for March 2000. An amendment, if approved, could allow unlimited casino gambling on Indian reservations. Governor Grey Davis, in an effort to both curtail the potential for unlimited gaming and to ensure the legality of tribal gaming, established twenty-year compacts with most of California's 107 tribes. These compacts allow most tribes to nearly double their existing amount of slot machines already in operation in exchange for their pledge to put some gaming limits on the proposed amendment.[74] If the amendment meets voter approval, big gaming, perhaps even to the scale of Las Vegas casinos will have a happy home in California.

Gaming Prosperity

As the situation in California illustrates, Indian tribes are unlikely to relinquish gaming rights without a fight. Across the nation, gaming has created an economic niche for Indian tribes. As one tribal council member put it. "We're not making baskets anymore. We're making money."[75] An estimated 310 gaming operations exist on Indian reservations in twenty-eight states.[76] More than 200 of the nation's 558 tribes operate some form of gaming.[77] These operations account for about 20 percent of all U.S. casino revenues.[78] The largest of these casinos is the Foxwoods Resort Casino in Connecticut, operated by the Mashantucket Pequot tribe. The Foxwoods Casino, which employs about 12,000 people, brings in an estimated $1.5 billion a year, making it one of the world's most profitable gaming operations.[79]

Most Indian tribes argue that this newfound gaming wealth has had a positive impact on their lives. Perhaps the most beneficial aspect of gaming has been a dramatic increase in employment opportunities. Between 1989 and 1995, unemployment has dropped an estimated 13 percent on reservations that operate casinos.[80] In Washington State, the Tulalip tribe's unemployment rate is down to 10 percent from 65 percent when it first opened casino operations in 1991.[81] The Oneida nation of Wisconsin reports even more dramatic numbers, with an unemployment rate below 10 percent, down from 80 percent in the 1960s.[82]

Many argue that gaming is also helping to restore Indian sovereignty by giving tribes economic opportunity, which in turn gives them political leverage and the ability to create educational opportunities.[83] The National Indian Gaming Association argues that Indian gaming is the only economic development tool that has ever worked on Indian reservations.[84] This may be largely because, unlike traditional commercial gaming, IGRA requires that profits go to governmental and charitable purposes that directly benefit the tribe. Gaming has thus been seen as a vehicle to combat many of the economic and social problems on reservations. For example, the Tulalip tribe plans to use casino revenues to build a new health clinic to help combat alcoholism.[85] The tribe is also planning on building its own school and opening a new business park.[86] In Michigan, the Grand Traverse Band of Ottawa and the Chippewa Indians are also planning on building new health facilities as well as creating new investment funds for its members.[87] The Oneida casino in Wisconsin used some of its gaming funds to build a $10-million hotel, establish a cattle farm, a testing laboratory, and shopping centers.[88] In Connecticut, the Mashantucket Pequot tribe has created a museum and research center to help preserve its heritage.[89] Indians are also quick to point out that many states are also benefiting from casino revenues. For example, in 1988, the State of Connecticut received $170 million from its quarter interest in the Mashantucket Pequot's slot revenues.[90]

The success of gaming in creating opportunities for Native Americans is encouraging. Native Americans have proven that gaming revenues can be utilized to promote prosperity among tribes. In addition, although IGRA has had problems, it has proven effective in striking the balance between legally sanctioning gaming on Native American lands while ensuring that profits are utilized responsibly and fairly. Congress should be encouraged by the fact that it can play an active role in managing gaming activities.

Because Native Americans have received such beneficial results from gaming, they are unlikely to welcome either increased regulation through IGRA or legalization of gaming in nontribal areas. Native American fears about losing the gaming niche, while understandable, is only speculative. The success of professionally run operations such as the Mashantucket Pequots' Foxwoods Casino would undoubtedly remain profitable should gaming be legalized across the nation. However, even if some operations lose business to more attractive operations, the ultimate winner is the American public. Fairly and competitively run gaming operations benefit both Native American and non-Native American consumers.

National Gambling Impact Study

In 1996, Congress created the National Gambling Impact Commission through Public Law 104169. The commission was to conduct a comprehensive study of both the social and economic impacts of gambling in America. The study examined six aspects of gaming in America: (1) a review of policies and practices of American Indian gaming; (2) an evaluation of crime and gaming; (3) an assessment of problems of pathological gambling; (4) a review of gambling's effects on the economy in general; (5) a review of how gaming promotes revenues for state, local, and Native American governments; and, (6) a review and assessment of Internet gambling. The nine-member panel held hearings throughout the country for two years, listening to testimony from various opponents and proponents of gambling.

The final report was made public on June 18, 1999, and included seventy-six recommendations for lawmakers to consider. Among the commission's recommendations were bans on college sports gambling, Internet gambling, credit card cash-advancement machines in casinos, and gambling for those under twenty-one years of age. The commission also criticized "convenience" gambling, operation of gaming machines in non-casinos such as gas stations and convenience stores. The commission also strongly urged that states curtail marketing lotteries to poorer citizens.

To help combat the problems of pathological gambling, the commission recommended that states and tribal governments adopt a gambling privilege tax and dedicate the revenues to create and support programs such as research of pathological problems, public awareness campaigns, and support for gambling addiction treatment facilities and treatment costs.

The commission report recognized the struggle between states and tribes over gaming and recommended that IGRA's classes of gambling be more clearly defined and that any Indian gaming be consistent with the state's gambling policies. In light of the controversies around the IGRA compacting provision, the report urges Congress to outline a clear process to resolve disputes between tribes and states. The report recommends empowering an impartial decision-maker to approve compacts into which states refuse to enter. Overall, in terms of Indian gaming, the report seems to simultaneously recognize the economic and political benefits of gaming for Indians and yet encourage a stronger role of federal regulation via the National Indian Gaming Commission.

The report's most controversial measure is an overall recommendation for a moratorium on the establishment of new gambling. The report concedes that gambling has become widespread throughout America, generating about 700,000 jobs and $21 billion in wages. However, the commission believed that a "pause" in the growth of gaming is necessary in order to "Encourage governments to do what, to date, few, if any, have done: to survey the results of their decisions and to determine if they have chosen wisely: to ask if their decisions are in accord with the public good, if harmful effects could be remedied, if benefits are being unnecessarily passed up."

Reactions to the impact study have been mixed. The report is not binding upon the gaming industry, but rather suggests issues to be addressed by the legislature. Senator Richard Bryan of Nevada adamantly denounces the commission's report: "[The commission] wasted $5 million in taxpayer funds to find out that Americans have known all along that a great majority of Americans, who choose to gamble, do so responsibly." Senator Bryan may have support for such an assertion in the impact study itself, which estimated that the pathological gamblers compose about one percent of the gambling population.[91] Senator Bryan also commented that "instead of Congress working on worthwhile legislative efforts needed by the American people, we will find Congress wasting time on the anti-gambling crusade which will undoubtedly manage somehow to use this report to fuel their campaign."[92] Indeed, as Senator Bryan predicted, opponents of gaming believe the report has dealt a blow to the gaming industry. Tom Grey, executive director of the National Coalition Against Legalized Gambling, has likened legalized gambling to the tobacco industry. Grey postulates that as the evidence of the problems of gaming are let out, such as in the recent impact study, big money may be made in suing an industry that he believes knowingly encourages addiction.[93] As Grey puts it: "You contain them, you constrain them, and ultimately they conquer themselves. That's basic infantry 101."[94]

Whether the impact study will substantively change gaming in American is debatable. Clearly, though, the issue is now a hot legal topic with political maneuvering on both sides. In 1998, for example, the casinos contributed $5.7 million to candidates and national party committees.[95] This struggle between proponents and opponents of legalized gambling is likely to continue until the federal government takes a clear stance on gaming. Many proponents offer little credence to the cause for legalization by failing to offer a consistent stance on the issue. The strange alliance between the Las Vegas casinos and the moral opponents of gaming in California's recent referendum is illustrative of the hypocrisy: they continue to condemn tribal gaming while reaping the benefits of unfair lottery practices.

The impact study should be a wake-up call to Congress to end both the political wrangling and the unfair and morally objectionable practices of both the states and many gaming operations. The impact study's recognition that gaming revenues can be taxed and used to combat the gambling purported problems seems a step in the right direction. If gaming problems are as widespread as gaming opponents claim they are, the potential availability of funds to help combat gaming's various social ills should be an inducement. Such taxes could indeed be mandated on a national level, but until the federal government gives legal sanction to gambling, the potential of any such tax will remain unrealized.

Two points should therefore be gleaned from the impact study. First, Congress should realize that gaming operations are profitable and beneficial in many respects. Second, Congress should realize that by taking advantage of the profitable nature of gaming by legalizing, regulating, and taxing operations, it could help combat the many social problems the impact study condemns.

NOTES

1. John Ashton, *The History of Gambling in England* (Montclair, N.J.: Patterson Smith, 1898, 1969) p. 2, cited by Ronald J. Rychlack, Lotteries, Revenues and Social Costs: A Historical Examination of State-Sponsored Gambling, 34 *B.C. L. Rev.* 11, 1992).

2. *Id.*, note 1, p. 14.

3. Rychlak *supra* note 1, pp. 16–17.

4. Mike Roberts, The National Gambling Debate: Two Defining Issues, 18 *Whittier L. Rev.* 579, 582, 1997.

5. Rychlack, *supra* note 1, p. 1.

6. Rychlack, *supra* note 1, p. 17.

7. Jason Kalish, Do the States Have an Ace in the Hole, or Should the Indians Call Their Bluff? Tribes Caught in the Power Struggle between the Federal Government and the States, 38 *Ariz. L. Rev.* 1345, Winter 1996.

8. William N. Thompson and Diana Dever, *Gambling Enterprise and the Restoration of Native American Sovereignty, Gambling: Public Policies and the Social Sciences* (William R. Eadington and Judy A. Cornelius, eds., Reno, Nev.: Institute for the Study of Gambling and Commercial Gaming, 1997), p. 295.

9. William N. Thompson, *History, Development, and Legislation of Native American Casino Gaming, Legalized Casino Gaming in the United States* (Cathy H. C. Hsu, ed., Binghamton, NY: Haworth Hospitality Press, 1999), p. 44.

10. *Cherokee Nation v. Georgia*, 30 U.S. (5. Pet.) 1, 20 (1831).

11. *Seminole Tribe of Florida v. Butterworth*, 658 F.2d 310 (5th Cir. 1981).

12. Thompson and Dever, *supra* note 8, p. 300.

13. Bryan v. Itasca County, Minnesota, 426 U.S. 373 (1976).

14. *Id.*, pp. 378–84.

15. *Id.*

16. *Id.*, p. 313.

17. *Id.*, p. 314.

18. *Id.*, p. 315.

19. *California v. Carbazon Band of Mission Indians*, 480 U.S. 202 (1987).

20. *Id.*, p. 206.

21. *Id.*, p. 216 (quoting from *New Mexico v. Mescalero Apache Tribe*, 462 U.S. at 333, 334).

22. *Id.*, pp. 221–222.

23. *Id.*, pp. 211.

24. *Id.*

25. Eric D. Jones, The Indian Gaming Regulatory Act: A Forum for Conflict Among the Plenary Power of Congress, Tribal Sovereignty, and the Eleventh Amendment, 18 *Vt. L. Rev.* 127, Fall 1993. See also Linda King Kading, State Authority to Regulate Gaming Within Indian Lands: The Effect of the Indian Gaming Regulatory Act, 41 *Drake L. Rev.* 317, 1992.

26. Pub. L. No. 100–497, 102 Stat. 2467 (1988). Codified at 25 U.S.C. §§2701–21 (1988); 18 U.S.C. §§1166–68 (1988).

27. 25 U.S.C. § 2702 (1).

28. 25 U.S.C. § 2702 (2).

29. 25 U.S.C. § 2703 (6).

30. 25 U.S.C. § 2703.

31. 25 U.S.C. § 2703 (A)(i).

32. 25 U.S. C §2703 (7)(A)(ii)(I)-(II).

33. 25 U.S.C. § 2703 (7)(A)(ii)(II).

34. 25 U.S.C. § 2703 (7)(B)(i).

35. 25 U.S.C. § 2703 (7)(B)(ii).

36. 25 U.S.C. § 2710 (b)(1)(A).

37. 25 U.S.C. § 2710 (b)(1)(B).

38. 25 U.S.C. § 2710 (b)(2).

39. 25 U.S.C. § 2710.

40. 25 U.S.C. § 2703 (8).

41. 25 U.S.C. § 2710 (d)(1)(A).

42. 25 U.S.C. § 2710 (d)(1)(B).

43. 25 U.S.C. § 2710 (d).

44. 25 U.S.C. § 2710 (d)(3)(A).

45. 25 U.S.C. § 2710 (d)(3)(C).

46. 25 U.S.C. § 2710 (d)(7)(B).

47. 25 U.S.C. § 2710 (d)(7)(A)(i).

48. 25 U.S.C. § 2710 (d)(7)(B)(iii)(I)-(II).

49. 25 U.S.C. § 2710(d)(7)(B)(iii).

50. 25 U.S.C. § 2710(d)(7)(B)(iv).

51. 25 U.S.C. § 2710 (d)(7)(B)(vii)(I)-(II).

52. Jones, *supra* note 25, pp. 135–147 (Jones argues that, although Congress may use its plenary powers to abrogate tribal sovereignty via the Indian commerce clause, it is limited by three factors. First, the abrogation must not be ambiguous. Second, the federal government must, under the "trust doctrine," protect tribal interests. Third, when tribal sovereignty is abrogated, it is not subordinate to the states wherein they reside, but rather to the federal government. Jones recognizes that the federal government may relinquish jurisdiction over the tribes to the state in some circumstances, but to do so it is limited by its trust responsibilities.).

53. Frank R. Pommersheim, Tribal-State Relations: Hope for the Future? 36 *S.D. L. Rev.*, 1991, note 333, at p. 4, cited in Rebecca Tsosie, Negotiating Economic Survival: The Consent Principle and Tribal-State Compacts Under the Indian Gaming Regulatory Act, 29 *Ariz. St. L.J.*, 95–96, Spring 1997.

54. Tsosie, *supra* note 53, p. 26.

55. Jess Green, Economic Development and Gaming, 9 *St. Thomas L. Rev.* 149, Fall 1996.

56. Keith David Bilezerian, Ante Up or Fold: States Attempt to Play Their Hand While Indian Casinos Cash In, 29 *New Eng. L. Rev.* 463, Winter 1995.

57. Kevin J. Worthen and Wayne R. Farnsworth, Who Will Control the Future of Indian Gaming? "A Few Pages of History Are Worth a Volume of Logic," 1996 *BYU L. Rev.* 407, 1996. See also, Bilezerian, *supra* note 56, pp. 474–483.

58. *Pennsylvania* v. *Union Gas,* 491 U.S. 1 (1989).

59. *Id.,* p. 19.

60. Bilezerian, *supra,* note 56, pp. 483–487.

61. *Seminole Tribe of Florida* v. *Florida et al.,* 517 U.S. 44 (1996).

62. *Id.,* p. 44.

63. *Id.,* p. 55.

64. *Id.,* p. 53.

65. *Id.,* p. 63.

66. *Id.,* p. 66.

67. Martha A. Field, The Seminole Case, Federalism, and the Indian Commerce Clause, 29 *Ariz. St. L. J.,* 20–21, Spring 1997.

68. Charles Flowers, Federal Impact Study Not Expected to Alter Tribal Gambling, *Knight-Ridder Tribune Business News: Indian Country Today,* Monday, June 28, 1999.

69. Jeff Testerman and Jo Becker, Florida Files Suit to Block Casino-Style Gambling, *St. Petersburg Times,* Tuesday, April 13, 1999.

70. Kalish, , *supra* note 7, pp. 1369–1371.

71. Worthen and Farnsworth, *supra* note 57, pp. 441–443.

72. Five states operate without compacts with the state. Dan Seligman, *The Winning Hand.* The $8 Billion Indian Gaming Industry Remains in Fierce Growth Phase. This Can't Be Good for Non-Indian Gamers, *Forbes,* Monday, July 26, 1999.

73. Dan Caesar, California and Nevada Keep Upping Ante in Battle to Be "Casino Center of the World," *St. Louis Dispatch,* Monday, September 27, 1999.

74. Lynda Gledhill, Tribe Signs Gambling Pact, *San Francisco Chronicle,* Wednesday, September 15, 1999. See also, Dan Morain and Tom Gorman, Davis and Key Gaming Tribe Reach Deal on Gaming, *Los Angeles Times,* Wednesday, September 15, 1999.

75. Larry Bivens, Indians Find Clout in Newfound Wealth: Awash in Casino Cash, They're Tackling Poverty and Economic Issues, *Detroit News,* September 12, 1999, quoting Carol Shanks, a tribal council member for the Chippewa Tribe in Michigan.

76. Charles T. Jones and Mark A. Hutchison, Indian Tribes Hit Jackpot with Gaming, *Sunday Oklahoman,* Sunday, September 12, 1999.

77. Jessica McBride, Gambling's Blessing and Curse, *Milwaukee Journal Sentinel,* Sunday, August 22, 1999.

78. Seligman, *supra* note 72.

79. Jones and Hutchison, *supra* note 76.

80. Mike Rogoway, The New Indian Economy, *The Columbian,* Sunday, September 5, 1999, p. 1.

81. Jones and Hutchison, *supra* note 76.

82. McBride, *supra* note 77.

83. Thompson and Dever, *supra* note 8, pp. 295–315.

84. National Indian Gaming Association, *Tribal Gaming Benefits the Reservations, Legalized Gambling.* (Rod L. Evans and Mark Hance, eds., Peru, Ill.: Open Court, 1998), p. 338.

85. Rogoway, *supra* note 80.

86. *Id.*

87. Bivens, *supra* note 75.

88. Thompson, *supra* note 9, p. 56.

89. Rachel V. Katz, A Tribe Rediscovers Its Heritage; Community: Once Nearly Extinct, Connecticut's Mashantucket Pequot Indians Have Built a Thriving Community Fueled by Highly Profitable Gambling Casino and Resort, *Baltimore Sun,* Thursday, August 5, 1999.

90. Gambling on the Future, *Economist,* Saturday, June 26, 1999.

91. Warren Cohen, Don't Bet on Gambling Reform Anytime Soon, *U.S. News & World Report,* June 14, 1999.

92. Government Press Releases by Federal Document Clearing House. June 18, 1999.

93. Gambling on the Future, *supra* note 90.

94. *Id.*

95. J. Scott Orr, Gambling Industry Confronts New Deal: Congress Examines Bills Aimed at Growth, *Harrisburg Patriot,* Monday, October 4, 1999. Chapter 6.

Chapter 6

Victimless Crimes and the Ninth Amendment

The history of the Bill of Rights, and in particular the Ninth Amendment, begins with the constitutional convention in Philadelphia in 1787. Similar to our modern two-party system in the United States, the framers of the Constitution were divided into two factions: the Federalists and Antifederalists. The main issue on which the parties differed was whether or not to include an enumerated list of individual rights in the document that was to guide a young nation into the future. When the convention began, the two factions each held a position as to whether a bill of rights was necessary and should be included in the constitution of the United States.

The Federalists claimed it was both dangerous and unnecessary. The Antifederalists argued that a document without these rights enumerated was an automatic relinquishment of individual rights to the federal government.[1] The answer to this debate was ultimately solved when the state constitutional conventions ratified the Constitution. A bill of rights would be added to the Constitution, and a specific amendment was written to address the issue at hand. The Ninth Amendment solved the debate between the two factions who authored the Constitution of the United States. It states, "The enumeration in the Constitution, of certain rights, shall not be construed to deny or disparage others retained by the people."[2]

However, the progression from the constitutional convention in 1787 to the states' ratifying conventions in 1788–91, tells the story of the bill of rights and why it was ultimately included in the Constitution of the United States of America.[3]

James Madison was often referred to as the father of the Constitution,[4] a label he deemed inaccurate.[5] Madison argued early in the convention that a bill of rights was unnecessary. The sovereign people, he pointed out, had made an explicit, quite narrow, delegation of power to the central government in the Constitution.[6] To allow the states to be independent, the framers vested the central government with "few and defined" powers, reserving to the states "all the objects, which, in the ordinary affairs, concern the lives, liberties and properties of the people."[7] In other words, the states' constitutional laws must protect individual rights, not the federal government. Madison would later change his position to carry out a promise to the Antifederalists, who would approve the constitution only if a bill of rights would later be added.

The Federalists voiced opposition to a bill of rights protecting individual rights from the early days of the constitutional convention to the last days of the state ratifying conventions. At the Massachusetts convention Mr. Peterson made the point that "...no power was given to the congress to infringe on any one of these natural rights of the people by this constitution; and, should they attempt it without constitutional authority, the act would be a nullity, and could not be enforced."[8]

This argument was supported by Alexander Hamilton, who had written years earlier in the *Federalist Papers*, "Why, for instance, should it be said that the liberty of the press shall not be restrained when no power is given by which restrictions may be imposed?"[9] Hamilton and other Federalists claimed the narrow scope of powers given to the central government was enough to protect individual rights, and as he argued in the *Federalist Papers*, the government could not infringe where they had not been delegated power.

Another area of Federalist concern with including an enumerated list of individual rights was the implication that rights not mentioned were deemed waived by the people and thus put into government hands. Refraining from listing rights allowed the government no power to infringe on an individual's liberty. Including a list of rights, however, brought into question the rights not listed.

James Wilson argued the danger of an enumerated list of rights and the insupportable danger of an incomplete list at the Pennsylvania convention. "In a government possessed of enumerated powers, such a measure would not be only unnecessary but preposterous and dangerous...if we attempt an enumeration, everything that is not enumerated is presumed to be given. The consequence is that an imperfect enumeration would throw all implied power into the scale of the government, and the rights of the people would be rendered incomplete."[10]

This common fear of an incomplete list of rights was also made in North Carolina's ratification convention and was voiced by future Supreme Court justice James Iredell. "[I]t would be not only useless, but dangerous, to enumerate a number of rights that are not intended to be given up; because it would be implying, in the strongest manner, that every right not included in the exception might be implied by the government without usurpation; and it would be impossible to enumerate every one. Let any one make what collection or enumeration of rights he pleases, I will immediately mention twenty or thirty more rights not contained in it."[11]

The Antifederalists were concerned with the power granted the new central government under the Constitution and viewed the enumeration of individual rights as a necessary part of the document. They feared that no mention of these rights would be considered an automatic relinquishment of these rights to the government.

At the 1787 constitutional convention, the Federalists defeated several Antifederalist attempts to include this list of rights in the constitution. Charles Pickney of South Carolina and Elbridge Gerry of Massachusetts tried on several occasions to have the rights included but were voted down by the Federalist-dominated convention.[12] Although the Federalist position of no bill of rights was the opinion at the 1787 convention, a constitution without a bill of rights would become the chief rallying point for opponents to the constitution during ratification debates.[13] In the end, the Antifederalists succeeded and a bill of rights was ultimately included in the Constitution of the United States.

The Antifederalists took the position that every other country with a constitution or similar outline for government included listing individual rights. Patrick Henry, a leading Antifederalist argued, "That all nations have adopted this construction—that all rights not expressly and unequivocally reserved to the people are impliedly and incidentally relinquished to rulers, as necessary inseparable from the delegated powers."[14]

A second attack on the Federalist opposition to a list of rights was directed at James Madison's argument in the *Federalist Papers*[15] where Madison said it would be up to the states to protect individual rights. Antifederalists feared that the Constitution's supremacy clause[16] would allow federal legislation to trump state law, which they interpreted to include any bill of rights in state constitutions that protected individual rights.

The Antifederalists had yet another argument to require a listing of enumerated rights. The Constitution, as it was already written, enumerated rights such as the right to a jury trial in criminal cases[17] and to writs of habeas corpus, and prohibitions against bills of attainder and ex post facto laws.[18] In attacking the Federalists' position, the Antifederalists asked why these rights were mentioned when it was "not only unnecessary...but would even be dangerous"[19] to enumerate individual rights in the Constitution. If an incomplete enumeration was dangerous and unnecessary as the Federalist argued, then the few rights already mentioned in the Constitution were indeed dangerous. Expanding this list, argued the Antifederalists, would therefore cause no harm.[20]

When this argument surfaced, it became clear that a bill of rights would be needed if the state conventions were going to ratify the Constitution. Many states, including Virginia, New York, North Carolina, and Pennsylvania included amendments to the Constitution to secure a listing of individual rights.

The Virginia proposal, considered the original model for the Ninth Amendment because it was the first ratified, passed on June 26, 1788.[21] Among the many proposed amendments Virginia submitted, the seventeenth stated, "That those clauses which declare Congress shall not exercise certain powers, be not interpreted in any manner whatsoever, to extend the powers of Congress; but that they be construed either as making exceptions to the specified powers where this shall be the case, or otherwise, as inserted merely for greater caution."[22] North Carolina's related amendment was almost a mirror image of Virginia's, and the other states had similar amendments voicing these concerns.

The states' proposed amendments were presented to the House of Representatives to be considered as part of the Constitution. When James Madison introduced the precursor of the Ninth Amendment in the House it stated, "The exceptions here or elsewhere in the constitution, made in favor of particular rights, shall not be construed as to diminish the just importance of other rights retained by the people; or as to enlarge the powers delegated by the Constitution; but either as actual limitations of such powers, or as inserted merely for greater caution."[23]

This form passed the House and Senate and was sent to the House select committee, who revised it into the present-day version of the Ninth Amendment. Unfortunately, no records have survived from the House select committee to explain the revised changes. The joint resolution of Congress proposing a bill of rights listed the amendment in its present-day form: "The enumeration in the Constitution, of certain rights, shall not be construed to deny or disparage others retained by the people."[24]

JURISPRUDENCE OF THE NINTH AMENDMENT

From its ratification in 1791 until 1965, the Supreme Court dealt with the Ninth Amendment on seven occasions.[25] The Court, however, did not provide its construction of the amendment in any of these cases. In most of the cases, the Court simply dismissed the petitioner's Ninth Amendment claims as not applicable to the issues raised. For example, in *United Public Workers* v. *Mitchell*[26] the Court said, "... when objection is made that the exercise of a federal power infringes upon rights reserved by the Ninth and Tenth Amendments, the inquiry must be directed toward the granted power under which the action of the Union was taken. If granted power is found, necessarily the objection of invasion of those rights, reserved by the Ninth and Tenth Amendments must fail...." The Court's discussion of the

Ninth Amendment in *Mitchell*,[27] like the other cases, provided little insight to what the amendment might mean.

This would change in 1965 when the Court decided *Griswold* v. *Connecticut*,[28] holding that a Connecticut law preventing married couples from using birth control violated the United States Constitution. Justice Douglas, writing for the majority, talked of specific provisions of the Bill of Rights having penumbras that give them substance.[29] According to the majority, some of the amendments, including the First, Third, Fourth, Fifth, and Ninth Amendments, create zones of privacy.[30] The Court based its decision on the fact that one of these zones of privacy protects the marital relationship, which rendered the statute unconstitutional.[31]

In a concurring opinion, Justice Goldberg, joined by Chief Justice Warren and Justice Brennan, emphasized the importance of the Ninth Amendment in the Court's recognition of a right of marital privacy.[32] Justice Goldberg argued that the Ninth Amendment's language and history reveal the framers of the Constitution's belief that additional fundamental rights, not just the rights listed in the first eight amendments, are also protected from governmental infringement.[33] Justice Goldberg discussed the historical aspects of the Ninth Amendment and the debates on whether a list of enumerated rights was necessary.[34]

The Ninth Amendment, according to Justice Goldberg, is not an independent source of rights.[35] It lends strong support to the view that the liberty clause in the Fifth and Fourteenth Amendments is not restricted to rights mentioned in the first eight amendments.[36] When applying Justice Goldberg's reading of the Ninth Amendment to the facts in *Griswold*,[37] to hold a state may violate a fundamental right such as marital privacy simply because the first eight amendments do not guarantee this right in so many words, would be to ignore the Ninth Amendment and to give it no effect whatsoever.[38] A judicial construction that a fundamental right has no protection in the Constitution, because it is not mentioned in explicit terms, would violate the Ninth Amendment.[39] Justice Goldberg, while discussing the Court's few occasions to interpret the Ninth Amendment, quotes Chief Justice Marshall in *Marbury* v. *Madison*, "it cannot be presumed that any clause in the constitution is intended to be without effect."[40] And the Court in *Myers* v. *Nebraska*: "real effect should be given to all the words it uses."[41] Justice Goldberg's point is simple: the Ninth Amendment was written to protect these unenumerated rights reserved by the people, and since 1791 it has been a basic part of the Constitution, which the Court is sworn to uphold.[42]

Justice Goldberg, in answering criticism from the dissent, mentioned several tests that prevent judges left at large to determine which rights are fundamental based on their personal and private notions.[43] Judges must look to the "traditions and collective conscience of our people"[44] to determine whether a principle is "so rooted [there]...as to be ranked as fundamental."[45] Judges must inquire whether the right involved "is of such character that it cannot be denied without violating those fundamental principles of liberty and justice which lie at the base of all our civil and political institutions."[46] Justice Goldberg also cited *Poe* v. *Ullman:*[47] "liberty also gains content from the emanations of...specific constitutional guarantees and from experience with the requirements of a free society."[48] Justice Goldberg, in listing these tests, argued that a judge's responsibility to determine whether a right is basic and fundamental is not based on unrestricted personal discretion.[49] Justice Goldberg said, "In sum, I believe that the right of privacy in the marital relationship is fundamental and basic—a personal right retained by the people within the meaning of the Ninth Amendment."[50]

In *Hardwick* v. *Bowers*,[51] the United States Court of Appeals for the Eleventh Circuit held unconstitutional a Georgia statute outlawing sodomy, ruling the statute infringed upon fundamental constitutional rights based upon the Ninth Amendment and the due process clause of the Fourteenth Amendment. The limitations of state power find their source in what has been termed the "right to privacy."[52] The court held that certain personal decisions affect an individual's life so keenly that the right to privacy prohibits state interference even in the likelihood of significant public consequences. The Supreme Court has held this right is not limited to conduct that takes place only in the private home[53] but it is the private activity of individuals that will be the focus. The right to privacy extends to some activities that would not normally merit constitutional protections simply because those activities take on added significance under certain limited circumstances.[54] The Court noted the constitutional right to privacy reaches its height when the state attempts to regulate activity in the home.[55]

The Eleventh Circuit in part based its holding on *Stanley* v. *Georgia*,[56] in which police officers executing a search warrant found obscene films and charged Stanley with possession of obscene materials. The Supreme Court held the state could not make the private possession of obscene materials a criminal offense. The Court said that, while a state may regulate obscenity when distributed or displayed in public, it may not prohibit private uses of obscenity.[57] Although *Stanley* was decided on First Amendment grounds, the privacy issue involved the absence of any public ramifications led the Eleventh Circuit to rely in large part on the holding of *Stanley*. The Eleventh Circuit viewed the interest asserted by *Hardwick* as at least as substantial as the interest in *Stanley*, being the fact that in both cases the activity is carried out in private bolster its significance.[58] The Eleventh Circuit, in relying on the Supreme Court decisions in *Griswold* v. *Connecticut*[59] and *Stanley* v. *Georgia*,[60] held the Georgia sodomy statute violated Hardwick's fundamental rights. The activity Hardwick hoped to engage in is a private matter and lies at the heart of an intimate association beyond the proper reach of the state.[61] The Ninth Amendment protects such a right, the Court held, and the notion of fundamental fairness embodied in the due process clause of the Fourteenth Amendment.[62]

The United States Supreme Court reversed the Eleventh Circuit Court of Appeals' decision in *Bowers* v. *Hardwick*,[63] holding the Georgia sodomy statute constitutional. Justice White, writing for the majority, held denied a constitutionally protected right to homosexual sodomy under the due process clause of the Fourteenth Amendment. The Court refused to accept *Hardwick's* reliance on *Stanley* v. *Georgia*,[64] stating the decision in *Stanley* was firmly grounded in the First Amendment. Justice White, in responding to *Hardwick's* reliance on *Stanley*, said the right being asserted had no similar support in the text of the Constitution, and it did not qualify for recognition under the prevailing principles for construing the Fourteenth Amendment.[65] The Supreme Court in *Bowers*[66] did not address the Ninth Amendment issue because Hardwick did not defend the judgment of the Eleventh Circuit Court of Appeals on this issue.

Justice Blackman, in his dissenting opinion in *Bowers*,[67] disagreed with the majority opinion on several issues. First, he argued that the case is not about a fundamental right to engage in homosexual sodomy, as the court purported,[68] but rather about "the most comprehensive of rights and the right most valued by civilized men" namely, "the right to be let alone."[69] Justice Blackman claimed that the Georgia statute denied individuals the right to decide for themselves whether to engage in particular forms of private, consensual sexual activity.[70] According to Justice Blackman, the fact that moral judgments expressed by statutes like the one in question might be "natural and familiar...ought not to conclude the court's judgment upon the question whether statutes embodying them conflict with the Constitution of the United States."[71]

Second, Justice Blackman disagreed with the majority's refusal to consider whether the Georgia statute in question violates the Ninth Amendment, in that Hardwick's complaint relied on the Ninth Amendment and the Court's decision in *Griswold* v. *Connecticut*.[72] Blackman argued that it is a well-settled principle of law that "a complaint should not be dismissed merely because a plaintiff's allegations do not support the particular legal theory he advances, for the court is under a duty to examine the complaint to determine if the allegations provide for relief on any possible theory."[73] According to this principle of law, Justice Blackman argued that even if Hardwick did not advance claims to the Supreme Court based upon the Ninth Amendment, his complaint should not be dismissed if the provision could entitle him to relief. Justice Blackman concluded his argument by stating, "The court's cramped reading of the issue before it makes for a short opinion, but it does little to make for a persuasive one."[74]

In 1981, the Ninth Amendment again found its way into the opinion of the Supreme Court. In *Richmond Newspaper Inc.* v. *Virginia*,[75] the issue of whether or not a criminal trial may be closed to the public without any demonstration that closure is required to protect the defendant's superior right to a fair trial was argued before the court. The defendant in a murder trial had been convicted of second-degree murder, but the Virginia Supreme Court overturned the conviction.[76] Second and third trials ended in mistrials and a fourth trial had begun when the trial judge granted the closure order.

Chief Justice Burger, joined by Justices White and Stevens, announced the opinion of the court holding that the First and Fourteenth Amendments guarantee the public the right to attend criminal trials. The Court discussed at great length the historical aspects of both criminal and civil trials being presumptively open to the public throughout English common law and colonial America. The Court explained this as not a quirk in history; rather, it has long been recognized as an indispensable attribute of Anglo-American trials.[77]

The Ninth Amendment surfaces to rebut the states' argument that the Constitution nowhere spells out a guarantee for the right of the public to attend trials, therefore, no such right is protected. Chief Justice Burger, responding to the states' argument, addresses the fact that the Constitution's draftsmen were aware of such an argument and in footnote fifteen of the *Richmond* decision[78] he relates the Ninth Amendment's purpose. Notwithstanding the appropriate caution against reading into the Constitution rights not explicitly defined, the opinion continues, the Court has acknowledged that certain unarticulated rights are implicit in enumerated guarantees.[79] The Court then listed several of these rights, including the rights of association and of privacy, the right to be presumed innocent, and the right to be judged by a standard of proof beyond a reasonable doubt in a criminal trial, as well as the right to travel.[80] None of these rights are mentioned in the Constitution or the Bill of Rights, yet these important unarticulated rights have nonetheless been found to share constitutional protections in common with explicit guarantees.[81] The concerns expressed by Madison and others have been resolved, the opinion concluded; the Court has recognized fundamental rights, even though not expressly guaranteed, as indispensable to the enjoyment of rights explicitly defined.[82]

FOURTEENTH AMENDMENT DUE PROCESS CASES

In 1923 the Supreme Court decided *Meyer* v. *Nebraska*,[83] holding that the due process clause of the Fourteenth Amendment protected parental choice in education concerning what language subjects could be taught to children. The Nebraska statute in question held it unlawful to teach subjects in any language other than English, and also the teaching of any other language until a pupil had attained and successfully passed the eighth grade. The state argued its purpose was to promote civic development by limiting the education of the immature in foreign tongues and ideals before they could learn English and acquire American ideals.[84] The state further argued that because the foreign population is so large and these communities continue to use a foreign language, following foreign leaders and so on, that the children are hindered from becoming citizens of the most useful type and public safety is imperiled.[85]

The Supreme Court, in an opinion by Justice McReynolds, held the statute went too far and violated rights held by the people. That the state may do much, goes far indeed, in order to improve the quality of its citizens physically, mentally, and morally, is clear; but the individual has certain fundamental rights that must be respected.[86] The Court acknowledged the state's desire to promote a homogeneous people who would hold American ideals and understand discussions of civic matters, however, the state's efforts to achieve this goal went too far. Justice McReynolds in the opinion states, "...the means adopted, we think, exceed the limitations upon the power of the state and conflict with rights assured to the plaintiff in error."[87]

The Supreme Court at no time prior to *Meyer* ever attempted to define with any exactness the liberty guaranteed by the due process clause of the Fourteenth Amendment. However, the due process clause had received plenty of attention by the Court in recognizing individual rights in many areas. Among these rights, the right of the individual to contract, to engage in any of the common occupations of life, to acquire useful knowledge, to marry, establish a home and bring up children, to worship God according to the dictates of conscience, and generally to enjoy these privileges long recognized at common law as essential to the orderly pursuit of happiness by free people.[88] The Court emphasized the established doctrine that liberty may not be interfered with under guise of protecting the public interest by legislative action, which is arbitrary, or without reasonable relation to some purpose within the competency of the state to effect.[89]

The American people have always regarded education and acquisition of knowledge as matters of supreme importance that should be diligently promoted.[90] The Court talked of the teaching profession as honorable, essential, and useful to the public welfare, an occupation to benefit all. Therefore, the teacher's right to teach and the right of parents to engage the teacher so to instruct their children are within the liberty of the Fourteenth Amendment.[91] The statute in question dealt only with teaching languages, leaving complete freedom as to other matters, which left the Court to conclude no adequate foundation in Nebraska's law to protect the child's health by limiting mental activities. It is well known that proficiency in a foreign language seldom comes to one not instructed at an early age, and experience shows that this is not injurious to the health, morals, or understanding of the ordinary child.[92]

The Supreme Court in 1925 revisited the issue of education and the liberty interest in parental choice as to what schools children could attend in *Pierce* v. *Society of Sisters.*[93] Oregon passed a statute requiring all children, with few exceptions, between the ages of eight and sixteen to attend public schools. Appellee, the Society of Sisters, a private corporation along with a companion case brought by Hill Military Academy, challenged the Oregon statute as a violation of the due process clause of the Fourteenth Amendment. The Society of Sisters alleged that the statute conflicted with the rights of parents to choose where their children will receive appropriate mental and religious training, the right of schools and teachers therein to engage in a useful business or profession[94]

The District Court for the District of Oregon held the statute violated the due process clause of the Fourteenth Amendment, and the Supreme Court agreed also noting its reliance on *Meyer* v. *Nebraska.*[95] The district court held the Fourteenth Amendment guaranteed appellees against the deprivation of their property without due process of law consequent upon the unlawful interference by appellants with the free choice of patrons, present and prospective.[96] The district courts also held the right to conduct schools was property and that parents and guardians, as part of their liberty, might direct the education of children by selecting reputable teachers and places.[97]

Justice McReynolds, writing for the Court, held under *Meyer* v. *Nebraska*[98] the Oregon Act unreasonably interfered with the liberty of parents and guardians to direct the upbringing and education of children.[99] The Court went on to state the fundamental theory of liberty upon which all governments in the Union repose excludes any general power of the state to standardize its children by forcing them to accept instruction from public teachers. The Court continued that the child is not the mere creature of the state and said those who nurture and direct their destiny have the right, coupled with the high duty, to recognize and prepare them for additional obligations.[100]

NINTH AMENDMENT ADJUDICATION

For the past 100 years, the standard for analyzing unenumerated constitutional rights has been the legal mechanism known as substantive due process. This mechanism was first clearly articulated by the Supreme Court in *Lochner* v. *New York.*[101] In *Lochner,* the Court held that an individual has a substantive right to enter into an employment contract without unwarranted interference through state involvement, and such a right is protected by the liberty clause of the Fourteenth Amendment. The Court changed the procedural imperative of the amendment, which originally set out to protect life and property from being taken without sufficient procedural legal safeguards, into a substantive form of due process that recognized rights not expressly mentioned in the text of the Constitution.[102] The Court first used substantive due process in relation to privacy matters in *Meyer v. Nebraska*,[103] which secured the liberty "to marry, establish a home and bring up children."[104] This due process right was expanded two years later in *Pierce v. Society of Sisters*,[105] which held that "the liberty...to direct the upbringing and education of children"[106] was also protected.

To understand why substantive due process analysis fails in the area of privacy, one must look at the questions the analysis itself poses. Is a history or tradition of the activity in question to be regulated? Second, the substantive due process mechanism considers the value-laden determinations of the propriety of the specific regulation in question. One of the Supreme Court's most important substantive due process cases, *Bowers v. Hardwick*, illustrates the inherent problems with substantive due process analysis and provides a useful demonstration of the benefits of Ninth Amendment analysis. *Bowers* provides the logic to determine privacy issues based upon the Ninth Amendment's guarantee of reserved rights.

In a law review article on this subject, Professor Mark C. Niles proposes a two-step Ninth Amendment adjudicative mechanism that replaces substantive due process in the realm of personal autonomy rights. Professor Niles asks two simple questions: is the activity involved substantially private? Does the activity threaten individuals or the public as a whole?[107] Instead of forcing the individual to identify a specific protected right, as substantive due process requires, this Ninth Amendment approach shifts the burden to the government to show a legitimate reason to regulate an activity. This burden-shifting approach requires identifying the issues as disputes over the legitimate extent of government power and the relationship of that power to personal freedom. A debate about the relative importance and historical significance of specific individual acts is no longer necessary or required.[108]

In *Bowers v. Hardwick*,[109] Michael Hardwick was arrested in the bedroom of his home for violating a Georgia statute outlawing sodomy. When the case reached the Supreme Court, the issue reviewed was "whether the Federal Constitution confers a fundamental right upon homosexuals to engage in sodomy." The Court held there was no such right.[110] Relying on substantive due process analysis, the Court held such a right was neither "implicit in the concept of ordered liberty" nor "deeply rooted in the nation's history and tradition."[111] *Bowers* is a clear case of the problem with substantive due process analysis, which fails to properly address the dispute between personal freedom and governmental regulation. The central issue under Ninth Amendment adjudication would not question if governments have traditionally had laws criminalizing sodomy, but if this law was a legitimate exercise of government authority.[112] As Professor Niles points out, substantive due process has two key flaws—its reliance on history and its lack of focus on the central conflict of personal auton-omy disputes—both of which are clearly shown in *Bowers*.[113]

Under the Ninth Amendment, Hardwick would not have been forced to assert positive rights to engage in sodomy, as did the substantive due pro-cess analysis require of him. Rather, Hardwick would assert that the activ-ity was substantially private and posed no threat to any individual or the community as a whole. Because the activity was private and posed no public threat, the government had no legitimate reason to interfere, and if it chose to do so, it must have proved a legitimate public interest. The government would have difficulty meeting this burden, indicating that the government has no place in regulating this type of private activity. The Ninth Amendment adjudication would secure privacy rights to the people and prevent the government imposing its will in areas beyond legitimate government concern. Enforcing an external moral code on an individual, to the extent that it limits freedom to act in ways that pose no reasonable threat of harm to others or the community is an invalid exercise of state power under the Ninth Amendment.[114] If the government's justification for the sodomy law is to survive Ninth Amendment adjudication, it must involve identifying a public harm from the action and a connection between the harm and the regulation involved.[115]

Another example of why substantive due process analysis fails in the privacy realm is *Washington* v. *Glucksberg*,[116] in which the Court denied a constitutional right to physician-assisted suicide. Under substantive due process analysis, the Court held the right to assistance in committing sui-cide is not a fundamental liberty interest protected by the due process clause. The Court noted that "for 700 years, the Anglo-American common-law tradition has punished or otherwise disapproved of both suicide and assisting suicide."[117] Suicide by a sane person was punishable as a felony under English common law. The American colonies adopted this approach as early as 1647 in what would later become Rhode Island. The Court found no support for assisted suicide in our country's history or tra-dition: "The history of the law's treatment of assisted suicide in this coun-try has been and continues to be one of the rejections of nearly all efforts to permit it."[118] The Court supports the holding in *Glucksberg* by also find-ing the state's interests in banning assisted suicide rationally related to legitimate government interests. Among the interests that the state pos-sesses, the Court notes the "unqualified interest in the preservation of human life,"[119] an interest in protecting the integrity and ethics of the med-ical profession, and an interest in protecting vulnerable groups—includ-ing the poor, the elderly and the disabled from abuse, neglect and mistakes.[120]

One can argue that no right is more private than one's choice to "control one's final days" or to "choose a humane, dignified death."[121] Unlike sub-stantive due process, the Ninth Amendment can protect this right from government interference. Substantive due process, and its reliance on history and tradition, will not allow legitimate privacy claims to survive inappropriate government intrusion. Simply because common law traditions have outlawed suicide (and sodomy, as in *Bowers*) for hundreds of years does not automatically include these activities within a legitimate government sphere of influence. Government's historical failure to protect certain individual rights does not indicate that these failures are, or ever were, legitimate. The government has never been required to provide legitimate reasons for interference with private citizens' rights, but its doing so for hundreds of years has legitimized substantive due process.

Applying the Ninth Amendment mechanism to *Glucksberg* would require the state to show two points. First, how assisted suicide is not a substantially private activity; second, how this activity threatens individuals or the public at large. A person's choice to end his or her life is unquestionably a private matter, arguably the most private of all recognized personal autonomy rights. The state must struggle to prove assisted suicide is a public matter and therefore worthy of state regulation under the guise of police power. Also, assisted suicide's threat is at best minimal to any individual, or the public, and is insufficient to legitimize government involvement. In *Glucksberg*, the state raised several interests to allow the ban on assisted suicide. Among these are the right to protect the integrity and ethics of the medical profession and protection of vulnerable groups, including the poor, the elderly, and the disabled. Protection of the medical field's integrity and ethics, as with other professional groups, should be left to the medical field, and not the state. In protecting vulnerable groups such as the poor, elderly, and disabled, the Court of Appeals for the Ninth Circuit characterized the state's concern that disadvantaged people may be pressured into assisted suicide as "ludicrous on its face."[122] The court of appeals clearly saw no threat to individuals or the public, whereby the state fails to show a legitimate government interest in regulating assisted suicide.

THE FOURTH AMENDMENT AND THE "WAR ON DRUGS"

The United States government has a long-time policy regarding drug use, namely that it is in our best interest for the government to intervene to protect us against ourselves.[123] In fighting the war on drugs, the United States government has spent billions of dollars, but this staggering price ignores a far greater price paid in sacrificing our constitutional rights. The war on drugs has severely eroded Fourth Amendments rights, with the Supreme Court's holdings in this area commonly known as "the drug exception to the Fourth Amendment."[124] Among these eroded rights is the relaxation of criteria that must be satisfied to secure a search warrant. The

Court has also permitted the issuance of search warrants based on anony-
mous tips and tips from informants, some of whom have proven corrupt
and unreliable;[125] permitted unwarranted searches of fields, barns, and
private property near a residence;[126] permitted unwarranted surveillance
of a home;[127] lowered the permissible ceiling for aerial unwarranted
searches to 400 feet; and upheld the use of evidence obtained with defec-
tive search warrants on the grounds that the officers executing the warrant
were acting in "good faith."[128] These and other cases reveal the court's
efforts to enhance the war on drugs at the expense of individual rights.
These examples of government action clearly show judicial willingness to
allow the government to act in a paternalistic manner when the government is at war, whether with another sovereign nation or with its own
people. As long as the fight against drugs is termed the "war on drugs,"
the government, with judicial backing, will continue to violate, erode, or
simply abandon individual liberty and autonomy. Recent history should
be a dire warning against both the soundness of this rhetoric and the kinds
of reactive measures it justifies the government to pursue.[129]

TWO ARGUMENTS FOR DRUGS: THE RIGHT TO
SELF-DETERMINATION AND THE HARM PRINCIPLE

The Right to Self-Determination

The government and courts' entrenched erosion of Fourth Amendment
rights regarding drug use, requires us to look elsewhere for constitutional
protection from government intrusion into individual privacy or autonomy. The Ninth Amendment provides such protection: "The enumeration
in the Constitution, of certain rights, shall not be construed to deny or disparage others retained by the people"[130] As Justice Goldberg noted in
Griswold, "The Ninth Amendment simply shows the intent of the Constitution's authors that other fundamental personal rights should not be
denied such protections or disparaged in any other way simply because
they are not specifically listed in the first eight constitutional amendments."[131] Justice Goldberg's comments and the historical review of the
Ninth Amendment provided earlier clearly show that Madison and the
founding fathers understood the importance of individual privacy and
personal autonomy. Thus, it is not surprising that James Madison
described protection of the diversity of human faculties as "the first object
of Government."[132] This object of government protecting individual rights
and personal autonomy is precisely why the Ninth Amendment is part of
the Constitution; it protects the diversity of human faculties. The government best protects these rights by keeping itself outside them.

The government has no place in determining an individual's self-definition; this principle is perhaps the most basic tenet of a republic style of

government. In certain areas of the privacy realm the courts have supported this notion and refused to allow the government to interfere. However, the courts have limited their support of this important principle to certain realms of privacy. Most notably in the sexuality context[133] but also in limited circumstances of other important privacy matters.[134] The privacy rights just discussed and that the courts have awarded protection from government intrusion, play a major role in an individual's self-definition. The choices an individual makes regarding sexual matters between self and a consenting adult intertwine with the concept of self-determination to a point that can and must exclude any government role. However, the government continues to interfere in certain aspects of this privacy right.[135] Another aspect the court has protected is that of family rights and the privacy matters that relate to them. The household you are raised in, the values you are taught, and the education provided for you are basic building blocks of self-determination, and the courts have recognized and protected these rights from government intrusion as well. Here the courts have drawn the line in restricting government interference with the concept of an individual's self-determination. The privacy doctrines supported by the courts under the guise of substantive due process and the limited application of the Ninth Amendment go no further than the rights just discussed. But self-determination involves far more than the limited rights protected by the courts, and the Ninth Amendment is the vehicle that provides protection for these other rights fundamental to an individual's self-determination.

An individual's decision to use drugs is one of these rights that go to the heart of the self-determination concept. Numerous other rights populate the self-determination realm. Most of them, however, like choices of what or how much food to eat or whether to eat at all, are less controversial and therefore receive little attention. The point is that the choice we make on how to affect our level or state of consciousness and the choice we make on eating habits both affect our bodies and appearance and should be treated as the same. Provided the choice affects only the individual, the government or society has no room to step in and make these choices for the individual. This is the most basic and fundamental principle of the self-determination concept, which includes an individual's right to privacy and autonomy. The principle of the right to privacy is not freedom to do certain acts determined to be fundamental through some ever-progressing normative lens. It is the fundamental freedom not to have life choices determined by a progressively more normalizing state.[136]

The Supreme Court is aware of this threat. Consider the words of Justice Jackson in *West Virginia State Board of Education* v. *Barnette*,[137] when during World War II, the Court held as unconstitutional a law requiring schoolchildren to salute the flag and profess allegiance to the United States. Justice Jackson held the following:

Struggles to coerce uniformity of sentiment in support of some end thought essential to their time and country have been waged by many good as well as evil men....As first and moderate attempts to attain unity have failed, those bent on its accomplishment must resort to an ever-increasing severity....Ultimate futility of such attempts to compel coherence is the lesson of every such effort from the Roman drive to stamp out Christianity...down to the fast failing efforts of our present totalitarian enemies.[138]

The *Barnette* holding and other court decisions are clear examples of the Court recognizing the problems of standardization and paternalism through intrusive government actions. This idea was clear in 1943 when *Barnette* was decided and has continued in recent years in *Roberts* v. *United States Jaycees*,[139] which cited the "ability independently to define one's identity that is central to any concept of liberty,"[140] and the *Bowers* dissent claiming the right to privacy is a right to "self-definition."[141] Although the courts recognize the problem, they have done little to fashion a solution.

The final argument to support the self-determination concept and its relationship to drug use is that of pervasiveness. In his 1992 book, *Our Right To Drugs: The Case for a Free Market*,[142] Professor Thomas Szasz concludes the pervasiveness argument supports the self-determination theory in the privacy and autonomy situations relating to drug use. Professor Szasz also notes that the Supreme Court in its historical privacy case of *Griswold* v. *Connecticut*[143] accepts the pervasiveness theory and the concurring opinion by Justice Goldberg in fact relies heavily upon it. In *Griswold*, Justice Goldberg refused to find the state's argument regarding anti-extramarital relations as the basis for the law as compelling in light of "admitted widespread availability to all persons in the state of Connecticut, unmarried as well as married, of birth-control devices for the prevention of disease...."[144] This widespread availability and implied public demand supports the Connecticut public's recognition of a right to nonprocreational sexual relations as a pervasive right, that is a right that a significant portion of contemporary society believes is inextricably connected with the inherent dignity of the individual.[145] Based upon this recognition, Professor Szasz provides two considerations that the right to self-determination, as with the right to use drugs, is a pervasive right recognized by society. The relationship between the exercise of an individual's free will to use drugs and the concepts of autonomy, dignity, and moral responsibility provides support for this claim. According to Professor Szasz, this recognition of the relationship satisfies the criterion of pervasiveness.[146] The second is the data on drug use in the United States, which provides ample support for the significant recognition of a right to use drugs. Both casual drug users and addicts alike are understood to be asserting a right to have drugs by their acts of defying present prohibitionist laws.[147] The twenty-one million to twenty-five million Americans who have used cocaine, and the seventy million Americans who have used some type of illegal drug can be counted in calculating the pervasiveness of this recognition of self-determination regarding the right to use drugs.[148] Widespread contraceptive availability in Connecticut in 1964 was viewed as significant support for the claim that the right to nonprocreational sexual relations was a pervasive right. Similarly, widespread availability and use of controlled and illegal drugs may be viewed as significant support for the claim that a larger portion of society recognizes the right to use drugs as fundamental.[149]

The Harm Principle

The concept or theory of the harm principle is traced back to John Stuart Mill's classic essay "On Liberty," in which he discusses the "harm to others" principle.[150] According to Mill's theory, individuals may locate within their personal domain self-regarding decisions, meaning decisions that primarily affect only the decision-maker. Beyond this sphere of personal domain are other-regarding decisions that affect other persons. Other-regarding acts have consequences for the public and can be regulated, therefore, the right to self-determination is not absolute, and only self-regarding acts should be allowed in a republic style of government. There is a gray area, but no fine line between these two concepts, as in many realms of law, theory, and policy. However, the gray area alone is not enough reason to discard the theory in its entirety. Professor Joel Feinberg,[151] in his book titled *Social Philosophy*,[152] provides an example of an individual performing self-regarding acts. Professor Feinberg expands Mill's theory relating to the harm principle in that no one should be punished simply for being drunk, but a policeman should be punished for being drunk on duty.[153] Feinberg writes of

...a hard working bachelor who habitually spends his evenings hours drinking himself into a stupor, which he then sleeps off, rising fresh in the morning to put in another hard day's work. His drinking does not *directly* affect others in any of the ways of the drunken policeman's conduct. He has no family; he drinks alone and sets no direct example; he is not prevented from discharging any of his public duties; he creates no substantial risk of harm to the interests of other individuals. Although even his private conduct will have some effects Mill would call "indirect" and "remote." First is spending his evenings the way he does, our solitary tippler is *not* doing any number of things that might be of greater utility to others. In not earning and spending more money, he is failing to stimulate the economy (except for the liquor industry) as much as he might. Second, he fails to spend his evening time improving his talents and making himself a better person.... Third, he may make those of his colleagues who liked him sad on his behalf. Finally, to those who know of his habits he is a bad example.[154]

This comment from Professor Feinberg is clearly the example of an individual committing self-regarding acts. As noted, the indirect or remote effects on outsiders is minimal and does not change the fact that the individual actions do not violate the "harm to others" principle of which Mill speaks. The basic contention of this concept is to examine the relationship between the individual and the state and who should make the decisions regarding the best interest of an individual. Mill answers this question by noting that even when the state acts in good faith, the action is self-defeating and an adult's own good is "best provided for by allowing him to make his own means of pursuing it."[155] In essence, the harm principle allows the individual the right to define oneself even in opposition to widespread, traditional, "normal" values,[156] assuming the defining acts are self-regarding.

The right to be let alone, which has become a standard phrase in privacy jurisprudence, should be circumscribed by the state only when the harm principle has been violated. However, this is not the case today, and under the guise of police power, the state violates this right, and the individual receives little protection from the courts. A few courts and judges have recognized this problem, but they remain the minority throughout the judicial system. In 1998, the Hawaii Supreme Court in *State v. Mallan*[157] held that the state constitution does not protect the right to possess marijuana as a right to privacy. Justice Levinson in his dissent wrote, "Legislative enactments intended to compel purely personal safety, health, morals or welfare, under pain of criminal punishment, constitute unreasonable exercises of the police power; and such legislative enactments are therefore unconstitutional."[158] Justice Levinson rejects the regulation of personal, private conduct under the state's police power absent a showing of harm or likelihood of harm to others. [159] The other boundary Justice Levinson mentioned in his dissent was that, once the right to privacy is implicated, the protection afforded to the individual can be impinged upon only when the state demonstrates a compelling interest to do so, using the least restrictive means possible.[160] This proposed standard rejects the rationale basis standard of review and would require the state to show far more in order to demonstrate a compelling interest. The point being, legislation that interferes with an individual's right to privacy by prohibiting activity that does not violate the harm rule should be considered unconstitutional. Although the *Mallan* case primarily focused on the privacy article of the state constitution of Hawaii, the argument can be made that the Ninth Amendment supports this contention at the federal level.

The harm principle, paternalism, self-determination, and personhood, are all theories about individual autonomy, personal liberty, and the right to privacy. These theories share a common theme; the state should play no role in certain matters pertaining to individual activity. The idea that the state knows what is best for individuals and should be allowed to govern under this principle goes against the ideals of our founding fathers and their beliefs in natural law. For the state to interfere would be an "almost un-American rationale for any type of government activity"[161] The framers explicitly acknowledged that individuals possess certain "unalienable rights"[162] not enumerated in the text of the Constitution and not contingent on the relationship between individuals and the federal government.[163]

By implementing the harm principle into our nation's legislative and judicial branches of government, the rights of individuals to maintain their lives by their own standards will again be a reality. This government was founded upon the principles of natural law, and for the past 100 years has strayed from this foundation to the current system of overreaching legislatures with the mindset that the few know what is right for the many. The harm principle in no way allows society to do as it pleases, it is simply a check on government to respect the individual's autonomy, liberty, and right to privacy. Drug use, for example, needs certain regulation, much like alcohol and tobacco, including age limits, quality standards and restrictions upon when and where these products may be used. The war on drugs has failed and will continue to fail; criminalizing drug use is not the answer. The governmental interest in the well-being of the drug user can be best served by controlling drug quality and labeling and by increasing the availability of drug treatment to those seeking such assistance.[164] Although drug use will always face opposition as immoral, this alone should not cloud the judgments of the legislature and the courts. In *Bowers v. Hardwick*[165] Justice Blackman in his dissent observed that, "Reasonable people may differ about whether particular sexual acts are moral or immoral, but we have ample evidence for believing that people will not abandon morality, will not think any better of murder, cruelty and dishonesty, merely because some private sexual practice which they abominate is not punished by the law."[166] The correlation can be made to the issue of drug use, and the moral disagreements of certain sections of society should not carry the day.

CONCLUSION

The Ninth Amendment adjudication model and the concepts of self-determination and the harm principle are the standards upon which privacy issues should be litigated. The Ninth Amendment model follows the true beliefs of our founding fathers and their adherence to natural law, autonomy, liberty, and the right to privacy. This model must replace the substantive due process analysis used by the Supreme Court in the realm of personal autonomy issues. In addition, the recognition of self-determination and the harm principle will provide individual rights with the constitutional protection our founding fathers thought imperative to our ordered liberty.

NOTES

1. Calvin R. Massey, *Silent Rights: The Ninth Amendment and the Constitution's Unenumerated Rights* (Philadelphia: Temple University Press, 1995), p. 58.

2. U.S. Const., amend. IX.

3. 2 *Elliot's Debates* 436.

4. Irving Brant, *James Madison: Father of the Constitution 1781–1800* (6 vols., 1950; 1941-61).

5. Madison's response to the oft-made remark was: "You give me credit to which I have no claim in calling me "the writer of the Constitution of the United States." This was not, like the fabled goddess of wisdom, the offspring of a single brain. It ought to be regarded as the work of many heads & many hands" Letter to William Cogswell, 10 March 1834, in 9 Gaillard Hunt, *Writings of James Madison* (G. P. Putnam's Sons, 9 vols., 1904), p. 533.

6. Massey, *supra* note 2, p. 56.

7. Federalist No. 45, pp. 237–38 (James Madison).

8. 2 *Elliot's Debates* 436, *supra* note 4, p. 162.

9. Federalist No. 84, *supra* note 1, pp. 513–514.

10. 2 *Elliot's Debates* 236, *supra* note 4, pp. 436–437.

11. 4 *Elliot's Debates* 167 (James Iredell, N.C., ratifying convention July 28, 1788).

12. Massey, *supra* note 2, p. 56.

13. Arthur E. Wilwarth Jr., The Original Purpose of the Bill of Rights: James Madison and the Founders' Search for a Workable Balance Between Federal and State Power. 26 *Am. Crim. L. Rev.* 1261, 1989.

14. 3 *Elliot's Debates* 440 (Patrick Henry Virginia Ratifying Convention, June 14, 1788).

15. Federalist No. 45 *supra* note 8. pp. 237–238.

16. U.S. Const. art. VI, § 2.

17. U.S. Const. art. III, § 2.

18. U.S. Const. art. I, § 9.

19. Federalist No. 84, *supra* note 1, pp. 439–440.

20. *The Bill of Rights in Modern America After 200 years* (David J. Bodenhamer and James W. Ely, Jr. eds., Bloomington: Indiana University Press, 1993).

21. Kelly, The Uncertain Renaissance of the Ninth Amendment, 33 *U. Chi. L. Rev.* 814, 1966.

22. *Debates and Other Proceedings of the Convention of Virginia* (2nd ed., 1805), p. 475.

23. 1 *Annals of Congress* 452 (Gales & Seaton, ed., 1834).

24. *Joint Resolution of Congress, 1789* (Original in National Archives, Washington, D.C.).

25. *Roth* v. *U.S.*, 354 U.S. 476 (1957); *Woods* v. *Cloyd W. Miller Co.*, 333 U.S. 138 (1948); *United Public Workers of America (C.I.O.)* v. *Mitchell*, 330 U.S. 75 (1947); *Tennessee Elec. Power Co.* v. *Tennessee Val. Authority*, 306 U.S. 118 (1939); *Ashwander* v. *Tennessee Valley Authority*, 297 U.S. 288 (1936); *Dred Scott* v. *Sandford*, 60 U.S. 393 (1856) (Campbell, J., concurring); *Livingston's Lessee* v. *Moore*, 32 U.S. 470 (1833) Not particularly clear, may mean Seventh Amendment jury trial right.

26. *United Public Workers of America (C.I.O.)* *supra* note 26, pp. 95–6.

27. *Id.*
28. *Griswold* v. *Connecticut* 381 U.S. 479 (1965).
29. *Id.,* p. 484.
30. *Id.*
31. *Id.,* pp. 485–86.
32. *Id.,* p. 487 (Goldberg, J., concurring).
33. *Id.,* p. 488.
34. *Id.,* pp. 488–89.
35. *Id.,* p. 492.
36. *Id.,* p. 492.
37. *Id.,* p. 29, (Goldberg, J., concurring).
38. *Id.,* p. 491.
39. *Id.,* p. 491.
40. *Marbury* v. *Madison,* 5 U.S. 137, 174 (1803).
41. *Myers* v. *Nebraska,* 272 U.S. 52, 151 (1926).
42. *Griswold* v. *Connecticut, supra* note 29 (Goldberg, J., concurring).
43. *Id.,* p. 493.
44. *Snyder* v. *Com. of Mass.,* 291 U.S. 97 (1934).
45. *Id.,* p. 97.
46. *Powell* v. *State of Ala.,* 287 U.S. 45, 67 (1932).
47. *Poe* v. *Ullman,* 367 U.S. 497, 517 (1961) (Douglas, J., dissenting).
48. *Id.,* p. 517.
49. *Griswold, supra* note 29, p. 493 (Goldberg, J., concurring).
50. *Id.,* p. 499.
51. *Hardwick* v. *Bowers,* 760 F.2d 1202 (1985).
52. *Id.,* p. 1211.
53. *Myers, supra* note 41.
54. *Hardwick, supra* note 52, p. 1212.
55. *Payton* v. *New York,* 445 U.S. 573 (1980).
56. *Stanley* v. *Georgia,* 394 U.S. 557 (1969).
57. *Id.,* p. 568.
58. *Hardwick, supra* note 52.
59. *Griswold, supra* note 29.
60. *Stanley, supra* note 57.
61. *Hardwick, supra* note 52.
62. *Id.,* p. 1212.
63. *Bowers* v. *Hardwick,* 478 U.S. 186.
64. *Stanley, supra* note 57.
65. *Bowers, supra* note 64.
66. *Id.,* p. 66.
67. *Id.*
68. *Id.,* p. 199 (Blackman, J., dissenting).
69. *Olmstead* v. *U.S.,* 277 U.S. 438 (1928) (Brandeis, J., dissenting).
70. *Bowers, supra* note 64, p. 199 (1986) (Blackman, J., dissenting).
71. *Roe* v. *Wade,* 410 U.S. 113 (1973) [quoting *Lochner* v. *New York* 198 U.S. 45, 76 (1905)].
72. *Griswold, supra* note 29.
73. *Bramlet* v. *Wilson,* 495 F.2d 714 (1974).

74. *Bowers, supra* note 64, pp. 202–203 (Blackman, J., dissenting).

75. *Richmond Newspapers, Inc.* v. *Virginia*, 448 U.S. 555 (1980).

76. *Stevenson* v. *Commonwealth*, 218 Va. 462, 237 S. E. 2d 779.

77. *Richmond Newspapers, Inc., supra* note 76, p. 569.

78. *Id.*, p. 579.

79. *Id.*, p. 579.

80. *Id.*, pp. 579–580.

81. *Id.*, p. 580 [quoting *National Ass'n. for Advancement of Colored People* v. *State of Ala. ex rel. Patterson*, 357 U.S. 449 (right of association)]; *Griswold* v. *Connecticut*, 381 U.S. 479 (1965) and *Stanley* v. *Georgia*, 394 U.S. 557 (1969) (right of privacy); *Estelle* v. *Williams*, 425 U.S. 501, 503 (1976) and *Taylor* v. *Kentucky*, 436 U.S. 478, 483–86 (1978) (presumption of innocence); *In re* Winship 397 U.S. 358 (1970) (standard of proof beyond a reasonable doubt); *U.S.* v. *Guest*, 383 U.S. 745, 757–59 (1966) and *Shapiro* v. *Thompson*, 394 U.S. 618, 630 (1969) (right to interstate travel).

82. *Richmond Newspapers, Inc., supra* note 76, p. 580.

83. *Meyer, supra* note 54.

84. *Id.*, p. 401.

85. *Id.*

86. *Id.*

87. *Id.*, p. 402.

88. Id., p. 399 (citing Slaughterhouse cases: 83 U.S. 36 (1872); *Butchers' Union Slaughter-House & Live-Stock Landing Co.* v. *Crescent City Live-Stock Landing & Slaughter-House Co.*, 111 U.S. 746 (1884); *Yick Wo* v. *Hopkins*, 118 U.S. 356 (1886); *Minnesota* v. *Barber*, 136 U.S. 313 (1890); *Allgeyer* v. *State of La.*, 165 U.S. 356 (1897); *Lochner* v. *New York*, 198 U.S. 45 (1905); *Twining* v. *State of N.J.*, 211 U.S. 78 (1908).

89. *Meyer, supra* note 54. pp. 399–400.

90. *Id.*, p. 400.

91. *Id.*

92. *Id.*, p. 403.

93. *Pierce* v. *Society of the Sisters of the Holy Names of Jesus and Mary*, 268 U.S. 510 (1925).

94. *Id.*, p. 532.

95. *Meyer, supra* note 54.

96. *Pierce, supra* note 94, pp. 533–534.

97. *Id.*, p. 534.

98. *Meyer, supra* note 54.

99. *Pierce, supra* note 94, p. 535.

100. *Pierce, supra* note 94. p. 534.

101. *Lochner, supra* note 89.

102. *Id.*

103. *Meyer, supra* note 54.

104. *Id.*, p. 399.

105. *Pierce, supra* note 94.

106. *Id.*, p. 534.

107. Mark C. Niles, Ninth Amendment Adjudication: An Alternative to Substantive Due Process Analysis of Personal Autonomy Rights. 48 *UCLA L. Rev.* 85, 2000.

108. *Id.*, p. 155.

109. *Bowers , supra* note 64.

110. *Id.*, p. 191.

111. *Id.*

112. *Id.*

113. *Id.*, p. 152.

114. *Id.*, p. 145.

115. *Id.*, p. 156.

116. *Washington* v. *Glucksberg*, 521 U.S. 702 (1997).

117. *Cruzan by Cruzan* v. *Director, Missouri Dept. of Health*, 497 U.S. 261, 294–295 (1990) (Scalia, J., concurring).

118. *Washington, supra* note 117, p. 728.

119. *Cruzan, supra* note 118 p. 282.

120. *Washington, supra* note 117, p. 731.

121. *Washington, supra* note 117, p. 722 (Brief for Respondents 7, 15).

122. *Compassion in Dying* v. *State of Wash.*, 79 F.3d 790, 825 (1996).

123. For example, the court justified its decision to permit pretrial preventative detention, in *U.S.* v. *Salerno*, 481 U.S. 739 (1987), by explicitly comparing the war on drugs to a war against another nation, ruling that in times of "war or insurrection…the government's regulatory interest in community safety can…outweigh an individual's liberty interest."

124. *Illinois* v. *Gates*, 462 U.S. 213 (1983); *McCray* v. *State of Ill.*, 386 U.S. 300 (1967).

125. *Oliver* v. *U.S.*, 466 U.S. 170 (1984).

126. *California* v. *Ciraolo*, 476 U.S. 207 (1986).

127. *Florida* v. *Riley*, 488 U.S. 445 (1989).

128. *Maryland* v. *Garrison*, 480 U.S. 79 (1987); *Massachusetts* v. *Sheppard*, 468 U.S. 981 (1984); *U.S.* v. *Leon*, 468 U.S. 897 (1984).

129. David G. Savage, House OK's Extra $400 Million to Internees, *L.A. Times*, Sept. 17, 1992, See *Toyosaburo Korematsu* v. *U.S.*, 323 U.S. 214 (1944).

130. U.S. Const. amend. IX.

131. *Griswold, supra* note 29, p. 492 (Goldberg, J., concurring).

132. James Madison, *The Federalist*, No. 10, (Max Beloff, ed., 1948), p. 42.

133. *Griswold, supra* note 29 (right of married couples to use of contraceptives); *Roe, supra* note 72 (right of a woman to terminate pregnancy); *Eisenstadt* v. *Baird*, 405 U.S. 438 (1972) (extending the holding in *Griswold* to unmarried couples).

134. *Moore* v. *City of East Cleveland, Ohio*, 431 U.S. 494 (1977) (zoning ordinance limiting occupancy of dwelling units to members of nuclear family); *Meyer, supra* note 54 (right of parents to direct education of their children); *Pierce, supra* note 94 (right of parents to choose schools their children will attend).

135. *Bowers, supra* note 64 (holding no constitutional right to homosexual sodomy).

136. Jed Rubenfeld, The Right of Privacy, 102 *Harv. L. Rev.* 737, 1989.

137. *West Virginia State Board of Education* v. *Barnette*, 319 U.S. 624 (1943).

138. *Id.*, pp. 640–41.

139. *Roberts* v. *U.S. Jaycees*, 468 U.S. 609 (1984).

140. *Id.*, p. 619.

141. *Bowers, supra* note 64, p. 205 (Blackman, J., dissenting).

142. Thomas Steven Szasz, *Our Right to Drugs: The Case for a Free Market* (New York: Praeger, 1992) (Professor Emeritus of Psychiatry, State University of New York Health Science Center, Syracuse, New York).

143. *Griswold, supra* note 29.

144. *Griswold, supra* note 29, p. 498 (Goldberg, J., concurring).

145. Massey, *supra* note 2, p. 331.

146. Honorable Robert W. Sweet & Edward A. Harris, Book Review: Just and Unjust Wars: The War on the War on Drugs—Some Moral and Constitutional Dimensions of the War on Drugs, 87 *Nw. U. L. Rev.* 1302, 1368, 1993.

147. *Id.*, pp. 1368–69.

148. Sweet and Harris, *supra* note 147, p. 1369.

149. *Id.*

150. John Stuart Mill, *On Liberty* (Indianapolis: Bobbs Merrill 1956). (This work was originally published in 1859.)

151. Joel Feinberg, A. B., 1949; M.A., 1951; Ph.D., 1957, University of Michigan, is a professor of philosophy at the University of Arizona.

152. Joel Feinberg, *Social Philosophy* (Prentice Hall, 1973), p. 32.

153. Mill, *supra* note 151, pp. 99–100.

154. Feinberg, *supra* note 153, p. 32.

155. Mill, *supra* note 151, p. 125.

156. Rubenfeld, *supra* note 137, p. 756.

157. *State* v. *Mallan,* 86 Hawaii 440, 950 (1998).

158. *Id.*, p. 464 (Levinson, J., dissenting).

159. *State, supra* note 158, p. 459 (Levinson, J., dissenting).

160. *Id.*

161. Huber, The Old-New Division in Risk Regulation, 69 *Va. L. Rev.* 1103, 1025, 1983.

162. Declaration of Independence, para. 1 (U.S. 1776).

163. Jeffrey S. Koehlinger, Substantive Due Process Analysis and the Lockean Liberal Tradition: Rethinking the Modern Privacy Cases 65 *Ind. L.J.*, 723, 731, 1990.

164. Joseph L. Galiber, A Bill to Repeal Criminal Drug Laws: Replacing Prohibition with Regulation 18 *Hofstra L. Rev.* 831, 1990.

165. *Bowers, supra* note 64.

166. *Bowers, supra* note 64. p 212 (quoting H. L. Hart, *Immorality and Treason, in The Law as Literature* (Louis Blom-Cooper, ed., 1961), p. 225).

Bibliography

BOOKS

American Social History Project. *Who Built America: Working People and the Nations Economy Politics Culture and Society.* New York: Pantheon Books, 1990.

Asbury, Herbert. *The Great Illusion: An Informal History of Prohibition.* Garden City, N.Y.: Doubleday, 1950.

Ashton, John. *The History of Gambling in England.* Montclair, N.J.: Patterson Smith, 1898, 1969.

Bachofen, J. J. *Myth, Religion, and Mother Right, Selected Writings of Bachofen.* trans. Ralph Manheim. Nos. 84, 86. Princeton, N.J.: Princeton University Press, 1967.

Basserman, Lujo. *The Oldest Profession: A History of Prostitution.* New York: Dorset Press, 1988.

Batties, J., R. W. Pickens, et. al. *National and International Perspectives, Needle Sharing Among Intravenous Drug Users,* monograph no. 80. Washington, D.C.: National Institute on Drug Abuse.

Beck, James, M. *The Revolt Against Prohibition.* Printed speech in the House of Representatives 1930. Washington, D.C.: Government Printing Office, 1938.

Beecher, Henry K. *Movement of Subjective Responses: Quantitative Effects of Drugs.* New York: Oxford University Press, 1959.

Black, Forrest Revere. *Ill-Starred Prohibition Cases: A Study in Judicial Pathology.* Boston: R.G. Badger, 1931.

Bloch, Iwan. *Die Prostitution.* Berlin: Louis Marcus, 1912.

Boaz, David, ed. *The Crisis in Drug Prohibition.* Washington, D.C.: Cato Institute, 1990.

Bodenhamer, David J., and James W. Ely Jr., eds. *The Bill of Rights in Modern America After 200 Years.* Bloomington: Indiana University Press, 1993.

Bonnie, Richard J., *Marijuana Use and Criminal Sanctions: Essays on the Theory and Practice of Decriminalization*. Charlottesville, Va.: Michie, 1980.

Booth, Robert, Steven Koestler, Charles Reichardt, and J. Thomas Brewster. *Quantitative and Qualitative Methods to Assess Behavioral Change Among Injection Drug Users in Drugs and Society*. New York: Haworth Press, 1993.

Brant, Irving. *James Madison: Father of the Constitution 1781–1800*. Vol. 3. Indianapolis: Bobbs-Merrill, 1950.

Brecher, Edward M., and editors of *Consumer Reports*. *Licit and Illicit Drugs: The Consumer Union Reports on Narcotics, Stimulants, Depressants, Inhalants, Hallucinogens, and Marijuana—Including Caffeine, Nicotine and Alcohol*. Boston: Little, Brown, 1972.

Briffault, Robert. *The Mothers: A Study of the Origins of Sentiments and Institutions*. Vol. 3. New York: Macmillan, 1927.

Bruere, Martha Bensley. *Does Prohibition Work? A Study of the Operation of the Eighteenth Amendment Made by the National Federation of Settlements*. New York, London: Harper Bros., 1927.

Bruun, Kettil, Lynn Pan, and Ingemar Rexed. *The Gentlemen's Club: International Control of Drugs and Alcohol*. Chicago: University of Chicago Press, 1975.

Bullough, Vern L. *The History of Prostitution*. New Hyde Park, N.Y.: University Books, 1964.

Bullough, Vern L., and Bonnie. *Sin, Sickness & Sanity: A History of Sexual Attitudes*. New York: Garland, 1977.

———*Women and Prostitution: A Social History*. Buffalo, N.Y.: Prometheus Books, 1987.

Cannabis. Report by the Advisory Committee on Drug Dependence, 1968.

Cashman, Dennis. *Prohibition: The Lie of the Land*. New York: Free Press; London: Collier Macmillan Free Press, 1981.

Chatterjee, Syamal Kumar. *Legal Aspects of International Drug Control*. Hingham, Mass.: Kluwer. 1981.

Clark, Norman H. *Deliver Us From Evil: An Interpretation of American Prohibition*. New York: W.W. Norton, 1985.

Coffey, Thomas M. *The Long Thirst: Prohibition in America, 1920–1933*. New York: W.W. Norton, 1975.

Cook, Philip J., and Charles T. Clotfelter. *Selling Hope: State Lotteries in America*. National Bureau of Economic Research Bill, Cambridge, Mass.: Harvard University Press, 1991.

Decker, John F. *Prostitution: Regulation and Control*. Publications of Criminal Law Education and Research Center, New York University, Vol. 13, Littleton, Colo.: Fred B. Rothman, 1979.

Diagnostic and Statistical Manual of Mental Disorders, 3d ed. Washington, D.C.: American Psychiatric Association, , 1987.

Dobyns, Fletcher. *The Amazing Story of Repeal*. Chicago: Willett, Clark, 1940.

Dorn, Nicholas, Jørgen Jepsen, and Ernesto Savona, eds. *European Drug Policies and Enforcement*. Houndsmill, Basingstoke, Hampshire: Macmillan; New York, N.Y.: Macmillan; St. Martin's Press, 1996.

Douglas, Emily Taft. *Margaret Sanger, Pioneer of the Future*. Garrett Park, Md.: Garrett Park Press, 1975.

Duke, Steven B., and Albert C. Gross. *America's Longest War: Rethinking Our Tragic Crusade Against Drugs.* New York: G. P. Putnam's Sons, 1993.

Eldridge, William Butler. *Narcotics and the Law: A Critique of the American Experiment in Narcotic Drug Control,* 2d ed., Chicago: University of Chicago Press, 1967.

Engels, Friedrich. *The Origins of the Family, Private Property and the State In the Light of the Researches of Lewis H. Morgan.* Reprinted, 4th ed. New York: International Publishers, 1942.

Erickson, Patricia G., et al. *The Steel Drug: Cocaine in Perspective.* Lexington, Mass.: Lexington Books, 1987.

Evans, Rod L., and Mark Hance, eds. *Tribal Gaming Benefits the Reservations, Legalized Gambling.* National Indian Gaming Association. Peru, Ill.: Open Court, 1998.

Farley, Aloysius James. *Jim Farley's Story: The Roosevelt Years.* Westport, Conn.: Greenwood Press, 1984.

Feinberg, Joel. *Rights, Justice, and the Bounds of Liberty: Essays in Social Philosophy.* Princeton, N.J.: Princeton University Press, 1980.

Feldman, Hermann. *Prohibition: Its Economic and Industrial Aspects.* New York, London: D. Appleton, 1930.

Fennell, Phil, ed. *Criminal Justice in Europe: A Comparative Study.* Oxford: Clarendon Press; New York: Oxford University Press, 1995.

Fisher, Elizabeth. *Woman's Creation: Sexual Evolution and the Shaping of Society.* Garden City, N.Y.: Anchor Press, 1979.

Gaillard Hunt. *Writings of James Madison,* Vol. 9. New York: G. P. Putnam's Sons, 1904.

Gamini Sallgado. *The Elizabethan Underworld.* London: J.M. Dent; Totowa, N.J.: Rowman and Littlefield, 1977.

GAP. *Drug Misuse: A Psychiatric View of a Dilemma.* New York: Charles Scribner's Sons, 1971.

Gellius, Aulus. *Attic Nights.* IV, iii, ed, and trans. John C. Rolfe, London: William Heinemann, 1952–1960.

Golberg, Ted. Demystifying Drugs: A Psychosocial Perspective. New York: St. Martin's Press, 1999.

Goode, Erich. *Drugs in American Society.* New York: Alfred Knopf, 1972.

Group for the Advancement of Psychiatry. *Drug Misuse: A Psychiatric View of a Dilemma.* Report 80. New York: Charles Scribner's Sons, 1971.

Hamm, Richard F. *Shaping the Eighteenth Amendment : Temperance Reform, Legal Culture, and the Polity, 1880–1920.* Chapel Hill: University of North Carolina Press, 1995.

Hamowy, Ronald. *Dealing with Drugs: Consequences of Government Control.* Lexington, Mass.: Lexington, Mass.: D.C. Heath, 1987.

Hamowy, Ronald, ed. *Pacific Studies in Public Policy.* Lexington, Mass.: Lexington Books. 1987.

Hardaway, Robert M. *Population, Law and the Environment.* Westport, Conn.: Praeger Publishers, 1994.

Harding, Christopher, et al. *Criminal Justice in Europe: A Comparative Study.* Oxford: Clarendon Press; New York: Oxford University Press, 1995.

Husak, Douglas N. *Drugs and Rights*. Cambridge, New York: Cambridge University Press, 1992.

Jones, Aphrodite. *Cruel Sacrifice*. New York: Pinnacle Books, , 1994.

Kaplan, John. *The Hardest Drug:Heroin and Public Policy*. Chicago: University of Chicago Press, 1983.

Kiester, Edwin Jr. *Crimes With No Victims, How Legislating Morality Defeats the Cause of Justice*. New York: Alliance for a Safer New York, 1972.

King, Rufus. *Gambling and Organized Crime*. Washington, D.C.: Public Affairs Press, 1969.

Koren, John. *Economic Aspects of the Liquor Problem*. Boston; New York: Houghton Mifflin, 1899.

Kraepelin, Emil. *One Hundred Years of Psychiatry*. New York: Philosophical Library, 1962.

Kraska, Peter, ed. *Altered States of Mind: Critical Observations of the Drug War*. New York: Garland , 1993.

Kyvig, David E. *Explicit and Authentic Acts: Amending the U.S. Constitution, 1776–1995*. Lawrence, Kans.: University Press of Kansas, 1996.

Levine, Harvey R. *Legal Dimensions of Drug Abuse*. Springfield, Ill.: Thomas, 1974.

Liebman, Jon, and Nina Mulia. *An Office Based AIDS Prevention Program for High Risk Drug Users in Drugs and Society*. New York: Haworth Press, 1993.

Luther, Martin. *Letters of Spiritual Counsel*. ed. and trans. Theodore G. Tappert. Philadelphia: Westminster Press, 1955.

Massey, Calvin R. *Silent Rights: The Ninth Amendment and the Constitution's Unenumerated Rights*. Philadelphia: Temple University Press, 1995.

Matheson, Douglas, and Meredith Davison. *The Behavioral Effects of Drugs*. New York: Holt, Rinehart and Winston, 1972.

McWilliams, Peter. *Ain't Nobody's Business If You Do: The Absurdity of Consensual Crimes in a Free Society*. Los Angeles, Calif.: Prelude Press, 1993.

Mill, John Stuart, *On Liberty*. Originally published in 1859. Indianapolis: Bobbs Merrill 1956.

Mill, John Stuart. *Utilitarianism, On Liberty, and Representative Government*. New York: Dutton, 1910.

Miller, Lawrence Richard. *The Case for Legalizing Drugs*. New York: Praeger, 1991.

Musto, David F., M.D. *The American Disease; Origins of Narcotic Control*. New Haven: Yale University Press, 1973.

Otis, Leah Lydia. *Prostitution in Medieval Society: The History of an Urban Institution in Languedoc*. Chicago: University of Chicago Press, 1985.

Parent-Duchatelet, A. J. B. *De la prostitution dans la ville de Paris*. Paris: J. B. Bailliere, Vol. 2, 1837.

Phelps, Edward B. *The American Underwriter*. New York.

Plato. *Symposium*. (211B), ed. and trans. W. R. M. Lamb, London: William Heinemann, 1953.

Ploscoe, Morris, et. al. *Organized Crime and Law Enforcement: The Reports, Research Studies and Model Statutes and Commentaries*. American Bar Association. New York: Grosby Press, 1952.

Pollard, Joseph Percival. *The Road to Repeal, Submission to Conventions*. New York: Brentano's, 1932.

Posner, Richard A. *Sex and Reason.* Cambridge, Mass.: Harvard University Press, 1998, 1992.

Posner, Richard A., and Katharine B. Silbaugh. *A Guide to America's Sex Laws.* Chicago: University of Chicago Press, 1996.

Quaife, Geoffrey Robert. *Wanton Wenches and Wayward Wives: Peasants and Illicit Sex in Early Seventeenth Century England.* New Brunswick, N.J.: Rutgers University, 1979.

Reynolds, Helen. *The Economics of Prostitution.* Springfield, Ill.: Charles C. Thomas 1986.

Roberts, Nickie. *Whores in History: Prostitution in Western Society.* London: Harper-Collins, 1992.

Robertson, David. *VIRGINIA. CONVIENTION, 1788* (sic). Debates and other proceedings. Richmond: Enquirer Press, 1805.

Rowell, Earl and Robert Rowell. *On the Trail of Marijuana: The Weed of Madness.* Mountain View, Calif: Pacific Press, 1939.

Rush, Benjamin. *The Drunkard's Emblem, or, An Inquiry Into the Effects of Ardent Spirits Upon the Human Body and Mind: With an Account of the Means of Preventing, and of the Remedies for Curing Them.* New-Market, Va: Ambrose Henkel, 1814(?).

Sanger, William W. *The History of Prostitution: Its Extent, Causes and Effects Throughout the World.* New York: Eugenics Publishing, 1937.

Scarne, John. *Scarne's New Complete Guide to Gambling.* New York: Simon & Schuster, 1986.

Scarne, John, and Clayton Rawson. *Scarne on Dice.* Harrisburg, Pa.: Military Service Publishing, 1945.

Schaler, Jeffrey A., ed. *Drugs: Should We Legalize, Decriminalize, or Deregulate?* Amherst, N.Y.: Prometheus Books, 1998.

Smith, Preserved. *The Age of Reformation.* New York: Henry Holt, 1920.

Sprull, L., N. Silverman, and D. Levine. *Urban Crime and Drug Availability.* Public Research Institute, Center for Naval Analysis, PRI 75–1, 1975.

St. Augustine, *De Ordine,* II, iv, 12, in Migne, *Patrologa Latina,* XXXII.

Stark, Cameron. *Illegal Drug Use in the United Kingdom: Prevention, Treatment and Enforcement,* ed. Cameron Stark, Brian A. Kidd, and Roger A. D. Sykes. Aldershot, England; Brookfield, Vermont: Ashgate, 1999.

Stone, Lawrence. *The Family, Sex and Marriage in England. 1500–1800.* London: HarperCollins, 1977.

Suetonius. *Gaius Caligula, Lives of the Caesars,* XL, ed. and trans. J. C. Rolfe, 2 vols. London: William Heinemann, 1950–51.

Szasz, Thomas Steven. *Our Right to Drugs: The Case for a Free Market.* New York: Praeger, 1992.

Thompson, William N. *History, Development, and Legislation of Native American Casino Gaming, Legalized Casino Gaming in the United States,* ed. Cathy H. C. Hsu. Binghamton, NY: Haworth Hospitality Press, 1999.

Thompson, William N., and Diana Dever. *Gambling Enterprise and the Restoration of Native American Sovereignty, Gambling: Public Policies and the Social Sciences.* Reno, Nev.: Institute for the Study of Gambling and Commercial Gaming, 1997.

Timberlake, James H. *Prohibition and the Progressive Movement, 1900–1920,* Cambridge, Mass.: Harvard University Press, 1963.

Trebach, Arnold. *The Great Drug War, and Radical Proposals That Could Make America Safe Again,* New York: Macmillan; London: Collier Macmillan, 1987.

Walker III, William O. *Drug Control in the Americas,* rev. ed. Albuquerque: University of New Mexico Press, 1989.

Weissman, James C., ed. *Criminal Justice and Drugs: The Unresolved Connection.* Port Washington, N.Y.: Kennikat Press, 1982.

Weissman, James C. *Drug Abuse the Law and Treatment Alternatives.* Cincinnati: Criminal Justice Studies, Anderson Publishing Co., 1978.

Wissowa, Pauly. *Real Encyclopaedie, der classichen Altertumwissenschaft.* Vol. XL. Stuttgart: J. B. Metzler, 1914–1961.

Wright, Hamilton. *Report on the International Opium Commission and on the Opium Problem as Seen Within the United States and Its Possessions.* In Opium Problem. Message from the President of the United States, 61 Cong., 2 sess., 1910, S. Doc. No. 61–377 1910.

PERIODICALS

Alexander, Bruce, Robert Coambs, and Patricia Hardaway. "The Effect of Housing and Gender on Morphine Self-Administration in Rats." *Psychopharmacology* 58 (1978): 175–178.

Annals of Congress. (1834) Vol. 1, p. 452.

Atlantic Monthly. Boston: Atlantic Monthly Co.

Bandow, Doug. "War on Drugs or War on America." *Stanford Law and Policy Review* 3 (Fall 1991): 242.

Barrett, Paul. "Strategic Muddle: Federal War on Drugs Is Scattershot Affair, With Dubious Progress." *Wall St. Journal,* August 10, 1988, A1.

Begley, Sharon, and Erika Check. "Sex and the Single Fly." *Newsweek,* August 14, 2000, 44.

Bilezerian, Keith David. "Ante Up or Fold: States Attempt to Play Their Hand While Indian Casinos Cash In." *New England Law Review* 29 (Winter 1995): 463.

Bivens, Larry. "Indians Find Clout in Newfound Wealth: Awash in Casino Cash, They're Tackling Poverty and Economic Issues." *Detroit News* (September 12, 1999).

Block, Walter. "Drug Prohibition: A Legal and Economic Analysis." *Journal of Business Ethics* 12 (1993): 696.

Bonnie, Richard J., and Charles H. Whitebread II. "The Forbidden Fruit and the Tree of Knowledge: An Inquiry Into the Legal History of American Marijuana Prohibition." *Virginia Law Review* 56 (1970): 971, 1010.

Boudreaux, Donald J., and A. C. Pritchard. "The Price of Prohibition." *Arizona Law Review* 36 (1994): 1.

Breslau, Karen. "Over Planned Parenthood: Ceausescu's Cruel Law." *Newsweek,* January 22, 1990, 35.

Brown, R., and R. Middlefell. "Fifty-Five Years of Cocaine Dependence." *British Journal of Addiction* (1989): 946.

Caesar, Dan. "California and Nevada Keep Upping Ante in Battle to Be 'Casino Center of the World.'" *St. Louis Dispatch* Monday, September 27, 1999.

Campbell, Carole A. "Prostitution, AIDS, and Preventive Health Behavior." *Social Science Medicine* 32 (1991): 1368.

Chavira, Ricardo. "The Rise of Teenage Gambling." *Time,* February 25, 1991, 78.

Cohen, Warren. "Don't Bet on Gambling Reform Anytime Soon." *U.S. News &World Report,* June 14, 1999.

Collier's. Crowell-Collier, Springfield, Ohio, (1908).

Cosmopolitan. Schlict & Field, Rochester, N.Y., (1908).

"Debates in the Convention of the State of North Carolina, on the Adoption of the Federal Constitution." *Elliot's Debates:* State of North Carolina. (The Debates in the Several State Conventions on the Adoption of the Federal Constitution). Philadelphia. 4 (July 21, 1788), 167.

"The Debates in the Convention of the State of Pennsylvania, On the Adoption of the Federal Constitution." *Elliot's Debates:* State of Pennsylvania. (The Debates in the Several State Conventions on the Adoption of the Federal Constitution). Philadelphia. 2 (November 20, 1787, 436.

Demleitner, Nora V. "Organized Crime And Prohibition: What Difference Does Legalization Make?" *Whittier Law Review* 15 (1994): 613.

Dubious Progress." *Wall St. Journal,* August 10, 1988, A1.

"Editorial, Illusions of a War against Cocaine." *New York Times,* Jan. 24, 1998, A14.

"The Effectiveness of Drug Abuse Treatment: Implications for Controlling, AIDS/HIV Infection." Congress of the U.S. Office of Technology Assessment, (Sept. 1990).

Field, Martha A. "The Seminole Case, Federalism, and the Indian Commerce Clause." *Arizona State Law Journal* (Spring 1997): 20–21.

Flowers, Charles. "Federal Impact Study Not Expected to Alter Tribal Gambling." *Knight-Ridder Tribune Business News: Indian Country Today,* Monday, June 28, 1999.

Foust, John. "State Power to Regulate Alcohol Under the Twenty-First Amendment: The Constitutional Implications of the Twenty-First Amendment Enforcement Act." *Boston College Law Review* 41 (May 2000): 664.

France, Steve. "The Drug War: Should We Fight or Switch." *American Bar Association Journal* 121 (February 1990): 5.

Galiber, Joseph L. "A Bill to Repeal Criminal Drug Laws: Replacing Prohibition With Regulation." *Hofstra Law Review* 18 (1990): 831.

"Gambling on the Future." *The Economist,* Saturday, June 26, 1999.

Ganin, Frank, and Herbert Kleber. "Abstinence Symptomatology and Psychiatric Diagnosis in Cocaine Abusers: Clinical Observations." *Archives of General Psychiatry* (1983): 43.

Garavelli, Mario. "Drug Abuse in Italy And Europe in a Comparative Context." *Indiana International and Comparative Law Review* 4 (1994): 277.

Gledhill, Lynda. "Tribe Signs Gambling Pact." *San Francisco Chronicle* Wednesday, September 15, 1999.

Green, Jess. "Economic Development and Gaming." *St. Thomas Law Review* 9 (Fall 1996): 149.

Greene, Rex. "Toward a Policy of Mercy: Addiction in the 1990s." *Stanford Law and Policy Review* 3 (Fall 1991): 227.

Griffin, Moira. "Wives, Hookers, and the Law." *Student Lawyer* 10 (January 1982): 21.

Hamilton, Alexander. "Certain General and Miscellaneous Objections to the Constitution Considered and Answered." *McLean's* New York. Federalist Papers. Federalist No. 84, (May 28, 1788).

Hardaway, Robert M., et al. "The Right to Die and the Ninth Amendment: Compassion and Dying After Glucksberg and Vacco." *George Mason Law Review* 7 (1999): 313.

Hart, H. L. "Immorality and Treason: In the Law as Literature." *Listener,* July 30, 1959, 211.

Henry, Patrick. Virginia Ratifying Convention. *Elliot's Debates* 3 (June 14, 1788): 440.

Huber, Peter. "The Old-New Division in Risk Regulation." *Virginia Law Review* 69 (1983): 1103, 1025.

Jaffe, Mark. "Lottery Frenzy Expands." *Philadelphia Inquirer,* July 31, 1983, G1.

James, A. "Prostitution and Addiction: An Interdisciplinary Approach." *Addictive Diseases: International Journal* 2 (1976): 607.

Jehl, Douglas. "U.S. Estimate of World Cocaine Output Up 94%." *Los Angeles Times,* March 2, 1990, A12.

Joint Resolution of Congress 1789. United States National Archives & Records Administration, Washington D.C.

Jonas, Steven. "Solving the Drug Problem: A Public Health Approach to the Reduction of the Use and Abuse of Both Legal and Illegal Recreational Drugs." *Hofstra Law Review* 18 (1990): 758.

Jones, Charles T., and Mark A. Hutchison. "Indian Tribes Hit Jackpot with Gaming." *Sunday Oklahoman,* Sunday, September 12, 1999.

Jones, Eric D. "The Indian Gaming Regulatory Act: A Forum for Conflict Among the Plenary Power of Congress, Tribal Sovereignty, and the Eleventh Amendment." *Vermont Law Review* 18 (Fall 1993): 127.

Kading, Linda King. "State Authority to Regulate Gaming Within Indian Lands: The Effect of the Indian Gaming Regulatory Act." *Drake Law Review* 41 (1992): 317.

Kalish, Jason. "Do the States Have an Ace in the Hole, or Should the Indians Call Their Bluff? Tribes Caught in the Power Struggle Between the Federal Government and the States." *Arizona Law Review* 38 (Winter 1996): 1345.

Kandall, Stephen R., and Wendy Chavkin. "Illicit Drugs in America: History, Impact on Women and Infants, and Treatment Strategies for Women." *Hastings Law Journal* 43 (1992): 615.

Katz, Rachel V. "A Tribe Rediscovers Its Heritage; Community: Once Nearly Extinct, Connecticut's Mashantucket Pequot Indians Have Built a Thriving Community Fueled by Highly Profitable Gambling Casino and Resort." *Baltimore Sun,* Thursday, August 5, 1999.

Kelly. "The Uncertain Renaissance of the Ninth Amendment." *University of Chicago Law Review* 33 (1966): 814.

Kleinman, Mark A. R., and Aaron J. Saiger. "Drug Legalization: The Importance of Asking the Right Question." *Hofstra Law Review* (1990): 527.

Koehlinger, Jeffrey S. "Substantive Due Process Analysis and the Lockean Liberal Tradition: Rethinking the Modern Privacy Cases." *Indiana Law Journal* 65 (1990): 723, 731.

Lasagna, Louis, John M. Von Felsinger, and Henry K. Beecher. "Drug Induced Mood Changes in Man: Observations on Chronically Ill Patients and Post Addicts." *Journal of the American Medical Association* 157 (1955): 1017.

Law, Sylvia A. "Commercial Sex: Beyond Decriminalization." *Southern California Law Review* 73 (March 2000): 523, 567.

Leigh, Carol. "A First Hand Look at the San Francisco Task Force Report on Prostitution." *Hastings Women's Law Journal* 10 (Winter 1999): 59–60.

Lippmann, Walter, *Vanity Fair* 1930.

Literary Digest. Funk & Wagnalls, New York, (1914).

Lorber, Leah L., "State Rights. Tribal Sovereignty, and the 'White Man's Firewater': State Prohibition Of Gambling On New Indian Lands." *Indiana Law Journal* 69 (1993): 255.

Madison, James. " The Alleged Danger from the Powers of the Union to the State Governments Considered." Federalist Papers, no. 5, *Independent Journal* (January 26, 1788).

Marsh, Dr. John. "Whole World's Temperance Convention." Speech, New York City, May 1853.

McAuliffe, William. "A Second Look at First Effects: The Subjective Effects of Opiates on Non-Addicts." *Journal of Drug Issues* 5 (1975).

McBride, Jessica. "Gambling's Blessing and Curse." *Milwaukee Journal Sentinel,* Sunday, August 22, 1999.

McClure's Magazine. New York; London: S. S. McClure Limited, (1908).

McLaughlin, Gerald T. "Cocaine: The History and Regulation of a Dangerous Drug." *Cornell Law Review* 58 (1973): 544.

Melillo, Wendy. "Early Skirmishes in the War on Drugs." *Washington Post,* November 4, 1986, Z14.

Milman, Barbara. "New Rules for the Oldest Profession: Should We Change Our Prostitution Laws?" *Harvard Women's Law Journal* 3 (September 1980): 1.

Moore, Marvin M. "The Case for Legitimizing the Call Girl." *Cooley Law Review* 5 (May 1988): 337.

Morain, Dan and Tom Gorman. "Davis and Key Gaming Tribe Reach Deal on Gaming." *Los Angeles Times,* Wednesday, September 15, 1999.

Musto, David, and Manuel Ramos. "A Follow-Up Study of the New Haven Morphine Maintenance Clinic of 1920." *New England Journal of Medicine* 304 (1981): 1075–76.

Nadelmann, Ethan A. "Drug Prohibition in the U.S.: Costs, Consequences, and Alternatives." *Science* 245 (1989): 944.

Nadelmann, Ethan A. "Yes." *American Heritage* (February/March 1993): 48.

National Highway Traffic Safety Administration, U.S. Department of Transportation. "Traffic Safety Facts 2000: Alcohol." *DOT HS.* 809 (2000): 323.

National Institute of Drug Abuse, DAWN (1984): 52.

New York Times, Jan. 3, 1937.

Niles, Mark C. "Ninth Amendment Adjudication: An Alternative to Substantive Due Process Analysis of Personal Autonomy Rights." *UCLA Law Review* 48 (2000): 85.

"Off With Their Heads? Thoughts From the Drug Czar." *Washington Post,* June 20, 1989, A1.

Ome, Nicolas. "The Reformation and the Red Light." *History Today,* March 1997, 40.

Orr, J. Scott. "Gambling Industry Confronts New Deal Congress Examines Bills Aimed at Growth." *Harrisburg Patriot.* Harrisburg, Penn. Monday, October 4, 1999.

Ostrowski, James. "A Symposium on Drug Decriminalization: The Moral and Practical for Drug Legalization." *Hofstra Law Review* 18 (1990): 607.

Ostrowski, James. "Thinking About Drug Legalization." *Cato Institute Policy Analysis* 121 (May 1989): 25.

Pearl, Julie. "The Highest Paying Customers: America's Cities and the Costs of Prostitution Control." *Hastings Law Journal* 38 (April 1987): 769.

Pinkard, Eric. "The Death Penalty for Drug Kingpins: Constitutional and International Implications." *Vermont Law Review* 24 (1999): 1, 14.

Pommersheim, Frank R. "Tribal-State Relations: Hope for the Future?" *South Dakota Law Review* 36 (1991): 4.

Popkin, James. "Gambling With the Mob?" *U.S. News & World Report,* August 23, 1993, 30.

Powell, John A., and Eileen B. Hershenov. "Hostage to the Drug War: The National Purse, the Constitution and the Black Community." *University of California at Davis Law Review* 24 (1991): 557.

Raustiala, Kal. "Law, Liberalization & International Narcotics Trafficking." *New York University Journal of International Law and Politics* 32 (1999): 89.

Reidy, Chris. "Gambling Has Become the Nice Vice." *Boston Globe,* Jan. 17, 1993, 69.

Reinhold, Robert. "Police Hard Pressed in Drug War, Are Turning to Preventive Efforts." *New York Times,* December 28, 1989, A1.

Reuter, Peter. "Hawks Ascendant: The Punitive Trend of American Drug Policy." *Daedalus* 121 (Summer 1992): 33–34.

Richards, David A. J. "Commercial Sex and the Rights of the Person: A Moral Argument for the Decriminalization of Prostitution." *University of Pennsylvania Law Review* 127 (May 1979).

Robbins, Leonard. "Casino Gambling." *Miami Herald,* July 19, 1986, A23.

Roberts, Mike. "The National Gambling Debate: Two Defining Issues." *Whittier Law Review* 18 (1997): 579, 582.

Rogers, Will and Joseph A. Stout, Jr. ed.,. *Cowboy Philosopher on Prohibition.* Stillwater: Oklahoma State University Press, 1975.

Rogoway, Mike. "The New Indian Economy." *The Columbian* (Sunday, September 5, 1999): 1.

Rubenfeld, Jed. "The Right of Privacy." *Harvard Law Review* 102 (1989): 737.

Rychlak, Ronald J. "Lotteries, Revenues, and Social Costs: A Historical Examination of State-Sponsored Gambling." *Boston College Law Review* 34 (December

1992): 11.

Schmoke, Kurt L. "An Argument in Favor of Decriminalization." *Hofstra Law Review* 18 (1990): 501.

Schultz, David. "Rethinking Drug Criminalization Policies." *Texas Tech Law Review* 25 (1993): 152.

Seligman, Dan. "The Winning Hand: The $8 Billion Indian Gaming Industry Remains in Fierce Growth Phase. This Can't Be Good for Non-Indian Gamers." *Forbes,* Monday, July 26, 1999.

Shereda, Joseph P. "The Internalization of the War On Drugs and Its Potential for Successfully Addressing Drug Trafficking and Related Crimes in South Africa." *George Washington Journal of International Law and Economics* 31 (1998): 297, 306.

Spaeth, Sidney J. "The Twenty-First Amendment and State Control Over Intoxicating Liquors: Accommodating the Federal Interest." *California Law Review* 79 (January 1991): 108.

Sutton, Lawrence R., "The Effects of Alcohol, Marijuana, and Their Combination on Driving Ability." *Journal of Studies on Alcohol* (1983): 442.

Sweet, Honorable Robert W., & Edward A. Harris. "Book Review: Just and Unjust Wars: The War on the War on Drugs—Some Moral and Constitutional Dimensions of the War on Drugs." *Northwestern University Law Review* 87 (1993): 1302, 1368.

Taylor, Jerry. "Laws Lax for 'Oldest Profession.'" *Boston Globe,* Feb. 27, 1988, 21.

Testerman, Jeff, and Jo Becker. "Florida Files Suit to Block Casino-Style Gambling." *St. Petersburg Times,* Tuesday, April 13, 1999.

Thies, Clifford F., and Charles A. Register. "Decriminalization of Marijuana and the Demand for Alcohol, Marijuana, and Cocaine." *Social Science Journal* 30 (1993): 389.

Thompson, William. "Gambling: A Controlled Substance." *Pittsburgh Post-Gazette,* August 14, 1994, E1.

Touns, Charles. "The Injury of Tobacco and Its Relation to Other Drug Habits." *Century* 83 (1912): 770.

Tsosie, Rebecca. "Negotiating Economic Survival: The Consent Principle and Tribal-State Compacts Under the Indian Gaming Regulatory Act." *Arizona State Law Journal* 29 (Spring 1977): 95–96.

United States Department of Justice, Office of Justice Programs, Bureau of Justice Assistance. *Addressing Community Gang Problems: A Practical Guide* (May 1998): 22.

United States Government Press Releases by Federal Document Clearinghouse. (June 18, 1999).

Urschel, Joe. "If We're Going to Tax Sin, Go Whole Hog." *U.S.A Today,* September 28, 1993, A10.

"U.S.A.: Las Vegas Remakes Itself." *The Economist,* March 26, 1994, A31.

Van Dyke, Craig, and Robert Byck. "Cocaine." *Scientific American* (1982): 246.

Vorenberg and Vorenberg. "The Biggest Pimp of All: Prostitution and Some Facts of Life." *Atlantic Monthly,* January 1977, 28.

Weil, Andrew T., Norman Zinberg, and Judith Nielsen. "Clinical and Psychological Efforts of Marijuana in Man." *Science* 12 (1968): 1234–42.

Wetzsteon, Ross. "Why Nice Guys Buy Sex." *Mademoiselle,* November 1984, 196–197.

Will, George F., "Gambling With Our Character." *Washington Post,* Feb. 7, 1993, C7.

Wilwarth Jr., Arthur E. "The Original Purpose of the Bill of Rights: James Madison and the Founders' Search for a Workable Balance Between Federal and State Power." *American Criminal Law Review* 26 (1989): 1261.

Wisotsky, Steven. "Exposing the War on Cocaine: The Futility and Destructiveness of Prohibition." *Wisconsin Law Review* 1 (1983): 1384.

Worthen, Kevin J., and Wayne R. Farnsworth. "Who Will Control the Future of Indian Gaming? A Few Pages of History Are Worth a Volume of Logic." *Brigham Young University Law Review* 407 (1996).

ELECTRONIC MEDIA

American Medical Directors Association. http://www.amda.com/.

Annals of Congress. 452 (1834). U.S. National Archives and Records Administration, Archives Library Information Center. http://www.archives.gov/research_room/alic/government_publications/administrative_history_congress ional_debates.html

Browne, Ph.D., Gregory M. *The Progressive Era,* http://www.yorktownuniversity.com/documents/progressive_era.pdf.

Canney, Donald L. *A Rum War: The U.S. Coast Guard and Prohibition,* http://www.uscg.mil/hq/g-cp/history/h_rumwar.htm.

Center for Disease Control. *A Call for Action: Surgeon General's Report, Reducing Tobacco Use* (CDC, April 11, 2001), http://www.cdc.gov/tobacco/sgr/sgr_2000/factsheets/factsheet_callforaction.html.

Detroit Historical Museum. http://www.detroithistorical.org/

Group for the Advancement of Psychiatry. *Drug Misuse: A Psychiatric View of a Dilemma,* GAP Report 80. http://www.groupadpsych.org/publica tions.htm.

Hamilton, Alexander. Federalist Papers. Federalist No. 84. http://www.founding-fathers.info/federalistpapers/fed84.htm.

Holcombe, Randall G. *The Growth of Federal Government in the 1920s,* CATO Journal, Vol. 16 no. 2, http://www.cato.org/pubs/journal/cj16n2–2.htm., fn 20.

Hoover, Herbert. Thirty-first U.S. president, acceptance speech for the presidential nomination in Chicago, Illinois. *History Channel dot com,* http://www.history channel.com/cgi-bin/frameit.cgi?p = http%3A//www.historychannel. com/speeches/archive/speech_1 29.htm.

Judicial History of the Orphan's Division. http://courts.phila.gov/cpojh.htm

Kraepelin, Emil. International Kraepelin Organization, Emil Kraepelin, http://www.kraepelin.org.futuresite.register.com/.

La Guardia, Fiorello. http://www.cohums.ohio-state.edu/history/projects/prohibition/laguardi.htm.

Madison, James. Federalist Papers No. 45. http://memory.loc.gov/const/fed/fed_45.html

Meretrix, Magdalene. *A Brief History of Medieval Whores,* 1 (1999), http://www.realm-of-shade.com.

National Institute on Alcohol Abuse and Alcoholism. http://www.niaaa.nih.gov/databases/armort01.txt, last accessed Feb. 12, 2001, citing Alcohol Epidemiologic Data System, F. Saadatmand, F. S. Stinson, B. F. Grant, and M. C. Dufour, *Surveillance Report #52: Liver Mortality in the United States, 1970–96.* Rockville, MD: National Institute on Alcohol Abuse and Alcoholism, Division of Biometry and Epidemiology, December 1999.

Prostitution: The American Occupation of Womanhood. http://www.pimpz.org/prostitution.

Reform Judaism (also known as Progressive Judaism). http://www.wikipedia.com/wiki/Reform+Judaism.

Rogers, Will. C-Span's American Writers, http://www.americanwriters.org/works/cowboy.asp.

Schaer, Sidney C. *How Alcohol Beat Last Call: Predictions From the Past That Haven't Come True...Yet,* http://future.newsday.com/5/fbak0514.htm.

Temperance & Prohibition. http://www.cohums.ohio-state.edu/history/projects/prohibition/Medicinal_Alcohol.htm.

United States Department of Justice. http://www.ncjrs.org/pdffiles/164273.pdf.

Vidal, Gore. *The Gore Vidal Index.* http://www.pitt.edu/~kloman/vidal frame.htm.

Volunteer Committee of Lawyers. The Original VCL (1927–33), http://www.vcl.org/History/orig_vcl_short.htm.

Washington, Reverend Eli. *Letters to E.W.J. Lindesmith on Catholic Prohibition League of America, 1903–1919,* Reverend Eli Washington, John Lindesmith Papers, http://libsrve.lib.cua.edu/archive/Lindesmith/.

Wickersham. *Records of the Wickersham Commission on Law Observance and Enforcement,* http://www.lexisnexis.com/academic/2upa/Aj/Wickersham Comm.htm.

Williams, Dr. Henry Smith. *Conference Report: To Users of Liquor* (102nd Semi-Annual Conference of the Church of Jesus Christ of Latter-Day Saints, October 1931), http://www.kingdomofzion.org/doctrines/library/lds/GC_Oct1931.txt.

Woll, Matthew. Testimony of Matthew Woll, The National Prohibition Law Hearings, April 5 to 24, 1926, Schaffer Library of Drug Policy, http://www.druglibrary.org/schaffer/history/e1920/senj1926/woll.htm.

Index

About the Author

ROBERT M. HARDAWAY is Professor of Law at the University of Denver College of Law. He has taught law and public policy at the University of California Hastings Law School and The George Washington University Law School in Washington, D.C., and also served in the Judge Advocate General's Corps of the United States Navy. His earlier nine book-length publications include *America Goes to School: Law, Reform and Crisis in Public Education* (Praeger, 1995) and *The Electoral College and the Consitution* (Praeger, 1994).